JOHN THE BAPTIST

A BIOGRAPHY

CHARLES CROLL

malcolm down

PUBLISHING

23 22 21 20 19   7 6 5 4 3 2 1

First published 2019 by Malcolm Down Publishing Ltd.
www.malcolmdown.co.uk

British Library Cataloguing in Publication Data
A catalogue record for this book is available from the British Library.

ISBN 978-1-912863-15-0

Cover design by Esther Kotecha
Art direction by Sarah Grace
Back cover photo by Nic Barlow

Printed in the UK

CONTENTS

PREFACE

He ordered them not to depart from Jerusalem, but to wait for the
promise of the Father, which, he said,
'you heard from me;
For John indeed immersed in water, but you will be immersed in
the Holy Spirit not many days from now.'
(Acts 1:4b-5[1])

As a teenager I considered myself an atheist. Then, much to my
surprise, I had a series of spiritual experiences in the early '70s, while
living on a Jewish kibbutz in Galilee. This completely changed my
perspective and kick-started my journey of faith. I became a lapsed
atheist, thank God.

That journey was also a literal one that took me on an overland
trip across Europe and the Middle East, a year-long on-and-off
pilgrimage that led back to the holy land, to a small Arab church in
Bethlehem and a life-altering sermon about the cross. That is where
I learned that Jesus died for me. It is where I found God's forgiveness
and cleansing and a new depth of relationship with him in the Holy
Spirit. That is where I was, to use Jesus' much abused phrase, born
again.[2]

The next day I first came into contact with John the Baptist's great
prophecy (referred to by Jesus in the text at the beginning of this
Preface). I was staying in Jerusalem and talking to a Pentecostal pastor
from Alabama, who urged me to be baptized in the Holy Spirit. He
showed me where to find this expression in the New Testament and
prayed – loudly and with his hands on my head – for this to happen.
Bless him. But even then I questioned that use of John's prophecy –
there seemed to me to be more to it than that. It did encourage me,
though, about ten days later, to ask God for the gift of speaking in

tongues, which I received the following evening in an upper room in Jerusalem.

Shortly after this I was baptized by the Bethlehem preacher and the Alabama pastor in a fresh water spring by the Dead Sea, just ten miles as the crow flies from the place where Jesus was baptized by John (access to the River Jordan was problematic at that time, just a few months before the Yom Kippur war).

Years later, in the late 1990s, as a minister in the United Reformed Church, I was preaching from that passage in the Gospels in which Jesus says that there has never been anyone greater than John.[3] It is an extraordinary accolade and it led me to study the man and his message during a sabbatical that was scheduled shortly afterwards. With a backpack loaded with a Bible, two books on John (borrowed from a college library) and some articles from academic journals, I set off for Israel and Jordan again, to spend time at the locations of John's annunciation, birth, baptisms and execution.

By then, I had two theological degrees, had studied in London, Cambridge and Birmingham and was well-versed in academia, but those books and articles were a disappointment to me. I had mistakenly imagined that they might answer the straightforward questions I had about John, like:

Why did Jesus think that this desert preacher was among the greatest people who have ever lived?

Why did John think that the best way to 'Prepare the way of the LORD'[4] was to immerse people in the River Jordan?

What is the baptism (immersion) in the Holy Spirit that John prophesied?

How can a better understanding of John's life and teaching help me to draw closer to God and live a better life in the twenty-first century?

Those books, however, were part of a sceptical quest for the historical John the Baptist, part of a broader and equally sceptical quest for the historical Jesus, that is more focused on answering different questions. It is a quest that is concerned with speculative ideas about who wrote what, what the sources of information about John in the Gospels could have been, and hypothetical hidden agendas that the authors might have had. It is, in truth, a conspiracy theory based on a highly questionable notion that substantial parts of the Gospels are in some way fraudulent or based on false information. First-century fake news.

This simply did not ring in any way true to me. So, still determined to get answers to my questions, I devoted many years of consuming research and another sabbatical to John and his message. It has been an extraordinary time, during which I read every book and article I could lay my hands on, did lots of Bible study, made another visit to Jordan and Israel, and spent a good deal of time praying and pondering. It was because my quest led me to such radically different conclusions that I decided to write this book. It is the book I would like to have read twenty years ago. It is not an academic book, refuting point-by-point the thesis of the sceptical quest, as it has a very different and much more positive purpose: to uncover John's extraordinary story in an accessible yet rigorous way. By telling his story like this, a very different thesis presents itself:

The Gospels were written by able, honest, trustworthy men who had either been among John's disciples, or who knew John, or who knew people who knew him well. Written by people who loved and respected John, the Gospels contain a beautiful, reliable, coherent account of this remarkable man's life and prophetic ministry.

The Gospel writers have my respect and gratitude, as do numerous others who have helped me in my quest:

The United Reformed Church, having brought together infant-baptist denominations with a believer-baptist denomination, requires all its churches to offer both forms to all its members. This has also made me think about the issues. I am indebted to the URC both for its baptismal policy and for its sabbatical programme.

I appreciate those scholars and authors who have gone before and who have written about John, perhaps especially those with whom I have disagreed, for they prompted me to write this book.

I am mindful of the congregations who have listened to me preach about John and his message. I hope it has blessed them as much as the process has helped me.

I am equally thankful for the constructive comments of friends, colleagues and the community of those who are fascinated by John and his message (Proverbs 27:6).

I am so grateful to Mark Stibbe, who gave me invaluable advice and help with the overall style of the book. And to Malcolm Down and his lovely team who have been wonderful in the way they have finally brought it to publication.

I am especially grateful for the indulgence of my family, without whom I could not have done this. Where would we be without family?

And I cannot forget all those other lovely people I met on my journey, including Louis, the French-Canadian backpacker I shared a room with in Egypt, who asked such searching questions as we climbed Mt Sinai together.

Most of all I want to thank our loving God – so beautifully revealed at Jesus' baptism as the Trinity – who reached out to me in such a tender way all those years ago. And who sent faithful John, the forerunner, with such a powerful and enduring message.

INTRODUCTION

> Among those born of women no one has arisen
> greater than John the Baptist.
> (Matthew 11:11)

Jesus spoke more highly of John than of anyone else: he declared that this wilderness preacher was among the greatest people who ever lived. Nobody is better able to make this claim than Jesus, but it is an extraordinary thing to say. And that is not the only extraordinary thing that can be said:

- He was Jesus' cousin and is one of only two people in history whose coming, like that of his cousin, was foretold by prophets and announced by angels.
- His birth was miraculous.
- As well as being hailed by Jesus among the greatest people who ever lived, Jesus also described him as a great prophet and 'more than a prophet'.[1]
- He was the first to recognise Jesus prophetically, in the womb and at the start of his ministry.
- His core prophecy was quoted by seven other towering figures of the New Testament: Jesus, Peter, Paul, Matthew, Mark, Luke and John.
- Jesus quoted John's prophecy among his last words on earth, at his ascension, to prepare his disciples for Pentecost (the original working subtitle of this book was *The Prophet of Pentecost*).
- The first words of Jesus' ministry, as Matthew recorded them, were also borrowed from John.
- With his core prophetic act of baptism in the River Jordan, John set the scene for the first and greatest Trinitarian event in

9

recorded history – the revelation and introduction of the Trinity to the world.

• He was the first martyr of the New Testament.

• He is the only saint with two saints' days in the West, and many more in the East, where he is revered almost on a par with Mary.

• He instituted a religious rite that has probably been experienced one way or another by more people in more parts of the world than any other in the history of the human race.

The different Johns

Who was he, then? Someone once said that there are many Johns, and there are. For while there is only one John, he is perceived by people in lots of different ways.

Let's start with *Orthodox John*. In the Eastern Orthodox churches, as I have already mentioned, John is venerated almost on a par with Mary, which is often reflected in icons, another unique feature of this tradition. Also different from typical Western Church traditions is the Eastern practice of baptism by immersion, of both infants and adults, which means that Eastern artistic representations of John baptizing Jesus are sometimes quite different from the ones we find for our second John, Western *Catholic John*.

Eastern *Orthodox John* and Western *Catholic John* have this in common: religious art and iconography in both traditions have been affected by stories about him that were written after the New Testament. For example, there are the legends about John that are found in the late second-century apocryphal Gospel of James that have affected images of John as a child. An even later tradition is reflected in a textual variant in Slavonic Josephus, which has influenced a stream of iconic images of John as a strange, unkempt man in ragged furry clothes – a wild-eyed desert ranter, no less (more on this in Chapter 2). *Orthodox John* and *Catholic John* have also both been influenced by *Hermit John*, who comes out of the ancient wilderness-dwelling hermit tradition, the forerunner of monasticism. In this context, John is regarded as a role model.

A Greek Orthodox Deësis icon
Christ in the centre is flanked by Mary on his right
and John on his left with hands raised in prayer.
(*Deësis* (δέησις) means prayer)[2]

Then came the Reformation in the West with its belief in *sola scriptura*. The Canonical Scriptures were to be the sole source of information on matters of faith, so later traditions – such as The Gospel of James – were rejected. *Protestant John*, then, is our third main category. Mainstream Protestantism continued what had become the Western tradition of baptizing infants by sprinkling and rejected the call of some of the radical reformers, labelled Anabaptists, for baptism by immersion.[3] The controversy around this issue became so sharp that, as we shall see later, it affected the way John's core prophecy was translated, and continues to do so to this day. *Anabaptist John* was widely suppressed.

In the latter half of the twentieth century there was an attempt at a serious revision of our understanding of John by some sceptical academics from various traditions in a quest for the historical John, a sub-strand of the ongoing highly critical quest for the historical Jesus. Since the 1950s there has been a succession of books and articles that progressively whittled away the biblical texts about John by the overapplication of a series of otherwise useful critical literary tools, so much so that there is not much left. One of these authors, having dispensed with the whole of Luke chapter 1 by these methods, declared that in the search for an account of John's infancy 'we may have to reconcile ourselves to a complete blank'.[4] By this process *Sceptic John* has almost become Non-John. He is certainly a diminished John.

Into this mix comes the nineteenth-century explorer H.B. Tristram who sought out the long-abandoned ruined hilltop fortress of Machaerus, where John was executed, and assumed – wrongly, as it transpired – that a Herodian water cistern he saw there was a subterranean dungeon in which John had been incarcerated. Oscar Wilde read about this and let loose his vivid imagination in a play called *Salome* in which his female protagonist visited John in his gloomy cell and tried to seduce him. She failed, becoming a vengeful scorned woman. This entertaining hokum has since been popularised through Richard Strauss's frequently performed operatic version of the play.

To *Opera John* we can add *Hollywood John*, and *Computer Game John*, and *Fiction John*, who appears in different guises in novels loosely based on his story. There is even a *Feminist John* or, more correctly, a feminist Salome (the victim, it is claimed, of a misogynist castration fantasy[5]).

In this veritable confusion of Johns, my book is an attempt at describing John as we find him in the pages of the New Testament, while taking a much more optimistic view of the honesty and reliability of the Gospel writers than those involved in the *Sceptic John* process. The Gospels were written by people who had either been a disciple of John, or who knew John, or who knew people who knew him well.

Time for a fresh look

This book sets out to tell John's story, trying to understand the man as well as his message, which is what the main text of the book contains. However, the telling of John's story can sometimes become a bit technical as there are occasional issues to do with translation, as well as controversies about dates, or what John meant when he told his hearers to repent, and the like. To make the book flow more easily, some of this detail has been consigned to a large number of endnotes and an appendix, containing all sorts of information that can either be studied or passed over as the reader chooses. Further material can be found in various articles on my website johnthebaptistbook.com. For ease of reference, the relevant Bible passages have been included (from the ESV unless otherwise stated) so you can read the original sources in context.

In the light of the rise of the Pentecostal and charismatic movements in the twentieth century, it is timely to take a fresh look at John's oft-quoted core prophecy in which he foresees Jesus baptizing (immersing) people in the Holy Spirit. In the process we will also examine the unhelpful, opaque, political way that this prophecy has often been translated since the Anabaptist controversy. A reappraisal is long overdue.

We are very fortunate to be looking afresh at John in the twenty-first century just as two new archaeological gems have recently become available to us. Firstly, the Archaeological Park on the east bank of the River Jordan at the actual baptism site, an exciting development made possible by the Israel-Jordan Peace Treaty of 1994. A dozen new churches are being built there. The second is the fascinating archaeological work that is currently being undertaken at the site of John's execution, which is also in Jordan. Thanks to some coins recently found in Armenia, we also, amazingly, have contemporary likenesses of Salome in her thirties and forties – the only contemporary likenesses of a women mentioned in the Bible.

On top of this, our knowledge of John's background has been greatly helped by the better understanding we now have of his priestly heritage and the first-century Jewish context in which he was raised, especially the widespread practice of ritual immersions in water. Added to the Bible witness, there is also some evidence from Josephus, the well-informed late first-century Jewish historian. He is useful to our story as he wrote directly about John and provides a good deal of background detail, including the place of his execution and Salome's name.

Everything John did and said was dedicated to his deeply felt calling to 'prepare the way of the LORD', the high point of which was, as we have noted, the first and greatest revelation of the Trinity in recorded history at Jesus' baptism.

It would fill John with joy if we, by thinking about his ministry and message, grow closer to the LORD he so faithfully served.

The one who has the bride is the bridegroom. The friend of the bridegroom, who stands and hears him, rejoices greatly at the bridegroom's voice. Therefore, this joy of mine is now complete. He must increase, but I must decrease.
(John 3:29-30)

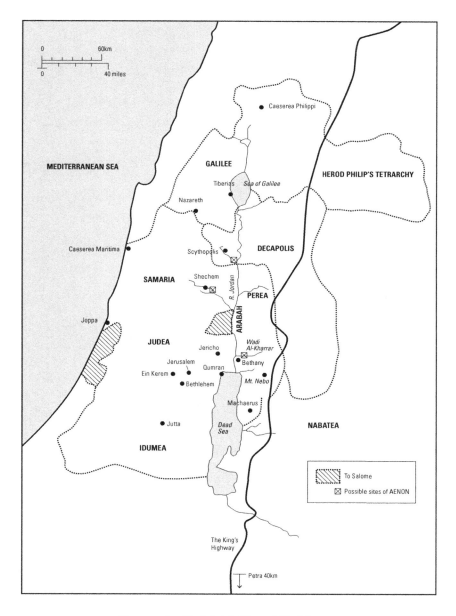

Drawn by D. McNeill and D. Negus

15

Part 1: ORIGINS

CHAPTER 1: MIRACULOUS BIRTH

The angel said to him, 'Do not be afraid, Zechariah, for your prayer
has been heard, and your wife Elizabeth will bear you a son, and
you shall call his name John.'
(Luke 1:13)

The opening scene of the New Testament features the priest Zechariah,
John's father, offering up the sweet-smelling fragrance of worship by
the Holy of Holies, the symbolic seat of God on earth.

The magnificent temple in Jerusalem had just been rebuilt – in
time for this event – on a massive scale by King Herod.[1] To run this
huge temple complex, which was considerably larger than either of
the two temples that preceded it, there was a roster of thousands
of priests and Levites, some of whom lived in the city, but most of
whom were village priests, like Zechariah, who served for a while in
their divisions and then went home.[2]

During their time on duty these priests were put on a rota, then
lots were drawn for special tasks, such as the lighting of incense
that was the culmination of the morning and evening rituals. These
rituals, which included burnt offerings on the altar of sacrifice and
the priests' ceremonial washings, ended when a priest chosen by lot –
Zechariah on this occasion – would gather embers from the altar
on a bronze shovel, and a mix of specially prepared spices, and take
them up the steps into the Holy Place, which was in the building at
the heart of the temple complex.

As he processed through the Holy Place the priest passed the table
of showbread to his right, then the seven-branched lampstand on his
left, and proceeded to the golden altar of incense that stood in front
of the curtain, or veil, that was decorated with cherubim, and which
closed off the Holy of Holies.[3]

It was here that Zechariah offered up the incense of worship and it was at this moment that the angel Gabriel, the angel of the visions of Daniel, suddenly appeared to Zechariah to the right of the golden altar. With that, the drama of the New Testament began.[4]

The Angel Appearing to Zacharias by William Blake, c. 1800.[5]

Behold, I send my messenger,[6] and he will prepare the way before me. And the Lord whom you seek will suddenly come to his temple; and the messenger of the covenant in whom you delight, behold, he is coming, says the LORD of hosts. (Malachi 3:1)

Struck dumb at the altar

Zechariah[7] was an older rural priest and, not surprisingly, was unnerved by Gabriel's dramatic appearing. After reassuring him, Gabriel told Zechariah that he was to become the father of someone of considerable significance who was to be called John. Like Mary, who was also to be visited by Gabriel in a little over five months' time, Zechariah asked how this could be. These questions were perfectly reasonable. Mary's was practical – about who was to be the father, given that she was a virgin and unmarried. Zechariah's, on the other hand, contained a doubt about whether what he had been told could happen, given his and his wife's age.

Zechariah's may not have been an unreasonable question, but the angel's message was not about reason: it was about faith. It reminds us of Genesis 15 where Abram was told that he and Sarai were to have a son in their childless old age. Abram 'believed the LORD, and he counted it to him as righteousness'.[8] For doubting him, Gabriel gave Zechariah a sign: he was rendered mute and was unable to speak until the child was born. Becoming dumbstruck when faced with an apparition of this kind is not unusual; it happened to Paul's companions on the road to Damascus. Zechariah's silence, however, was a public event that was to last nine months.

We must remember that many people would have come to the temple each day to observe these rituals, in something of the same way that people do today at, for instance, the daily incense burning ceremonies in the Church of the Holy Sepulchre in Jerusalem, the traditional site of the crucifixion and resurrection. In the temple complex in Zechariah's day, however, only men were allowed into the Court of Israelites, and only priests could enter the Court of Priests that surrounded the central building and contained the altar of sacrifice.[10] The central building was only accessible to priests performing their duties.

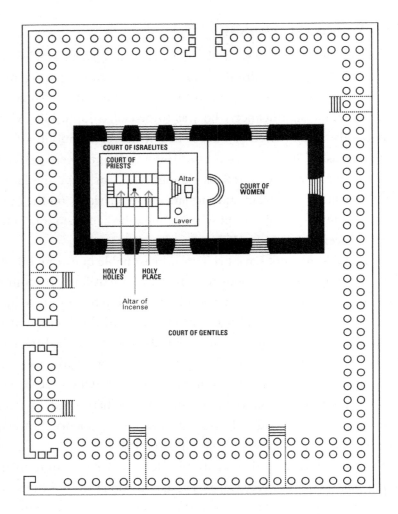

Plan of the temple at the time of Jesus.[9]

It was only priests, therefore, who would have seen this ceremony up-close and most of them would have had to wait outside while Zechariah lit the incense. It did not normally take long to perform the practised task of preparing the smouldering embers, then carefully placing the sacred mix of incense spices on the golden altar, so we can imagine this angelic encounter delaying Zechariah and the crowd of worshippers waiting outside beginning to wonder what had happened. They were startled when he did appear and was unable to speak; they knew that something dramatic had occurred.

In the days of Herod, king of Judea, there was a priest named Zechariah, of the division of Abijah. And he had a wife from the daughters of Aaron, and her name was Elizabeth. And they were both righteous before God, walking blamelessly in all the commandments and statutes of the Lord. But they had no child, because Elizabeth was barren, and both were advanced in years. Now while he was serving as priest before God when his division was on duty, according to the custom of the priesthood, he was chosen by lot to enter the temple of the Lord and burn incense. And the whole multitude of the people were praying outside at the hour of incense. And there appeared to him an angel of the Lord standing on the right side of the altar of incense. And Zechariah was troubled when he saw him, and fear fell upon him. But the angel said to him, 'Do not be afraid, Zechariah, for your prayer has been heard, and your wife Elizabeth will bear you a son, and you shall call his name John. And you will have joy and gladness, and many will rejoice at his birth, for he will be great before the Lord. And he must not drink wine or strong drink, and he will be filled with the Holy Spirit, even from his mother's womb. And he will turn many of the children of Israel to the Lord their God, and he will go before him in the spirit and power of Elijah, to turn the hearts of the fathers to the children, and the disobedient to the wisdom of the just, to make ready for the Lord a people prepared.' And Zechariah said to the angel, 'How shall I know this? For I am

an old man, and my wife is advanced in years.' And the angel answered him, 'I am Gabriel. I stand in the presence of God, and I was sent to speak to you and to bring you this good news.[11] And behold, you will be silent and unable to speak until the day that these things take place, because you did not believe my words, which will be fulfilled in their time.' And the people were waiting for Zechariah, and they were wondering at his delay in the temple. And when he came out, he was unable to speak to them, and they realized that he had seen a vision in the temple. And he kept making signs to them and remained mute. And when his time of service was ended, he went to his home. After these days his wife Elizabeth conceived, and for five months she kept herself hidden, saying, 'Thus the Lord has done for me in the days when he looked on me, to take away my reproach among people.'
(Luke 1:5-25)

Mary and Elizabeth

How did Zechariah tell his wife the news of her forthcoming pregnancy if he could not speak? It is not hard to imagine Zechariah writing it down, as he later wrote down that his son's name was John. It is not hard either to imagine that it was an extraordinary, joyful and prayerful occasion.

From then on, conception took place in the normal way. Unlike in Jesus' case, the miracle consisted of the fact that John's mother, Elizabeth, was past the normal age for bearing children. Like her husband, Elizabeth was of priestly stock and must have lived with the shame attending childlessness in those days. However, she somehow kept her condition to herself for five months, taking special care of herself and the child at home.[12]

Tradition places this home in Ein Kerem, a village in the hill country of Judah, on the fringe of the wilderness, about seven kilometres west of the old city of Jerusalem.[13] The town of Juttah (aka Yata), eight kilometres south of Hebron and more desert-like than Ein Kerem, is also thought by some to be where they lived. Although Ein Kerem is better attested, we will never know for sure because the only written record of the birthplace of John tells us that it took place in 'a town in Judah', in 'the hill country'. In trying to piece together John's life, we are going to assume he was born in the better attested place: Ein Kerem. Being only an hour and a half's walk from the temple, it is an ideal location for a rural priest to live; close enough to Jerusalem for Zechariah to be able to fulfil his temple duties, but far enough away to be out of reach of the bustle, the politics and the corruption of the city. Today, although it is still a distinct and pretty village, it is on the edge of the sprawling municipality of modern Jerusalem.

The modern village of Ein Kerem is dominated by two churches marking two significant events that took place within three months of each other.[14] The Church of the Visitation commemorates the visit Mary paid to her relative Elizabeth after the annunciation in Nazareth, during which Mary had been told that Elizabeth was also expecting a child.

And behold, your relative Elizabeth in her old age has also conceived a son, and this is the sixth month with her who was called barren. For nothing will be impossible with God.
(Luke 1:36-37)

For five months Elizabeth kept her pregnancy well concealed, so when Gabriel told Mary that Elizabeth was in her sixth month (that is, between five and six months), she was among the first to be told. It would seem, then, that God respected Elizabeth's need for privacy. Later we learn that Mary stayed with Elizabeth and Zechariah for three months before John's birth, which means that she must have arrived in Ein Kerem when Elizabeth was about six months pregnant, within a month of Jesus' annunciation.[15]

We cannot be certain about Mary and Elizabeth's relationship. The Greek word used in the Bible, *syngenes*, could be translated 'relative', 'cousin' or 'kin'.[16] In ancient times *syngenes* could just mean someone from the same tribe. However, if Jesus' genealogy in Luke 3 is about Mary's side of the family (which is one of the explanations for the differences between Luke's genealogy and the genealogy in Matthew 1), she was descended from David of the tribe of Judah while Elizabeth, as we have seen, was a descendant of Aaron of the tribe of Levi. This would mean that the connection between them was more than tribal. Since they were closely enough related to each other for Elizabeth to be identified to Mary simply as 'your relative Elizabeth', with no further explanations or patronymics, it is commonly assumed that they were cousins of some kind.

One possible scenario is that a sister of one of Mary's parents married a man from the tribe of Levi and this couple became Elizabeth's parents, which would make Mary and Elizabeth first cousins. Or, given the age difference, it could have been a sister of one of Mary's grandparents who married a Levite, which would make Elizabeth a first cousin of one of Mary's parents, making Mary and Elizabeth first cousins once removed.[17] This sort of scenario would make Elizabeth 'from the daughters of Aaron', as Luke says, but still related to Mary.[18]

The visitation

Matthew records some of the concerns that Joseph felt when Mary recounted her story to him. She was now a teenage unmarried mother. In a religious community like Nazareth in first-century

Galilee, she could have been stoned for having sexual intercourse before marriage.[19] Joseph's first reaction was that he could not marry her, but that he would take care of her in the time-honoured way, by sending her away to have the baby. It was not until God sent him a dream to reassure him that he and Mary did get married.

Matthew's Gospel, which recounts this story, says he 'took his wife', but does not tell us when the wedding took place. Luke's Gospel tells us that they were still betrothed when they were in Bethlehem.[20] Given this, it is a reasonable assumption that the marriage took place on the quiet at some point while they stayed there, where they had extended family. As a priest, Zechariah, who lived just eight kilometres from Bethlehem, could easily have made the arrangements for them. Having heard the angel mentioning Elizabeth's news at the annunciation, Mary will have urgently wanted to go and see her, and by sending Mary away to stay with Elizabeth, Joseph – presumably with the agreement of her parents – was protecting her in the prudent way that had originally occurred to him.

When Mary arrived at Elizabeth's house she had had a very emotional and exhausting time: the annunciation, sorting matters out with Joseph, planning with him what to do, not to mention embarking on a journey which, even travelling the most direct route via Samaria and Jerusalem, is more than 100 kilometres. All this while in the early stages of pregnancy. As she journeyed south she must have mulled all these things over and over in her mind, trying to make sense of it all. After her experience with Joseph she must also have wondered what sort of reception she would get when she arrived in Ein Kerem. What she really must have needed was some reassurance in the form of a welcoming and secure home-from-home with people who perfectly understood her situation. She got all that and more while staying with Elizabeth and Zechariah. It was their early contribution to preparing the way of the LORD.

In those days Mary arose and went with haste into the hill country, to a town in Judah, and she entered the house of Zechariah and greeted Elizabeth. And when Elizabeth heard the greeting of Mary, the baby leaped in her womb. And Elizabeth was filled with the Holy Spirit, and she exclaimed with a loud cry, 'Blessed are you among women, and blessed is the fruit of your womb! And why is this granted to me that the mother of my Lord should come to me? For behold, when the sound of your greeting came to my ears, the baby in my womb leaped for joy. And blessed is she who believed that there would be a fulfilment of what was spoken to her from the Lord.'
(Luke 1:39-45)

This meeting of the mothers, known as the visitation, is one of the most tender moments recorded in Scripture. Elizabeth's beautiful, uplifting and encouraging greeting contained one of the most profound, insightful and joyous prophecies in the whole Bible. It was the perfect reassurance for Mary. This prophecy was prompted by John's reaction in the womb; he leaped, which surely signifies something more than a normal foetal movement. This unborn child, filled with the Spirit while still in his mother's womb, as Gabriel had said at his annunciation, was the first unprompted person to recognise the Christ, who was himself unborn. It was this Spirit-filled greeting from John and Elizabeth that provided the setting for Mary's inspirational outpouring that we know as the Magnificat.[21]

The Magnificat

And Mary said, 'My soul magnifies the Lord, and my spirit rejoices in God my Saviour, for he has looked on the humble estate of his servant. For behold, from now on all generations will call me blessed; for he who is mighty has done great things for me, and holy is his name. And his mercy is for those who fear him from generation to generation. He has shown strength with his arm; he has scattered the proud in the thoughts of their hearts; he has brought down the mighty from their thrones and exalted those of humble estate; he has filled the hungry with good things, and the rich he has sent away empty. He has helped his servant Israel, in remembrance of his mercy, as he spoke to our fathers, to Abraham and to his offspring for ever.' (Luke 1:46-55)

If you visit the Church of the Visitation in Ein Kerem you will find in the courtyard a moving modern statue depicting this meeting of Mary and Elizabeth. You will also find scores of wall mosaics, each one with the Magnificat in a different language.

It is left to our imagination to wonder what it was like in Zechariah's household for the last three months of Elizabeth's pregnancy. Between their everyday domestic and community responsibilities, the expectant Mary and Elizabeth will surely have done a lot of praying and talking about their soon-to-be born sons. Zechariah was unable to speak, but he was an experienced priest who had been theologically trained so one can imagine him poring over the Scriptures – housed in the local synagogue – and contributing to the discussion by pointing out the many prophecies about the Messiah and his forerunner. This is a process that must have begun with John's annunciation and conception. They were insightful, prophetically gifted, Bible-drenched, prayerful people and this time together will have given them the opportunity to try to gain some understanding of what God's plan might be for Mary's child and his forerunner. It must have been a time of rich reflection and constant wondering.

Church of the Visitation, Ein Kerem. [22]
Mercy and truth have met together;
righteousness and peace have kissed.
(Psalm 85:10 NKJV)

What's in a name?

The other major church in Ein Kerem today is the Church of Saint John the Baptist, which was built to commemorate his birth.[23]

Eight days after he was born, his naming ceremony took place at his circumcision, where there was something of a debate about the choice of his name. When the angel Gabriel had appeared before Zechariah to announce the coming of John, he had been very specific: 'You shall call his name John.' John is *Yohanan* in Hebrew, or *Ioannēs* when transliterated into the Greek of the New Testament.[24] When it came to the naming, Elizabeth was obedient to the angel and said that his name was to be John, but then their neighbours and relatives protested that it was not a family name and insisted on checking with Zechariah. The village priest was still dumbstruck. He therefore asked for writing equipment. 'His name is John,' he insisted,[25] whereupon he was suddenly able to speak again. Filled with the Holy Spirit, he launched into the prophetic outpouring that we know as the Benedictus.

The narrative leaves us in no doubt that the name is important, so let us examine it. The name of Elijah, the Old Testament prophet in whose spirit John was to conduct his ministry, has a bearing on John's name. In Elijah's day, the greatest challenge he faced was the encroachment of idolatry into the religious life of the northern kingdom of Israel during the days of the divided monarchy. His name (*Eliyahu* in Hebrew), which means 'My God is Yahweh (or Jehovah)', is a clear statement of intent concerning his prophetic ministry. It sent an unmistakable signal about Elijah's loyalties.

John's prophetic role was to prepare the way of the LORD, and since 'the LORD' is 'Yahweh' (or 'Jehovah') in the Hebrew of Isaiah 40:3, and the LORD was to usher in an age of grace, *Yohanan* means 'Yahweh (or Jehovah) brings grace'.[26]

In the same way that Elijah's name was indicative of his ministry, so John's name can be seen as a pointer to his prophetic role as the forerunner and the herald of the one who was to usher in the age of grace.[27]

These stories about John were often repeated in the communities in the hill country round about as folk speculated about the nature of the child who had just been born in such startling circumstances.

> And Mary remained with her about three months and returned to her home.
>
> Now the time came for Elizabeth to give birth, and she bore a son. And her neighbours and relatives heard that the Lord had shown great mercy to her, and they rejoiced with her. And on the eighth day they came to circumcise the child. And they would have called him Zechariah after his father, but his mother answered, 'No; he shall be called John.' And they said to her, 'None of your relatives is called by this name.' And they made signs to his father, enquiring what he wanted him to be called. And he asked for a writing tablet and wrote, 'His name is John.' And they all wondered. And immediately his mouth was opened and his tongue loosed, and he spoke, blessing God. And fear came on all their neighbours. And all these things were talked about through all the hill country of Judea, and all who heard them laid them up in their hearts, saying, 'What then will this child be?' For the hand of the Lord was with him.
> (Luke 1:56-66)

It is a curious idiosyncrasy of the style of Luke's Gospel that, for reasons that suit his wider narrative, he tells us that John was incarcerated before he records Jesus' baptism,[28] and here he tells us that Mary returned to her home before he records John's birth. However, just as John was, of course, present at Jesus' baptism before he was arrested, we also know that Mary arrived in Ein Kerem when Elizabeth was about six months into her pregnancy and then stayed for three months, which means that it is very likely that she was present at John's birth, before going home. Given all that had happened she would certainly want to be there for the birth – why else did she stay until Elizabeth had reached full term? Mary and Elizabeth must have grown very close during their time together and it will have been perfectly natural for Mary to have been present at the birth as a kind of birth partner; it will have helped her to prepare for giving birth in five months' time.

Birth of John: the child being bathed, by Pinturicchio (1454-1513)[29]

A father's blessing

The walls of the courtyard of the Church of Saint John the Baptist are covered with mosaics in many languages containing Zechariah's Benedictus, that other great paean of praise from this story, which to this day is included in many liturgies of morning prayer.[30]

The Benedictus[31]

And his father Zechariah was filled with the Holy Spirit and prophesied, saying, 'Blessed be the Lord God of Israel, for he has visited and redeemed his people and has raised up a horn of salvation for us in the house of his servant David, as he spoke by the mouth of his holy prophets from of old, that we should be saved from our enemies and from the hand of all who hate us; to show the mercy promised to our fathers and to remember his holy covenant, the oath that he swore to our father Abraham, to grant us that we, being delivered from the hand of our enemies, might serve him without fear, in holiness and righteousness before him all our days. And you, child, will be called the prophet of the Most High; for you will go before the Lord to prepare his ways, to give knowledge of salvation to his people in the forgiveness of their sins, because of the tender mercy of our God, whereby the sunrise shall visit us from on high to give light to those who sit in darkness and in the shadow of death, to guide our feet into the way of peace.'
(Luke 1:67-79)

This utterance is another beautiful and profound prophecy. It has a strikingly Old Testament feel to it and it is clear, and not surprising, that Zechariah did not fully understand at this point what his son was later to say and do, although he clearly understood that he was to be a prophet and the one who was to prepare the way of the LORD, as he quotes from the relevant text from Isaiah.[32]

When Zechariah talked about God remembering his covenant he was referring to the old covenant (or testament) as we now understand it, and this is the only time the word 'covenant' is used in the Gospels in relation to the old covenant. John, however, was going to be the herald of the new covenant prophesied by Jeremiah.[33] John must have learned much from his parents, but his prophetic work had far-reaching implications that were going to change Zechariah's world and the covenant that he valued so much.

There is an article on the website johnthebaptistbook.com that describes a scenario in which Mary went to live in Bethlehem after John's birth rather than returning to Nazareth, which would allow her to stay within just two hours walking distance of Elizabeth and Zechariah, as well as stay well out of the way of gossip and danger in Nazareth. It is a scenario that is worth considering, but whether Mary did spend the last five months of her pregnancy with relatives in Bethlehem, close by her older cousin Elizabeth, or whether she really did make the Christmas-card journey on a donkey from Nazareth to Bethlehem while heavily pregnant, John and Jesus were born just five months and five miles apart within the same extended family, and Jesus, while in Mary's womb, was very likely present at the birth of John.

Two unique births

It is Luke's Gospel that gives us the interwoven infancy narratives of both Jesus and John with deliberate parallels between the two. For instance, 'you shall call his name John' (1:13) is echoed by, 'you shall call his name Jesus' (1:31) and both boys 'grew and became strong' (1:80 and 2:40)[34] and both have angelic annunciations.

While it is flattering for John to be compared to Jesus, there are significant differences in the two accounts as well. For example, Jesus is conceived by the Holy Spirit in a virgin and born to the accompaniment of angels and awestruck shepherds (and a star and worshipping Magi in Matthew's Gospel). Mary's faith at the annunciation is impeccable while Zechariah is struck dumb, and there is considerably more detail for Jesus.

John's birth was a miraculous birth, just as Isaac's, Samson's and Samuel's were, he was 'a man sent from God',[35] but there was something else that set it apart from anyone else's. Of all the people known to us in history – and remember, Jesus said there is none greater than John[36] – only two have had their coming foretold hundreds of years in advance. One of these, of course, is Jesus himself, about whom there were scores of prophecies about many details in his life. The other is John the Baptist. The prophecies relating to him all concern his role as the person who was to prepare the way of the LORD and they played a powerful part in shaping his life and ministry. The core texts are these:

Behold, I send my messenger, and he will prepare the way before me. And the Lord whom you seek will suddenly come to his temple; and the messenger of the covenant in whom you delight, behold, he is coming, says the LORD of hosts. (Malachi 3:1)[37]

Behold, I will send you Elijah the prophet before the great and awesome day of the LORD comes. And he will turn the hearts of fathers to their children and the hearts of children to their fathers, lest I come and strike the land with a decree of utter destruction. (Malachi 4:5-6)[38]

The voice of one crying in the wilderness: 'Prepare the way of
the LORD;
Make straight in the desert
A highway for our God.
Every valley shall be exalted
And every mountain and hill brought low;
The crooked places shall be made straight
And the rough places smooth;
The glory of the LORD shall be revealed,
And all flesh shall see *it* together;
For the mouth of the LORD has spoken.'
The voice said, 'Cry out!'
And he said, 'What shall I cry?'
'All flesh is grass,
And all its loveliness is like the flower of the field.
The grass withers, the flower fades,
Because the breath of the LORD blows upon it;
Surely the people are grass.
The grass withers, the flower fades,
But the word of our God stands forever.'
O Zion, you who bring good tidings,
Get up into the high mountain; O Jerusalem,
You who bring good tidings,
Lift up your voice with strength,
Lift *it* up, be not afraid;
Say to the cities of Judah, 'Behold your God!'
(Isaiah 40:3-9, NKJV)[39]

The first part of the book of Isaiah deals with issues that were mainly
contemporary to the prophet, but then, from chapter 40 onwards, the

style and subject matter of his prophecy both change as the idea of the suffering servant is introduced.[40]

It is no coincidence that John's commissioning text comes at the very beginning of this section that introduces the suffering servant in Isaiah just as John himself introduced the suffering servant in real life.

As we shall see, these prophecies played a major part in preparing John for his life's work.

He was 'The voice' who was to prepare the way for 'the Word'.[41] The 'word of our God will stand for ever'.[42]

CHAPTER 2: THE WILDERNESS YEARS

And the child grew and became strong in spirit,
and he was in the wilderness until the day of
his public appearance to Israel.
(Luke 1:80)

All we know about the life of John during the thirty or so years after his infancy is contained within this last verse of Luke chapter 1 (above). Not surprisingly, this has led to endless speculation, this one verse becoming a magnet for mythmakers.

For example, there is a legend, found in a section of the less than reliable late second-century apocryphal Gospel of James – a section that is thought by some not even to be part of the original text – that claims that Herod's troops also tried to kill John when they looked for the infant Jesus, but Elizabeth whisked him away from Ein Kerem and hid with him in a cave in what is now called Even Sappir, about three kilometres away as the crow flies.[1] This is largely uncultivated hill country that just about qualifies as Judean wilderness. In this legend, Zechariah refused to tell the soldiers where to find John, so they killed him. John then grew up in the cave with his mother. Even Sappir is an evocative place and there are several caves there: one was, until recently, occupied by an eremite; another, with claims to be where Elizabeth is buried, has a crusader building above it which currently houses a silent order of nuns; another has a monastery above it.[2]

Another version of John's story is that his parents, being older, died when he was young. John was then dramatically cast adrift to grow up in the wilderness alone. There are numerous artistic impressions of a wild and solitary young John in the wilderness. More recently, some have speculated that some Essenes may have adopted the orphaned

John and raised him in an Essene wilderness community, perhaps Qumran.[3] This is the interpretation preferred by those who advocate a strong link between John and Qumran, which is discussed later in this chapter.

Was John an orphan?

The idea that John was orphaned and either grew up alone in the wilderness or was taken in by Essenes has weaknesses, one being that the normal way of taking care of orphans in first-century Jewish society, as it is in most societies, was for the extended family to take them in. We know that John's extended family included Mary and Joseph but was wider than just them.[4] If John's parents died when he was young he would have been looked after by his family.

Having said that, is there anything in the text to suggest that John was orphaned? This brings us to the question of Zechariah and Elizabeth's life expectancy. In the ancient world people generally lived shorter lives than in the developed world today, but there were people who lived to a great age. Elizabeth must have been at least in her mid-forties when John was conceived because Luke describes her as 'barren' and 'well advanced in years'.[5] Zechariah was probably just as old. They will have been at least in their mid-sixties if they lived until John was twenty, and this is perfectly feasible. They could have made it to their three score years and ten, or even older.

Then there is the question of whether John lived in the wilderness all his life. The grammar of the Greek text of Luke 1:80 does not tell us how the first part of the verse, which describes John as a child, is linked to the last part of the verse, which describes him as an adult in the wilderness. Some say that John lived in the wilderness all his life, and others say he went there as an adult to prepare for his public ministry, having not been there as a child. While we can never know for sure, we do know that John was the son of a priest and that he was born in the family home, probably in Ein Kerem. To which we can add a bit of often overlooked internal evidence suggesting that he had an ongoing strong relationship with his father. John's commissioning text in Malachi 4:6 stresses the importance of the relationship of fathers to sons and sons to fathers, and so did Gabriel at John's annunciation. Since our family loving God went to such trouble to have the priestly Zechariah as John's father it seems very likely that he arranged it so that John had a good relationship with him as he grew up. At his annunciation the angel told his father that John, 'Will be a joy and delight to you', and we can think of him like that as he grew up with his parents in Ein Kerem.[6] It makes more sense of John's eventual message and ministry, as we shall see, if he came from this sort of background and intentionally chose to go to the wilderness himself as an adult. There was no need for him to have gone when he was younger, and it is more probable that he did not.

Legends about John

Given that the tale about John being orphaned appears in a late second-century document, we should pause to consider later witnesses to the life of John. There is good reason for putting aside these later stories when trying to discern the details of John's life and message, beyond simply the *sola scriptura* principle mentioned in the Introduction. This is because they are late, more than a century after the events, and in some cases several centuries. They are too far removed from the actual events to be considered reliable.

The Quran briefly mentions John, and the Mandeans, a Middle Eastern gnostic sect, have some writings about him, but both of these texts are from a much later period – more than half a millennium later.[7]

Josephus has some useful information that adds to our knowledge, even though he was born after John's time.[8] However, there is some additional material in some fifteenth and sixteenth-century manuscripts of Josephus' *Jewish War* in the Slavonic (Old Russian) translation, thought to date from the twelfth or thirteenth century, that describes John as a 'wild man', 'like a wild animal' and clothed with 'animal hides on his body everywhere'.[9] These emendations are certainly not authentic, but they have nevertheless inspired some striking images of John in a strand of the Russian icon tradition. There are other artistic representations of John wearing fur that predate this Russian medieval myth and these have together shaped the way that he has sometimes been portrayed in more recent art and films. It is an artistic tradition that has unhelpfully influenced the popular romanticised perception of John as a wild, fur-clad, unkempt man. We shall see later in the chapter that John's camel-hair coat was very different to this.

I mentioned in the Introduction that Catholic and Orthodox religious art and iconography of John have sometimes been influenced by later, extra-biblical traditions. And we have just seen an example of how the medium of art has in turn come to affect popular perceptions of John. If you are interested in this process there is an article on 'The Symbolism John the Baptist in Art' on my website johnthebaptistbook.com.

These later legends are colourful and have their adherents, but there is nothing in the record of John's early life to suggest that he was raised other than as the much-loved, only son of older, godly parents in the picturesque village of Ein Kerem, and this is what I propose in this chapter. In what follows, we are going to look at the life influences that John probably experienced in that setting, and at the way those life influences appear to have impacted his message and ministry. It was from this environment that God called him to put aside his personal life – the chance of marriage and children – and drew him away from the relative comfort of home life in Ein

Kerem to go off instead to the rigours of the wilderness and the dangers of a prophetic ministry. Like Elijah, who suddenly appeared out of the desert and proclaimed a drought to King Ahab, or like the enigmatic Melchizedek who just appeared from nowhere to be a priest to Abraham, John just appeared one day in the wilderness.[11]

Saint John the Baptist
by El Greco (Doménikos Theotokópoulos), c. 1600.[10]

John's priestly background

What were the life influences that prepared John for such a calling? He was an only son, yes, but he was also part of the social life of the village. We catch a glimpse of this when we see the people of the village involved at John's circumcision and naming ceremony. This shows that he most likely grew up in this setting, with the other children of the village.

John also had an extended family. Elizabeth, as discussed in the previous chapter, most likely had a mother or grandmother from the tribe of Judah, related to Mary's family, who married a priest from the tribe of Levi. John 19:25 tells us that Mary had at least one sibling – a sister – and as Mary's family roots appear to be in Bethlehem it is possible that Elizabeth had extended family there too, not least because Bethlehem is just eight kilometres from Ein Kerem. As already noted, we learn from Luke 1:58 that Elizabeth's relatives, wherever they lived, were present at John's circumcision. Zechariah's family may well have come from Ein Kerem and whatever extended family he may have had will also have played a part in John's upbringing.

John's mother and father, and other family members and friends, would have told John at some appropriate time about the stories of his birth as recorded in Luke chapter 1. He would also have known Mary and Joseph and heard their stories about the infancy of Jesus, and he will have known Jesus all his life; the families will almost certainly have spent time together when they attended the three annual festivals at Jerusalem – Passover, Pentecost and Tabernacles.[12] These stories cannot fail to have had a major influence on John and his thinking. For example, the angel Gabriel at his annunciation told Zechariah that John would go in the spirit and power of Elijah, and his father's prophecy, the Benedictus, says that John would be a prophet going before the Lord to prepare his ways, a reference to Isaiah 40, John's commissioning text.[13]

Since Jesus and John knew each other all their lives, and their families will have come together several times a year, it does not take much imagination to picture them as two little boys of a similar age running round together at these family gatherings. It does not take much imagination either to see that John – an only child – could have thought of Jesus as the brother he never had: his brother from another mother, as the saying goes. As teenagers and young men in their twenties and early thirties they had plenty of opportunity to hang out together (for the ages of John and Jesus when they began their ministries, see the Appendix). Surely, at times they discussed theology, prophecy, the kingdom of God and the like. It may be speculative to say this, but it is very likely.

John's family was a priestly family. As well as his father, he may have had uncles who were priests. At least one of his grandfathers had been a priest, quite possibly both since Luke 1:5 suggests that Elizabeth was born to a priestly family. John had a priestly heritage and there would therefore have been an expectation that he would follow his father into the priesthood. In fact, it would have been unusual in those days for an eldest son – in this case the only son – not to follow his father's profession. Turning his back on his duty to continue the priestly line was not a decision he will have taken lightly.[14]

There is a possibility, even a probability, that John may have begun his priestly training. He certainly would have been very familiar with the various duties, customs and practices of the priesthood. He would have known the local synagogue very well, in which his father will have played an important part as the village priest. He will have known the temple too, with all its glories and corruptions. By the time he began his ministry, the high priesthood had become a political appointment by the Romans.[15] To a diligent and upright man like John's father, and to John himself, these corruptions – and no doubt there were others too, along the lines of Malachi's lament – would have been a real disappointment, but by living in rural Ein Kerem rather than in the city he could distance himself from these problems.[16]

While we are thinking about the priestly background of John's family, we should consider the angel's instruction at his annunciation that 'he must not drink wine or strong drink.'[17] There are commentators who assume from this that John was a Nazirite, and this is sometimes reflected in artistic representations of John.[18] Nazirites are described in Numbers 6:1-21, and verse 3 includes the instruction that a Nazirite, 'shall separate himself from wine and strong drink'. It is also sometimes suggested that there are (faint) echoes of Samson's and Samuel's birth narratives in John's, and that they too were Nazirites. The flaw in these assumptions is that it is never stated about Samson or Samuel – or John – that they were Nazirites. And it is a big leap from an instruction not to drink wine or strong drink to assuming that John was a Nazirite. A much better explanation, one that Zechariah would have understood well as he stood in the heart of the temple, is the instruction in Leviticus 10:9 to Aaron, and to all priests that follow him, that they should, 'Drink no wine or strong drink ... when you go into the tent of meeting ...' This is especially so as the angel's words as recorded in Greek are almost a direct quote from that Leviticus verse as found in the third-century BC Septuagint Greek version of the Old Testament. John may not have become a priest, but he was to follow this priestly instruction and live his whole life as if he were a priest on duty in the temple.

A culture of ritual washing

In the inner court of the temple, where the altar of sacrifice was found, there was a huge bronze laver for the ritual cleansing of priests.[19] By New Testament times these cleansings had become a highly ritualised part of a priest's daily life while on duty; priests would bathe after any kind of ritual impurity and even before meals. It is very likely that Zechariah would have explained the ritualism and symbolism of all this to John, who was no doubt fascinated by it all. Just as interesting to John, though, and very relevant to his later prophetic baptisms, will have been the ritual immersions in water that were practised by the wider Jewish population. They were the regular, even daily practice of many observant Jews of his day. A river was perfect for these immersions, but if none was available, they took place in a *mikvah*, which is not dissimilar in form to what we would call a baptistery, although the function is very different. Archaeologists have unearthed scores of these from this period in Jerusalem and all over the country.[20]

As with all things Jewish, there were numerous regulations concerning the proper construction of a *mikvah*: it had to be in contact with the ground (so it cannot be a bath on legs) and should contain at least forty *se'ahs* of water (which is about 750 litres, although estimates vary) and the water had to be running water.[21] This last requirement meant that drawn water would not do and there were elaborate rituals that had to be performed if the water became contaminated, and so forth. The baptismal pool at the Monastery of St John of the Desert in Even Sappir,[22] close to Ein Kerem – being constantly filled by a crystal-clear spring – is ideal. A person entering a *mikvah* must be naked, although Josephus recorded the practice of preserving modesty in a public *mikvah* by keeping some garments on.[23] Communal *mikva'ot* had rails to separate those coming out from those going in, to reduce the chance of being made impure by bodily contact. Ritual immersion is known as *tevilah* in Hebrew.

First-century communal *mikvah* in the Jerusalem
Archaeological Park.[24]

The genesis of the practice is found in the first five books of the Bible
that the Jews call the Torah – in Leviticus 11-15 in particular – and
is to be understood in the context of ritual impurity. Ritual impurity
was, and still is, important to Jews, with different traditions placing
more or less importance on it. As some branches of Judaism have
added all sorts of extra regulations, it has become a somewhat
complicated subject.[25] The essential idea behind it is that there are
some things that are thought to be distasteful to God, therefore one
should wash oneself ritually clean of them before expecting to come
into his presence.

Ritual impurity is not the same as moral impurity (sin). It is also
unavoidable. For example, a woman becomes impure during her

monthly cycle and after childbirth. A man is impure after emitting semen. One also becomes impure after contact with a corpse, or when contracting certain skin conditions, or by simply touching someone else who is impure, which is why in Jesus' day many observant Jews would wash after going to the market just in case such contact had taken place.[26]

It was also common for people to immerse themselves before going to the temple. Priests were required to be fastidious about these things, hence the huge laver. It is thought, too, that the rituals of the Day of Atonement (*Yom Kippur*) were partly to do with cleansing the temple from any incidental ritual uncleanness of the previous year.[27] Some impurity conditions required more than just *tevilah;* they required a blood sacrifice in which the sacrificial carcass was then burned in a fire as a burnt offering. Childbirth and leprosy are examples of blood and fire being needed for full ritual cleansing, and there is reference to both in the New Testament.[28]

This concept of ritual impurity, as well as the practice of immersion in water for cleansing, was deeply imbedded in the Judaism that John and Jesus imbibed as they grew up. These ideas are strange for Christians because, as we shall see in Chapter 4, John changed both the practice and our understanding of water immersion, and then Jesus changed our whole approach to purity.

The custom of fasting

John would have learned about fasting from his observant priestly family and very probably made a practice of it himself as he grew up. He certainly did during his ministry, and while we do not know the details, we do have a record that he taught his disciples to fast as did the Pharisees.[29] Whether this means that they fasted and so did the Pharisees, or that they fasted in the same way that the Pharisees fasted, is a moot point. If it was the latter we know from Luke 18:12

of a Pharisee who fasted twice a week, but we do not know if this was the normal practice of all Pharisees, although there is some later evidence to suggest that it was a fairly widespread custom.[30] We cannot, therefore, say that John taught his disciples to fast twice a week, just that he might have done. His own diet was the austere fare of a wilderness dweller, to which he added the rigours of fasting, and it is entirely likely that, like Moses, Daniel and Jesus, he also engaged in a long period of fasting in preparation for his ministry.

After his baptism, Jesus fasted for forty days in the wilderness. Nevertheless, he was very aware that his followers would not feel the need to fast while he was with them, so he taught them that while he – the bridegroom – was with them they should not do so. The time would come when people would fast, which was after he was taken from them.

Fasting is an age-old spiritual discipline and an important one for Christians who follow Jesus' example and teaching, which was that people should, on occasion, fast when they pray.[31] Some follow the pattern of John and the Pharisees and fast in a regular disciplined way, such as on Fridays and in Lent, while others follow the example that Jesus seemed to set and are more flexible, fasting as the need arises. Some do both.

Now John's disciples and the Pharisees were fasting. And people came and said to him, 'Why do John's disciples and the disciples of the Pharisees fast, but your disciples do not fast?' And Jesus said to them, 'Can the wedding guests fast while the bridegroom is with them? As long as they have the bridegroom with them, they cannot fast. The days will come when the bridegroom is taken away from them, and then they will fast in that day.' (Mark 2:18-20, cf. Matthew 9:14-15; Luke 5:33-35)

Was John an Essene?

Since the discovery of the Dead Sea Scrolls in 1947, Qumran has gripped the imaginations of many people. Qumran is generally, although not universally, thought to be an Essene community and opinions are divided about whether John had anything to do with them or not. There are those who maintain that he was a member of the community, or at least a novice. Others think he had nothing to do with the community at all. Then there are those in-between who think he probably had some contact with the community, or with individual members of it, or some other Essene group at some point, but whatever contact he had was irrevocably broken by the time he began his ministry.

It is likely that John would have made it his business at least to know about Essenism, as he would have made it his business to know about every branch of first-century Judaism. An effective communicator needs to understand the thinking, practices and language of his audience, and Qumran was just half a day's walk from the place where John carried out his baptisms.

It is thought that the Essenes exercised a brief period of influence in the temple during the early stages of Herod the Great's reign and John's father was probably old enough to remember this. Herod favoured the Essenes since the time when he was a boy and an Essene called Menahem addressed him prophetically as 'King of the Jews'.[32]

The more that we know about the community at Qumran, however – and the literature covering it is vast – the more we can see that any similarities with John are superficial. In summary, the similarities that have been noted are:

Immersions in water: At Qumran these were self-administered, normally without clothes on, by initiates after being at the community for a year, and thereafter regularly before each meal like the temple priests (Qumran meals were communal affairs open only to those who were fully part of the community, and in good standing). Although ritual purity of this kind was already common among Jews of John's time, the Essenes were, in general, much stricter about it. In contrast, John's baptism was open to all. Following repentance, it was administered in some way by John. It may (or may not) have been a once-only baptism, and it had a symbolic meaning to do with the work of the one who was to come – or the Coming One as some translators render it – as we shall see in the next chapter.

Holy Spirit: It was the Essenes who first taught that the Holy Spirit was somehow a separate entity from God and had detached itself from the temple, because of corruption, to be where their community was. The Qumran literature also includes the idea of the Spirit being poured out. John went further than this and taught that the Coming One would immerse people in the Holy Spirit (a sign of which was water immersion). This was a major difference, one that would lead ultimately to the doctrine of the Holy Spirit as the third person of the Trinity.

The wilderness and Isaiah 40:3-5a:

The voice of one crying in the wilderness:
'Prepare the way of the LORD;
Make straight in the desert
A highway for our God.
Every valley shall be exalted
And every mountain and hill brought low;
The crooked places shall be made straight
And the rough places smooth;
The glory of the LORD shall be revealed ...'
(NKJV)

The Qumran community saw itself as the voice of Isaiah 40 crying in the wilderness to prepare the way of the LORD, just as John did. The Qumranites, however, were expecting people to join them, whereas John wanted people to repent, return to their homes and occupations and to prepare for the Coming One. John's was a voice crying in the wilderness, 'Prepare the way of the LORD ...', whereas the Qumran community was a voice crying, 'In the wilderness prepare the way of the LORD ...'[33] The fact that John identified Jesus, a man, with the expected LORD of Isaiah 40, i.e. with Yahweh (or Jehovah), is a definite departure from anything anyone else in Judaism could have done, including the Qumranites, and makes John the first to see the divine/human nature of Jesus.

Messiah: The people of Qumran expected a Messiah to come soon, one who was to set up a new kingdom with Elijah as his herald. But while the Qumranites expected the kingdom to come imminently to vindicate them, John proclaimed that it had already come near and expected it to focus on the Coming One, whom he identified at his baptism as Jesus.

Community: The Qumranites thought that the road to salvation lay in joining their community. There were other Essene communities that taught a similar thing and only a few Essenes continued to live in towns in families. In contrast, John taught people to live ethical lives and return to their own communities to expect the Coming One. Although he had disciples, he did not try to start an exclusive movement.

Diet: One theory about John is that he was two years into his noviciate when he decided to leave the community.[34] Because of the vows he would have already taken by this stage this meant he could not eat with others and had to survive through his own self-sufficiency in the wilderness.[35] This, so the theory goes, explains his strange diet of locusts and wild honey. There are, however, other explanations for his diet, as we shall see. Qumran community meals were of bread and wine but, according to Jesus, John ate neither bread nor wine.[36]

Geography: John baptized only fourteen kilometres from the Qumran site, half a day's walk. Both chose this area for biblical reasons, especially Isaiah 40:3, and Ezekiel 47, which describes a visionary river that was to flow into the Arabah, where both sites were located. John's reasons were more complex, however, as we shall see in the next chapter.

Celibacy: Many Essenes were celibate, but not all. Some say it was this Essene influence on John that caused him to be celibate, although there are other reasons for such a man to remain unmarried.[37]

Predestination: This is where John parts company with the Qumranites in a big way. They were strict predestinarians and judged people by their lifestyle as well as their physical characteristics and according to a person's astrological birth sign. There was no way for someone who was predestined to be of the House of Darkness to become a member of the House of Light. This is diametrically opposed to John's inclusive view and his preaching of a message of repentance to everyone, although he recognised that some were not going to heed his message.

As we can see above, not one of these superficial similarities connects John to Qumran. To this list we can add the fact that the people of Qumran wore white while John wore a camel-hair garment. One commentator summed it up by saying, 'None of the [Qumran] scrolls contains writings that could be said to relate to John's activities in any way.'[38]

As well as the Essenes and the Pharisees, Sadducees, Zealots and Herodians – who we know from the pages of the New Testament – there were numerous other sects in first-century Judaism. Among these there were some groups that focused on immersion in water, mainly around the River Jordan. The Essenes fall into this general category, including Qumran, but there were non-Essene water-immersionist groups as well. Epiphanius (who may not be entirely reliable) mentions a sect of the Nasarenes (not to be confused with the Christian Nazarenes), and another group known as the Hemerobaptists. Hegesippus makes passing reference to the Masbotheans, and the Talmud (written years later) refers to the morning bathers, a group of strict ritual immersionists. There were other baptist groups after John's time, such as the one led by Banus, who influenced Josephus, and the Ebionites.[39] As with the Qumranites, John would probably have known about these groups and been familiar with their teachings, but he was quite distinct from them. It is significant that he was the only one, as far as we know, to have been called 'the Baptist', by both Christians and Jews, which is an indication of the uniqueness of his ministry.[40]

The development of a prophet

John's upbringing would have been literate; he would have been well-versed in Scripture and the written and oral rabbinic traditions of his day through his father, his family and others in his home town, especially in the synagogue, and in Jerusalem. He would have been very aware of biblical passages such as Isaiah 40 and Malachi 3 and 4, for example, which had a particular influence on him, and he is very likely to have discussed these at length with his priestly father. Very probably with Jesus as well. He would also have been familiar with other imagery connected with the temple and the priesthood, such as the vision of the river flowing from the heart of the temple (where his annunciation took place) recorded in Ezekiel 47, for this almost certainly had an influence on his choice of baptismal site. We have already seen how this text influenced the location of Qumran, and we will discuss it more in the next chapter.

On top of all the family, priestly, religious and scriptural influences on John's life, Luke tells us that he was also a prophet full of the Holy Spirit from his mother's womb.

Jesus said that John was 'more than a prophet' and that there was no greater prophet, while his father said he was to be the prophet of the Highest and Gabriel said he was to go 'in the spirit and power of Elijah'.[41] He had a prophetic nature; his personal genetic make-up was such that he was predisposed to the kind of life he adopted. God made him to be what he was and breathed into him his fiery Spirit and his Word, which gave John a divine compulsion to say the things he said, even if it brought him into real danger and made him unpredictable and sometimes uncomfortable to be around. He was not, as Jesus remarked, 'A reed shaken by the wind'.[42] A prophet, of course, has a dual role of predicting the future and as a speaker of difficult truths to the people of his day, and John did both.

A garment of camel hair

His clothing – the famous camel-hair garment with the leather belt – was chosen consciously to identify him as a prophet.[43] Elijah's equally famous ninth-century BC mantle was described as 'a garment of hair', and the prophet Zechariah spoke of prophets wearing 'a robe of coarse hair'.[44] The camel-hair cloth of John's garment fitted this description, which will be why the New Testament records it.

The cloth used to make his garment is not to be confused with the cloth used to make modern camel-hair coats – which is a smooth cloth made from a mixture of wool and the undercoat of Asian two-humped, bactrian camels. The hair on Middle Eastern dromedaries is shorter and coarser, but the outer guard hair was until recently plucked, spun and woven into a rough homespun that was used for traditional Bedouin tents. The material closes up when wet, becoming water resistant, allowing air to pass through when dry, making it ideal for this purpose. Using the hair of camels, designed as it is for desert conditions, is the logical thing for traditional desert dwellers to do. It is also hard-wearing and was employed widely for saddles, saddle bags and the like. Right up until the twentieth century it was also used to make the thick, coarse, burnous-type outer garment that was valued for protection from wet and cold weather. It was often used by shepherds to sleep in at night.

In 1907, James Neil wrote this in Palestine:

Over the kemise, in wet or cold weather, and during the night, the shepherd, like all peasants, wears a thick, warm, sleeveless, sack-like outer garment, made of camel's hair, invariable as to material, shape, and colour, the latter being dark brown of different shades, with whitish perpendicular stripes. This is the common overcoat of the agricultural labourer and of all the working classes of the country districts.[45]

It is thought that camels were domesticated in this part of the world as early as the third millennium BC and at some time during this period someone must have worked out how to make cloth from the little over 2kg of hair that a camel sheds each year. Archaeology has not yet produced examples of ancient camel-hair cloth from the Middle East, so we do not know exactly how they spun and wove the cloth in the first century. John's clothing appears to be the earliest literary record of camel-hair cloth.

Palestinian camel-hair coat.[46]

Clothing styles will have varied over the centuries, but probably not very much for this sort of garment, which is fairly primitive. In all likelihood this was the sort of thing that John wore, or a variation of it, with or without the stripes. The notion that he had something specially fashioned for him is not one that sits well with his character as we know it. The Old Testament Hebrew word for Elijah's mantle is *adderet*, which, as well as meaning a cloak, also means wide, and it is easy to see from the photographs above why his mantle could also have been this type of garment. It is entirely possible that John wore regular first-century linen clothes under the camel-hair outer garment in the way that Elijah evidently wore regular clothes under his mantle. Camel-hair cloth has thermal qualities that make it ideal for cooler conditions at night, but desert-dwellers also keep such an outer garment on in warmer weather to contain body moisture, which is otherwise lost in evaporation more quickly. For the same reason, John will have worn a head covering during the heat of the day. While we cannot know for certain that this was the kind of garment that John wore, or Elijah, what we can emphatically say is that he did not wear something made from camel skin and fur as is often quite wrongly portrayed in art and in films. Similarly, when we bear in mind the desert conditions in which he lived, where the heat can be lethal, the torn raggedy kind of garment in which John is sometimes portrayed also cannot be right; his skin would have become very burnt and he would have become dehydrated and suffered from sunstroke.[47]

There are two other reasons for John to choose such a garment. One is to identify with the poor, which he did with his whole lifestyle, as Jesus noted when he compared John's clothing to that of the ruling elite: 'What then did you go out to see? A man dressed in soft clothing? Behold, those who are dressed in splendid clothing and live in luxury are in kings' courts.'[48] The garb of a prophet is the garb of the poor. The other reason is practical. John was going to live in extreme conditions and like most people who do this sort of thing he would have wanted the best kit, and this type of garment was tried and tested.

There were usually no fastenings on such a robe and a belt would be used to tie it closed. John used a leather belt like Elijah, who used his to gird up his loins for his epic run from Mount Carmel to Jezreel after the confrontation with the prophets of Baal.[49] By so doing John identified with the prophet Elijah, knowing that the Jews of his day expected Elijah to return as the herald of the coming Messiah (and they still do). John will have known that his actions were a fulfilment of prophecy and that people would take notice. Having said that, although it was the garment of a prophet, this sort of garment, if it is what he wore, will also have been common among the local peasant population so it will not have been overconspicuous. It sounds exotic to us in the West but was an everyday garment in the wilderness in times past.

A diet of locusts and wild honey

When people are asked what they know about John the Baptist the most common answer is that he ate locusts and wild honey. We also know that he fasted frequently, abstained from alcohol and apparently, according to Jesus, from eating bread, although he may not have meant this literally. Here are the texts:

Now John wore a garment of camel's hair and a leather belt round his waist, and his food was locusts and wild honey. Then Jerusalem and all Judea and all the region about the Jordan were going out to him, and they were baptized by him in the river Jordan, confessing their sins.
(Matthew 3:4-6)

John appeared, baptizing in the wilderness and proclaiming a baptism of repentance for the forgiveness of sins. And all the country of Judea and all Jerusalem were going out to him and were being baptized by him in the river Jordan, confessing their sins. Now John was clothed with camel's hair and wore a leather belt round his waist and ate locusts and wild honey.'
(Mark 1:4-6)

And he must not drink wine or strong drink, and he will be filled with the Holy Spirit, even from his mother's womb.
(Luke 1:15b, the annunciation)

For John came neither eating nor drinking, and they say, 'He has a demon.' The Son of Man came eating and drinking, and

they say, 'Look at him! A glutton and a drunkard, a friend of tax collectors and sinners!' Yet wisdom is justified by her deeds.
(Matthew 11:18-19)

For John the Baptist has come eating no bread and drinking no wine, and you say, 'He has a demon.' The Son of Man has come eating and drinking, and you say, 'Look at him! A glutton and a drunkard, a friend of tax collectors and sinners!' Yet wisdom is justified by all her children.'
(Luke 7:33-35)

Then the disciples of John came to him, saying, 'Why do we and the Pharisees fast, but your disciples do not fast?' And Jesus said to them, 'Can the wedding guests mourn as long as the bridegroom is with them? The days will come when the bridegroom is taken away from them, and then they will fast.'
(Matthew 9:14-15)

Now John's disciples and the Pharisees were fasting. And people came and said to him, 'Why do John's disciples and the disciples of the Pharisees fast, but your disciples do not fast?' And Jesus said to them, 'Can the wedding guests fast while the bridegroom is with them? As long as they have the bridegroom with them, they cannot fast. The days will come when the bridegroom is taken away from them, and then they will fast in that day.'
(Mark 2:18-20, cf. Luke 5:33-35)

The land of the Bible was famously described in Exodus 3:8 as 'flowing with milk and honey', which may be a bit of hyperbole but does indicate that honey was not rare. There were certainly enough flowering plants and trees in what was in times past called 'the jungle of the Jordan' to sustain colonies of wild bees, and we find examples in the Old Testament of Samson and Jonathan finding wild honey, and references in the Psalms and the song of Moses to God blessing the people with honey.[50] Josephus reports that bees were plentiful in the area and the Damascus Document from nearby Qumran hints at eating honey, while Philo records Essenes keeping domestic bees for honey.[51]

The idea of John being a locust eater troubles the more squeamish, but in truth they were common desert fare. They are allowed in Old Testament dietary laws. There are references in the *Mishnah* to the kinds of locusts that can be eaten, as well as in the Damascus document at Qumran to eating locusts if they are properly roasted.[52] It is dieticians who throw up the main question about John's diet because if it consisted only of locusts and honey he would have had no vitamin C and not enough carbohydrates and would probably have contracted scurvy. We must therefore ask whether the texts claim that locusts and wild honey were all that he ever ate and, of course, they do not say that. It is hard to conclude from the evidence that he never ate anything else, just as you would not conclude from Matthew 11:18 (see above) that he ate and drank nothing at all. It could well be that he was content to grub around and live on this desert fare when necessary, but equally content to eat other food provided by well-wishers, for he did, after all, teach people to share their food.[53]

There does not seem to be any discernible reason, symbolic or otherwise, for John to adopt such a diet, other than that it was the austere diet of a man who lived the extreme, ascetic and at times self-sufficient life of a holy man in the wilderness. And judging by comments recorded in Matthew 11 and Luke 7 (see above) that is how Jesus saw it too.[54] John was the arch-practitioner of the simple lifestyle.

John's working environment

John was a man of the wilderness. Earlier we saw how he was probably raised in Ein Kerem and deliberately chose to go into this uncultivated environment, and there can be little doubt that he went there because of his commissioning text that says he was to be the 'voice of one crying in the wilderness'.[55] His father's working environment was the temple and the synagogue but John chose the wilderness for his, connecting with a more ancient spirituality.[56] By living the desert lifestyle he was following a long tradition that included, among others, Abraham, Isaac, Jacob, Moses, Joshua, David, Jeremiah and especially Elijah.

In the Jewish tradition the wilderness is a mystical place and John's time there must have made a deep impression on him. The desert can be a place of awe and majesty, and a place of lonely barrenness and silence, a place of encounter with God and a place of revelation, where one can listen to God without distractions. It is not a place for the fainthearted or for the unprepared. Somehow John learned the skills and self-discipline necessary to live in this hostile environment. Luke 1:80 says he went into the wildernesses – plural (Greek: ἐρήμοις) – which suggests that he travelled round before ending up at Bethany beyond the Jordan, where he baptized. In the next chapter, we speculate about where he might have gone.

For those not familiar with this environment it varies hugely, from rolling sand dunes to dramatic rocky landscapes to scrubland where shepherds roam with their small flocks of sheep and goats. Some say that the Hebrew word for wilderness – *mid'var* – stems from a word meaning to guide or to lead and refers to a place where the only use for the land is to lead flocks of sheep from place to place. In the Greek of the New Testament the word is *eremos*, from which we get the word eremite to describe a desert hermit, which has the same etymological root.[57]

There is a dark side to the wilderness as well; it is the place where the scapegoat was led on the Day of Atonement and it is the place where Jesus sent an evil spirit to wander.[58] Jesus noted in Matthew's and Luke's Gospels (see above) that John had some detractors who said that his extreme wilderness diet indicated that he had a demon, but they had completely misunderstood John.

Luke 3:2 records that 'The word of God came to John son of Zechariah in the wilderness'.[59] He used his wilderness years well. He was a holy man in the best tradition, 'a man sent from God'.[60]

Part 2: MINISTRY

CHAPTER 3: BAPTISM IN WATER

For this is he who was spoken of by the prophet Isaiah
when he said,
'The voice of one crying in the wilderness:
'Prepare the way of the Lord; make his paths straight.'
(Matthew 3:3, quoting Isaiah 40:3)

John's prophetic mission was guided by his commissioning text from Isaiah: 'Prepare the way of the LORD.'[1] As English-speaking Christians it is very easy to read this and think that John was to prepare the way of Jesus because we are used to referring to Jesus as 'the Lord'. John, however, was a Hebrew-speaking, first-century Jew and when he read this text in Isaiah he did not read 'the LORD', as it is usually translated in Isaiah 40, or 'the Lord', as it is usually translated in most versions of the Gospels, he read יהוה, the sacred name for God that we call the Tetragrammaton.[2] Because of a fear of offending God and taking his name in vain, Jews refuse even to pronounce יהוה, and to make it harder to do so they have deleted the original vowels. When Hebrew readers encounter the Tetragrammaton they will commonly say 'Hashem', which is Hebrew for 'The Name'.[3]

In an attempt to pronounce the resulting unpronounceable יהוה Christians have taken another approach and used Jehovah, or more recently Yahweh, but translators of the Old Testament commonly render it as LORD, using upper case letters. When a biblical text containing יהוה was translated for the third-century BC Septuagint Greek version of the Old Testament, it was usually rendered *kyrios* (κύριος), the Greek word for lord. The Gospel writers followed the same convention. *Kyrios* is usually translated into English as Lord, using lower case letters, which means that when our text from Isaiah is quoted in the Gospels it is usually translated 'Prepare the way of the Lord', as we can see in the quote at the head of this chapter, which makes English speakers even more likely to think that it refers to Jesus.[4]

The difference between LORD and Lord is a subtlety that can easily be missed, but even that is often not available to English readers of the Gospels. The point is that John expected to prepare the way of יהוה – Yahweh/Jehovah – and, as we shall see in this and the next three chapters, his choice of water baptism was an extraordinarily effective way of doing this, culminating as it did in the first and greatest overt revelation of the Trinity in recorded history. In preparing the way of Yahweh/Jehovah, he prepared the way of the Trinity.

In the spirit of Elijah

John had to prepare the way of the LORD in the spirit of Elijah and he had to work out how to do this in the most effective way. One of the things he must have done was to learn everything he could about Elijah in the holy texts and by listening to teachers. He may also have visited the various places associated with Elijah – places like Tishbe in Gilead, Mount Carmel and Jezreel, and he may even have followed in his footsteps to Mount Horeb.[5] He must have visited the place where it was thought Elijah was carried up into heaven in a whirlwind with the chariot of fire, where the double portion of his spirit fell on his successor Elisha, where Elijah's mantle was passed on to Elisha, where both Elijah and Elisha used the mantle to part the water of the River Jordan and pass through, and where some thought Elijah would return, for the place where all this was believed to have happened is right beside where John preached and baptized.[6] It is also close to where the Brook Cherith was believed to be, where Elijah was fed by ravens.[7] Elijah's Hill, as the place of his ascension is known today, is only about a kilometre and a half from the baptism site, so it would be incredible if he did not go there, both before he started baptizing and during his period of ministry.[8] It can be no coincidence that John began his ministry at the place where Elijah had ended his, where his spirit fell on his successor and where Elijah was expected to return.

As we have already seen, John probably went into the wilderness as an adult and not as a child and this may well have happened in his twenties. The current best estimate for the date of Jesus' nativity is in the spring of 5 BC, which means that John was born in the late autumn of 6 BC and this would mean that he turned twenty in the autumn of AD 15.[9] The date of the start of his public ministry is the only sure date we have been given in the New Testament: according to Luke 3:1-3 it started in the fifteenth year of the emperor Tiberius. When we say 'sure date', as with all dates in the ancient world there are some disputes. These are to do with the date of the beginning of Tiberius' rule and which calendar Luke was using. Having said that, we can be reasonably sure that Luke was talking about the year AD 29. There is more detailed information about the calculation of theses dates in the Appendix.

In the fifteenth year of the reign of Tiberius Caesar, Pontius Pilate being governor of Judea, and Herod being tetrarch of Galilee, and his brother Philip tetrarch of the region of Ituraea and Trachonitis, and Lysanias tetrarch of Abilene, during the high priesthood of Annas and Caiaphas, the word of God came to John the son of Zechariah in the wilderness.[10] And he went into all the region around the Jordan, proclaiming a baptism of repentance for the forgiveness of sins.
(Luke 3:1-3)

This means that John was about thirty-four years old when he began his public ministry, leaving him plenty of time to think about Elijah and to visit the places associated with him.[11] He had plenty of time to sit on Elijah's Hill to fast and pray and meditate on how he was to prepare the way of the LORD. As the Israelites of old sat by the river of Babylon and wept,[12] so one can imagine John sitting for many an hour here, by the River Jordan, praying, fasting, reading, meditating on the texts and pondering his calling.

John the Baptist Meditating in the Wilderness
by Geertgen tot Sint Jans, c. 1490.[13]

Elijah's Hill lies at the southern end of the dramatic and historic Jordan River valley in the Moabite Plain, almost due east of Jerusalem and just nine kilometres to the north of the Dead Sea, the lowest point on the surface of the earth. Rising above it to the west are the Judean hills and to the east the hills of Moab, and standing prominently among those is Mount Nebo, where Moses went to die at the end of the epic forty years of Exodus wilderness wanderings. Before he died he looked over the Jordan valley to the Judean hills and beyond as God famously showed him the Promised Land. Famously also, we are told in the last chapter of Deuteronomy that God buried him there in secret, so that no one would know where the grave was. So, as John meditated on Elijah's Hill, under the place where Elijah enigmatically went into heaven, he would also have been aware that he was under the gaze, so to speak, of that other towering figure from the Old Testament whose departure from this world was equally enigmatic. This was an auspicious place, especially as these are the two men most associated with messianic expectations – the Old Testament ends with a reference to them both:[14]

> Remember the law of my servant Moses, the statutes and rules that I commanded him at Horeb for all Israel.
> 'Behold, I will send you Elijah the prophet before the great and awesome day of the LORD comes. And he will turn the hearts of fathers to their children and the hearts of children to their fathers, lest I come and strike the land with a decree of utter destruction.'
> (Malachi 4:4-6)

A prophetic landscape

We have just speculated that John may have visited Mount Horeb, where, of course, he would again have felt the influence of these two men so closely associated with the mountain.[15] And they were the ones who later, after John's execution, were to appear together with Jesus on another mountain, the mount of transfiguration, where Jesus confirmed to his disciples that John was Elijah.[16]

As John pondered these things he will have remembered how Moses led the children of Israel through the wilderness to the Moabite plain where he now was, and how he prepared the way for his successor Joshua to lead the Israelites from there into the Promised Land, passing through the River Jordan at that very place (Jericho is in plain sight, just eight kilometres away to the west). And being a Hebrew/Aramaic-speaker, he would have pronounced Joshua's name *Yeshua*,[17] which is the same name given to his cousin, whom we know better as Jesus. The name Jesus is the English transliteration of *Yēsou*, which in turn is the Septuagint's and the Greek New Testament's transliteration of the Hebrew *Yeshua*. Joshua and Jesus have the same name. John had not yet received the prophetic sign that God had promised him that was to confirm Jesus as the Coming One (we will look at this in the Chapter 6), but he did know him and the stories about him, and will have expected him to be the one, so this coincidence of names will not have been lost on him. As Moses prepared the way for Joshua at this place, John was about to do the same for his namesake. Also, as Moses did not live to enter the Promised Land, John did not live to see the kingdom come as it did on the day of Pentecost, which he prophesied (as we shall see in Chapter 4). And as Joshua led the people of Israel through the River Jordan here into the Promised Land, so John was baptizing people here and pointing to the Coming One – Jesus – who was to lead people into the kingdom of heaven that he had announced.[18] Joshua and the Israelites (and, years later, Elijah and Elisha) crossed the river here on dry ground, but for John it was different as he wanted people to be immersed in the water because of its prophetic symbolism.[19]

It is very likely too that John remembered the striking visions that the prophet Ezekiel saw while in exile in Babylon after the destruction of the first temple – visions of a rebuilt temple in Jerusalem, that were well-known to John's contemporaries. Ezekiel's visionary temple was a symbolic one, which was never meant to be built. And right at the end of the vision he described a similarly symbolic river that flowed east out of the heart of the temple, past the altar and out of the east gate, all the while getting bigger and bigger until it filled the Arabah.[20] The Arabah is a term used to describe the Jordan valley, including the Dead Sea.[21] This is where Elijah's Hill is found and the place where John chose to do his baptizing, which, as has been noted, lies to the east of the temple. Arabah is also the Hebrew word for 'desert' in Isaiah 40:3, which is where John was to 'make straight … a highway for God'. Ezekiel's river was to bring life and healing wherever it went, and Christians have traditionally interpreted this as a vision of the Holy Spirit flowing from the Father (symbolically represented by the Holy of Holies) and the Son (symbolically represented by the altar). It is a Trinitarian vision. Ezekiel's river, then, is like a watery Trinitarian prophetic finger pointing away from the temple, from the place of John's angelic annunciation, to the place of his baptisms, where that greatest of all Trinitarian manifestations was to take place. This vision of the Holy Spirit as a river must have affected John's view of the place he was in, and affected his message, which focused on people being immersed in water in a river. They were then told that there was one to come who would immerse them not in water as he had done but in the Holy Spirit, his great prophecy of Pentecost (as we shall see in the next chapter).

In this way, John found the stretch of the River Jordan in the wilderness, close to a crossing point that made access easy, where he was to conduct his ministry and his baptisms, which, we learn in the Gospel of John, was called Bethany beyond the Jordan.[22] He had found the perfect site, but now he had to work out *how* he was going to prepare the way of the LORD. We can picture him regularly in the river practising ritual immersion as an observant Jew, with images in his mind of Moses, Elijah, Joshua, Ezekiel's river, his commissioning texts from Isaiah and Malachi and the prophetic words of Gabriel at the annunciation, of his mother Elizabeth at the visitation and of his father Zechariah in the Benedictus, and we can see how his own idea of baptism (immersion) might have formed in his mind, guided by the Holy Spirit. When the time was right he took a common Jewish religious ritual and infused it with new meaning.

The word of God came to John the son of Zechariah in the wilderness. And he went into all the region around the Jordan, proclaiming a baptism of repentance for the forgiveness of sins.' (Luke 3:2b-3)

In those days John the Baptist came preaching in the wilderness of Judea, 'Repent, for the kingdom of heaven is at hand.' (Matthew 3:1-2)

John appeared, baptizing in the wilderness and proclaiming a baptism of repentance for the forgiveness of sins. (Mark 1:4)

John's early preaching

There are three big ideas in the early preaching of John that we need to think about:

- What did John mean when he announced, 'The kingdom of heaven is at hand'?

- What did John mean by 'repent' and 'repentance'?
- And what were John's baptisms?

When John made his announcement about the kingdom of heaven he was talking about the kingdom of God. The two terms are interchangeable. Heaven, in this instance, was a euphemism used by religious people to avoid any possibility of breaking the third commandment not to defile God's name. For example, in Mark's version of Jesus' trial before the Sanhedrin, the high priest used the term 'the Blessed' instead of saying 'God'. This was a convention prevalent at the time, which John evidently followed.[23]

This pioneering prophet was the first in the New Testament to declare the arrival of the kingdom of God. Indeed, John's message was significantly different to anyone else's. And, according to Matthew's Gospel, the words that John chose to begin his ministry – 'Repent, for the kingdom of heaven is at hand' – were identical to the first words that Jesus used to begin his ministry – another example of John preparing the way for his more illustrious cousin.[24] The Greek word commonly translated 'at hand' is ēngiken (ἤγγικεν), which is the perfect tense of the verb engizō (ἐγγίζω) and literally means 'has come near', i.e. it is something that has already taken place. The kingdom of heaven that John proclaimed had been at hand since the incarnation because the King was at hand, something John had been aware of since he leaped in the womb at Jesus' presence. At the point of John's declaration, the King was about to start his work, and the kingdom was yet to become even more present at Pentecost. From that time, the kingdom has not just been 'near' but 'here'.[25] Standard Jewish eschatological preaching was along the lines, 'If we repent the kingdom of heaven will arrive',[26] but for John the kingdom of heaven was already at hand – not just something to be hoped for in the future. This was something that people should realise and for that reason change their way of thinking and living.

Contemporary Jewish expectations about the kingdom of heaven were of a political realm, ruled by a King David-like messiah. It was to be a kingdom in which the Jewish nation became great and powerful. One in which roles would be reversed, so that instead of being a vassal state of the Roman Empire the nations would bow down to Israel. John, however, declared something radically different, and it was going to take a mind-shift for people to grasp this, as we shall see.

What did John mean by repent?

Working out what John meant by repent and repentance is a complex and somewhat controversial process. Despite almost every Bible translation in English using the words 'repent' and 'repentance,' there is a good case for a different translation that conveys John's meaning more clearly. If you ask someone what repentance means they will very likely talk about feeling guilty and saying sorry to God, or to a person they have hurt, generally with a commitment not to repeat the guilty act. But, as we shall see, this is not what John actually said. Since we are talking about John's first recorded word, carefully and prayerfully chosen after thirty-four years of preparation, the first recorded word of a canonical prophet after four centuries of prophetic silence - and the first word, according to Matthew, in the ministry of his more exalted cousin, Jesus - we need to make sure that we understand it correctly.

We should first remind ourselves that the goal of repentance is to restore one's relationship with God and live a kingdom life. To this end, the core idea of repentance in both the Old and New Testaments is turning (or returning) to God and away from sin.[27] Sometimes the emphasis is on turning to God and sometimes it is on turning from sin, but both are essential for true repentance. For James, 'faith without works is dead': for John, turning to God without turning from sin is equally dead. John said, 'Bear fruit in keeping with repentance' and that people who did not bear fruit were 'vipers'.[28] The Hebrew verb for turning is *shuv* (שׁוּב[29]), the Greek New Testament verb is *epistrephō* (ἐπιστρέφω[30]) and in the Latin Vulgate, the hugely influential version used widely in Europe for more than a millennium, the verb *converto* was used (from which we get 'convert'). As the goal of repentance is to have a restored relationship with God and to live a righteous life, and as the means by which we do this is to turn (or return) to God and away from sin, the New Testament describes three factors that lead a person to reorientate their life in this way:

1. Remorse
Sometimes the process is led by feelings of remorse or sorrow for something we have done or said, heartfelt feelings that impel us to turn to God for forgiveness, with a determination not to repeat the guilty act. The Hebrew verb for this is *nicham* (נָחַם), the Greek verbs are *metamelomai* (μεταμέλομαι) or *lupeō* (λυπέω). The Latin Vulgate verb is *paeniteo* (the noun is *paenitentia*), which is the root word for 'repent', which may explain in part why remorse is so commonly associated with repentance in the Latin-influenced Western Church.

2. Revelation
Sometimes people are led to turn to God because they have a direct spiritual experience, like the vision that Paul had on the road to Damascus, or the dream that Cornelius had in Caesarea that led him to send for Peter.[31] Dreams, visions, angelic visitations and the like are all experiences that lead people to reorientate their lives. It is how my conversion began.

3. Realisation
Sometimes it is the realisation of a new truth that changes the direction of a person's life. A person is travelling through life when

they have a light bulb moment and begin to see the world differently. For his mission, John chose to appeal, in the first instance, to people's minds in this way. The Greek verb used in Matthew 3:2 to record him saying 'Repent' is *metanoeō* (μετανοέω) and it means to have a change of mind. The Greek noun used in Mark 1:4 and Luke 3:3, translated 'repentance', is *metanoia* (μετάνοια), which means a change of mind.

Here is a simple summary of the six Rs of repentance:

```
┌─────────────────────────────────────────────────────────┐
│                                                          │
│                      Repentance                          │
│                                                          │
│   Relationship – the goal of repentance                  │
│                                                          │
│   Reorientation – the core idea of repentance            │
│                                                          │
│    • Remorse (paenitentia)        ⎤   Factors that       │
│    • Revelation                   ⎬   lead to            │
│    • Realisation (metanoia)       ⎦   repentance         │
│                                                          │
└─────────────────────────────────────────────────────────┘
```

It cannot be helpful to our understanding of John's message to translate what he said with a word that is commonly understood to mean remorse (and is derived from the Latin for remorse) when John said something that means realisation.[32] There must be a better way of doing it. This is especially so as John, and later Jesus, used the imperative form of the verb to begin their ministries.[33] Repent in the imperative is such a frowny, finger-wagging, reproachful word and we should ask ourselves whether Jesus and John really began their preaching in this way. Did they really say, in effect, 'Be remorseful, for the kingdom of heaven is at hand'? No, they did not.

Metanoeō and *metanoia* are compound words made up of *meta*, which can mean a number of things in compounds, usually 'with' or 'after', and the verb *noeō*, which means 'understand' or *noia*, which comes from the noun *nous* (from which we get the English word nous), which means 'mind'. The core lexical meaning of *metanoeō* is to change one's mind, as we have seen, in the sense that what one thinks *after* receiving some information (like being told that the kingdom of heaven is at hand) is different to what one thinks *before*, i.e. a realisation takes place.[34] In the ancient world, 'mind' did not necessarily mean exactly what we mean today and could include feelings, so *metanoeō* should not be thought of simply as an intellectual exercise.[35] And John did not preach *metanoia/metanoeō* as an intellectual truth on its own, but as a truth that should lead to a change of behaviour, saying, as we have seen, 'Bear fruits in keeping with [*metanoia*]'.[36] In this context, an intellectual truth that does not affect the way we live is a vanity.

Greek, Latin and Hebrew

Why is it so common to translate *metanoia/metanoeō* with repentance/repent? We have to go back a long way to find the answer. In the post-apostolic Church, in a process that can be seen as early as in the second century *Shepherd of Hermas*, there was a growth in emphasis on the remorse route to turning as opposed to the realisation route, including the idea of doing penance.[37] By the time of Jerome's definitive translation of the Bible into Latin (the fourth-century Vulgate), the emphasis was all on remorse, in a guilt-driven form of Christianity, hence Jerome's use of *paeniteo* to translate *metanoeō* and *paenitentia* to translate *metanoia* in all contexts. This may also have had something to do with Jerome being racked with guilt about earlier homosexual encounters. Unfortunately, as we have seen, the Vulgate's influence on the translation of *metanoeō* and *metanoia* is still felt today. There are other words that Jerome might have used that would have been more helpful, but sadly he didn't use them.

If the Latin tradition hasn't been altogether helpful, there is a current trend to say that John was a Jew and thought like a Jew and preached in either Hebrew or Aramaic, so he must have used the Old Testament Hebrew word for turn (*shuv*) when he preached.[38] This assertion is backed up by the observation that the angel at his annunciation said that John will 'turn (*epistrephō*) many of the children of Israel to the Lord their God' and will 'turn (*epistrephō*) the hearts of the fathers to the children', which is reflected in John's commissioning text in Malachi.[39] And we find that when the Old Testament was translated into Greek in the third century BC (the Septuagint), the Hebrew verb for turn (*shuv*) was sometimes translated using *metanoeō*. This was only in certain contexts and was because a change of mind (*metanoeō*) should lead to a change of behaviour and orientation, i.e. a turning. By the time of the New Testament, after more than three centuries of the influence of Greek language, culture and thought, Greek-speaking Jews were using *metanoeō* sometimes to mean turn and sometimes to mean to have a change of mind, as is evidenced in the writings of Philo and Josephus.[40] It would be a mistake, therefore, to say that it should always mean one thing or the other. A more nuanced approach is called for and one should always look at words in context. And, with reference to the angel's prophecy about John turning the children of Israel to the Lord and the hearts of fathers to the children, we should note that people did turn as a result of his ministry, but that does not mean he actually said 'turn' (*epistrephō*). What he said was have a *metanoia* that bears fruit. If we were to follow the suggestion that we should use the Hebrew idea of turning to translate John's use of *metanoia/metanoeō* we would be repeating the mistake that Jerome made when he used the Latin *paeniteo/paenitentia*.[41] Turning is an implied consequence of what he said, but it is not what he actually said.

There is a big clue to John's use of *metanoia/metanoeō* in the Acts of the Apostles where Peter, who had been a disciple of John, and Paul, who spoke about John and quoted him, both used *metanoeō* and *epistrephō* (turn) in the same sentence when addressing Hebrew audiences, making a distinction between the two. In Acts 3, Peter, speaking in the temple, said, '*metanoeō* therefore, and *epistrephō* (turn)'.[42] Later in Acts, Paul reported at his hearing in Caesarea that his preaching to both Jews and Gentiles included an exhortation to '*metanoeō* and *epistrephō* (turn) to God, performing deeds in keeping with their *metanoia*'.[43] In other words, both Peter and Paul used *metanoeō* to mean change of mind, and both of them exhorted their Jewish audiences to take the realisation route to turning. John in his context, like Peter and Paul in those passages above, used *metanoeō/metanoia* to mean change of mind.[44] Also, like Peter and Paul, *metanoeō* for John was distinct from the idea of turning, but led to it.

John was a Jew and he preached to Jews, but he was a prophet, and was beginning the proclamation of something radically different, something that was going to need a mind-shift on the part of those who heard him. In that context, *metanoeō* and *metanoia* are the right words for him to use. The assertion that we should use 'turn' (*shuv*) to translate John's words might seem superficially plausible but it would be a mistake to do so. The point is that John could have said, 'Turn (*epistrephō*) to God and away from sin, for the kingdom of heaven is at hand', and the Gospel writers would have recorded him doing so, but he did not. He could have said, 'Be remorseful, or sorrowful (*metamelomai* or *lupeō*), for the kingdom of heaven is at hand,' but he did not say that either. He said something much more revolutionary, and the Gospel writers put a lot of thought into the way they represented his revolutionary words in Greek.

The New Testament has been given to us in Greek, reaching out beyond the confines of the Hebrew world, and it is to the Greek text that we should look first for our understanding. There are times when a knowledge of Hebrew and Aramaic can guide us, but not in this instance.[45] We need to liberate these prophetic words of John's and free them from the tendency to make them conform to either Latin (*paeniteo*: repent) or Hebrew (*shuv*: turn). 'Repent' and 'repentance', with their overtones of remorse, are not the best loan-translation words to use when rendering John's message in English, for they do not convey the right impression of what he was trying to say. Neither does 'turn'. The Gospel writers have given us an excellent Greek word that perfectly expresses John's meaning in the context he so carefully chose. There is no good reason not to use it.

Preaching *metanoia*

John said, '*Metanoeō*, for the kingdom of heaven is at hand', using the imperative mood of the verb, and he said that for a reason. What John wanted people to do was to grasp this revolutionary truth: that the kingdom of God was at hand – a truth that should change them. John deliberately chose to preach the realisation route for people to turn to God and away from sin, and we do not do his message justice if we translate his words in a way that does not recognise this.

It is hard to find a single word or even a phrase in English that will do justice to John's prophetic cry. 'Reconsider' may be the best single word, but it seems a bit weak, lacking the imperative forcefulness of John's language. As noted above, the core lexical meaning of *metanoeō* is to change one's mind, so here are the texts again using that phrase, followed by a paraphrase translation for the first one, and an amplified translation for the second.[46]

CHAPTER 3: BAPTISM IN WATER

In those days John the Baptist came preaching in the wilderness of Judea,

> ... ['Change your mind], for the kingdom of heaven is at hand.'
> ... 'Rethink your understanding of the kingdom of heaven, for it has now drawn close.'
> (Matthew 3:1-2)

John appeared, baptizing in the wilderness and proclaiming

> ... a baptism of [a changed mind] for the forgiveness of sins.
> ... a baptism (immersion) of a changed mind (that should bear fruit that leads to a turning to God and away from sin) for the forgiveness of sins.
> (Mark 1:4 [cf. Luke 3:3])

Metanoia is increasingly being used as an English word in religious circles, although its definition is not identical to the way John used it. [47] It may, however, be a better loan-translation word than repent. Using it might make readers think, which is what John wanted his hearers to do, so we are going to see the texts one last time below, using *metanoia*. This is not some sort of quibble about semantics; *metanoeō* and *metanoia* were deliberately chosen to record what John said and they were the right words to use in those circumstances – they were the right words to use as he proclaimed a new era and a new vision of God and his kingdom. A revolution was being proclaimed and a new way of thinking was required.

In those days John the Baptist came preaching in the wilderness of Judea, ['*Metanoy*[48]], for the kingdom of heaven has come near.' (Matthew 3:1-2)

> John appeared, baptizing in the wilderness and proclaiming a
> baptism of [*metanoia*] for the forgiveness of sins.
> (Mark 1:4, cf. Luke 3:3)

John's baptisms were immersions of *metanoia* – a *metanoia* that
was in response to his preaching and that, with the turning and
confession of sins that accompanied it, resulted in the forgiveness
of sins. It is important to understand the relationship between
metanoia, forgiveness of sins and baptism in John's preaching, for it
is easy to get confused. It was never the case for John that baptism
led to forgiveness of sins. John's baptism was a baptism of *metanoia*
and it was the *metanoia*, with the turning to God and away from sin
and the confession that accompanied it, that led to the forgiveness of
sins, not the baptism. His was a baptism of *metanoia* for forgiveness,
not a baptism of forgiveness.[49] As Jesus commanded: '[*Metanoia*] and
forgiveness of sins should be proclaimed in his name to all nations'.[50]

> And you, child, will be called the prophet of the Most High;
> for you will go before the Lord to prepare his ways, to give
> knowledge of salvation to his people in the forgiveness of their
> sins ...
> (Luke 1:76-77 [from the Benedictus])

> Then Jerusalem and all Judea and all the region about the Jordan
> were going out to him, and they were baptized by him in the
> river Jordan, confessing their sins.
> (Matthew 3:5-6, cf. Mark 1:5)

Three *metanoias*

There were three *metanoias* that John proclaimed, a progression of
metanoias, one leading on from the other. He began his ministry by

announcing that the kingdom of heaven was at hand, which was so different from the standard Jewish expectations of the kingdom that it required a *metanoia*. This was the first *metanoia* in his preaching, the *metanoia about the kingdom*. There then followed two baptismal metanoias, one before people went into the river and the second as they came out, or after they came out of the water. What John wanted was for those who grasped his message about the kingdom being at hand to respond by turning to God and confessing their sins, and he wanted them to do this as they immersed themselves in his carefully selected and heavily symbolic stretch of the River Jordan. This immersion was not a standard Jewish *tevilah* for cleansing from ritual impurity, but was for the cleansing of their souls through confession. This was so different from standard Jewish practice, that another *metanoia* had to occur. That was John's second *metanoia*, the *metanoia of confession and forgiveness*. It was because John's baptisms were not about purity, and were therefore different from normal Jewish immersions, that it caused people to comment, as we can see in the incident recorded below. This must have happened hundreds of times, and it was the sort of thing that John wanted to happen.

> Now a discussion arose between some of John's disciples and a Jew over purification.
> (John 3:25)

In this way the scene was now set for John's third *metanoia*, the *metanoia about the Coming One*, the King. The people were now shriven and ready for his core prophetic oracle, for it was when they emerged from the water with their minds prepared and their sins forgiven that he told them about the Coming One.[51] As his father had prophesied in the Benedictus, John gave the knowledge of salvation to God's people in the forgiveness of their sins. He told them the

Coming One was in their midst, that he was great and that he would immerse them not in water, as he had done, but in 'the Holy Spirit and fire'. We will be looking at what this means in the next chapter.

> I indeed immerse (baptize) you in water for a *metanoia*, but the one who is coming after me is mightier than I, whose sandal I am not fit to carry: he will immerse (baptize) you in (the) Holy Spirit and fire.
> (Matthew 3:11,[52] cf. Mark 1:7-8; Luke 3:16; John 1:26-27,32-33)

> Paul said, 'John immersed (baptized) with an immersion (baptism) of *metanoia*, telling the people that they should believe in the One coming after him – that is, in Jesus.'
> (Acts 19:4)[53]

Commentators will sometimes say that John's preaching and baptizing were designed to get people to turn to God and away from sin in order to make them ready for the at-hand kingdom that he proclaimed. There is truth in this, but it is not the whole truth. John wanted people to understand that the kingdom he proclaimed was not just at hand but was of a very different sort to the one commonly expected: that the King – the Coming One – was already in their midst and was about to immerse people in the Holy Spirit and fire. John was preparing the way of the LORD, who was soon gloriously to be revealed as the Trinity.

Gabriel said that John would make a people prepared for the Lord, and this is how he did it.[54]

> ... it was so that he might be revealed to Israel that I came immersing (baptizing) in water.
> (John 1:31b)[55]

John's understanding of baptism

The third big idea in John's preaching is, of course, baptism, and John's baptism was one of a series of baptisms that are described in the Bible, each one building on the one that came before.

1. The first baptisms are the Old Testament ritual immersions, *tevilah*, which were to do with ritual purity. These baptisms evolved over the centuries and provided the essential backdrop for John's baptisms.[56]
2. John's baptisms were a tool that took the well-known imagery of Old Testament ritual immersions and used it to proclaim a new message. They were prophetic baptisms of *metanoia* and revelation.
3. During his ministry, Jesus' disciples, under his direction, baptized people.[57] We know little about these baptisms, but they may have been a development of John's practice during a different phase in the evolution of baptism.
4. Christian baptisms on the Day of Pentecost and subsequently contain a new set of meanings – they are baptisms of initiation overlaid with symbolic meaning to do with *metanoia* and, as we shall see in the next chapter, the Holy Spirit. They are the fruition of what went before.

As we saw earlier, there was some fuss at the time of John's circumcision concerning his name. Just as the name John (meaning 'Yahweh [or Jehovah] brings grace') was significant both for the way it pointed to the work of the Coming One, and because of the echoes of Elijah's name that it contained, his nickname 'the Baptist' was also important as it was a focal point of his ministry and preaching. In Hebrew his name is *Yohanan ha-Matvil*, and *Matvil* is related to *tevilah*, the Hebrew word for immersion. In the Greek of the New Testament his name is

Ioannēs ho Baptistēs[58] and *Baptistēs* comes from a family of Greek New Testament words transliterated into English as 'Baptist' (*baptistēs*), 'baptism' (*baptisma, baptismos*) and 'baptize' (*baptizō*). These come from the ancient Greek root word *baptō*. This family of words has a variety of meanings such as dipping, immersing, submerging, sinking, drowning, plunging and in ancient Greek it could be used in expressions like 'to go under', 'to go in over one's head', 'to be overwhelmed' and 'sink into sleep'. Similarly, a dyed cloth – one that has been soaked in a vat of dye – is a *bapta* in Greek. On one occasion in the New Testament, *baptismos* is used for the ritual washing of dishes.[59] A good English rendering of his name would be 'John the Immerser'.

John decided that he would, in part, use symbolism to proclaim his message, which can be very eloquent when trying to communicate great and wonderful ideas. Some of his symbolism was to do with the place where he conducted his ministry, with reference to Elijah, Elisha, Isaiah, Ezekiel, Moses and Joshua as described above, but his principal symbolism was to take something that was well-known to all observant Jews of his day, *tevilah*, and give it a new and powerful meaning. In that context immersion in water was a potent visual prophetic tool.

What John did was exhort those who had responded to his preaching, who had experienced a *metanoia*, to go into the River Jordan and be immersed in the water: a *tevilah*. Exactly what then happened is a bit opaque. Before we try to envisage it, we need to acknowledge that the way we might visualise him administering those immersions will be coloured by two millennia of varying Church traditions. It is, therefore, important to put those preconceptions aside and try to understand what happened in its historical and prophetic context. He might have been in the water with them physically immersing them, which is how we tend to imagine it, as we are used to a minister or a priest actively baptizing people in

Christian baptism, but this would be very unlike Jewish *tevilah* in which bodily contact was strictly avoided. He might have been in the water with them without touching them, while they immersed themselves in the Jewish style. Or he might equally have been on the riverbank, encouraging and overseeing the process and giving it his blessing. This is how it is commonly represented in the earliest Christian art and would be more in line with Jewish practice, the prophetic context of his baptisms. This is one of the imponderables of our text. For, although the verb *baptizō* is in the active mood when John is described baptizing someone and, conversely, the passive mood is employed to describe a person being baptized, that would be true of any of these three scenarios. And in the story of Philip baptizing the Ethiopian eunuch, both men went into the water, but this was Christian baptism and does not necessarily indicate the way that John baptized.[60]

If John did accompany people into the water he may not have kept his camel-hair outer garment on, as that way it would have soaked up a lot of water and have taken a long time to dry, even in the heat of the Jordan valley.

Because Jews are normally naked for a *tevilah* there are those who suggest that people may have been unclothed at John's baptisms. To preserve modesty in such a public place, however, this was almost certainly not the case. Josephus records the practice among the Essenes of women wearing a dress and men a loincloth in a public *mikvah*,[61] and John is often portrayed wearing a loincloth. Having said that, Orthodox Churches baptize people without clothes, claiming an early tradition. We do not know whether these baptisms included some sort of liturgy, but we do know that they confessed their sins prior to being baptized, which is a liturgical act of sorts even if it was extempore and, if John did pronounce a blessing over them, or spoke some other words, that is also a form of liturgy.[62]

Sixteenth-century icon: *Theophany of the Lord*, by
George the Cretan.[63]

In the twenty-first century the River Jordan is muddy and not very wide at the place where John baptized. It was wider at the time of the New Testament when not so much water was abstracted for irrigation, but the banks were still muddy.[64] This is often a surprise to people as it is quite different from the way it is usually portrayed in art or in films with a rocky riverbank. There is an easily accessible site just to the south of the Sea of Galilee that tourists in Israel are shown, which is more like the picture-book image, and baptisms are frequently conducted there. The lack of mud and the less polluted water make it more agreeable, but it has a very different feel to it, as well as being some distance from the real site.

The baptism site in the days before the flow was reduced and pollution became a problem.[65]

The baptism site in the twenty-first century.[66]

Remains of a 5th/6th century church at the baptism site. The river has changed course and this is now some distance from it.[67]

In this way John immersed people in the River Jordan. But, as we shall see in the next chapter, he also had something very important to say to them when they came up from the water, perhaps when they were standing on the riverbank again.

CHAPTER 4: BAPTISM IN THE HOLY SPIRIT

> I indeed immerse you in water; but one mightier than I is coming,
> the thong of whose sandals I am not fit to loosen. He will immerse
> you in the Holy Spirit and fire.
> (Luke 3:16)[1]

John the Baptist is best known for immersing people in the water of the River Jordan, but he was also known as a great prophet. In the next two chapters we will consider John as a prophet, beginning here with what people said about him in this role. We will start with Jesus.

We know Jesus considered John to be among the greatest people who had ever lived:

> Truly, I say to you, among those born of women there has arisen no one greater than John the Baptist.
> (Matthew 11:11a)

> I tell you, among those born of women none is greater than John.
> (Luke 7:28a)

This is an extraordinary accolade, but there is a variation in the Greek manuscript tradition at this point in Luke. Most English versions, like the ESV above, say that there is no greater *person* than John, but most surviving ancient Greek manuscripts record Jesus saying that there is no greater *prophet* than John, as does the Greek Orthodox Bible. A small number of English versions favour this:

JOHN THE BAPTIST – A BIOGRAPHY

For I say to you, among those born of women there is not a
greater prophet than John the Baptist ...
(Luke 7:28a, NKJV)

It is a matter of judgement which manuscript tradition is to be
preferred; textual criticism is not an exact science.[2] Jesus certainly
said that there is no greater person than John, and there is a very real
possibility that he also said that there is no greater prophet than John,
which would mean that in Jesus' estimation John is to be esteemed
in the same way as Isaiah, Jeremiah, Elijah, and others. Elsewhere,
when talking to a crowd about John, Jesus said, 'What then did you
go out to see? A prophet? Yes, I tell you, and more than a prophet.'[3]

Jesus was not alone in thinking of John as a prophet. At his
annunciation, Gabriel said that John was to go before the Lord 'in the
spirit and power of Elijah'. In his Benedictus, Zechariah said that his
new-born son was 'the prophet of the Most High'.[4] When Jesus asked
his disciples, 'Who do people say that the Son of Man is?' they replied,
'Some say John the Baptist, others say Elijah, and others Jeremiah or
one of the prophets.'[5] On four other occasions, the Gospels record
that his contemporaries popularly believed that John was a prophet:

[Herod Antipas] feared the people, because they held him
[John] to be a prophet.
(Matthew 14:5b)

[The chief priests and elders were] afraid of the crowd, for they
all hold that John was a prophet.
(Matthew 21:26b)

[Chief priests, scribes and elders] were afraid of the people, for they all held that John really was a prophet.
(Mark 11:32b)

[Chief priests, scribes and elders say] all the people … are convinced that John was a prophet.
(Luke 20:6b)

Bust of *St John the Baptist Preaching* by Auguste Rodin, 1878.[6]

John's core prophetic oracle

John was indeed a great prophet, the first since Malachi to rekindle the prophetic flame. In the last chapter, we looked at John's series of three *metanoias*, the last of which was his great core prophetic oracle – a prophecy recorded in all four Gospels, and repeated by Jesus, Peter and Paul. For when those being baptized emerged from the water, either standing in the river, or on the riverbank, John explained the symbolism of what they had just experienced when he said, 'I immerse you in water, but there is one who is to come, now living among you, who is mightier than me – I am not even worthy to untie his sandal straps, or even to carry them – he will immerse you in the Holy Spirit and fire.' This is a saying attested by eight towering figures of the New Testament: Jesus, John the Baptist, Peter, Paul, Matthew, Mark, Luke and John.

Since this is John's core prophetic oracle, it is important we understand what he meant by it. And since there are some controversies surrounding its translation, here the four Gospel passages, both in the original Greek, and in a very literal translation produced for this book:

Matthew 3:11

Ἐγὼ μὲν ὑμᾶς βαπτίζω ἐν ὕδατι εἰς μετάνοιαν· ὁ δὲ ὀπίσω μου ἐρχόμενος ἰσχυρότερός μού ἐστιν, οὗ οὐκ εἰμὶ ἱκανὸς τὰ ὑποδήματα βαστάσαι· αὐτὸς ὑμᾶς βαπτίσει ἐν πνεύματι ἁγίῳ καὶ πυρί.

'I indeed immerse (baptize) you in water for a *metanoia*, but the one who is coming after me is mightier than I, whose sandal I am not fit to carry: he will immerse (baptize) you in (the) Holy Spirit and fire.'

Mark 1:7b-8

...Ἔρχεται ὁ ἰσχυρότερός μου ὀπίσω μου, οὗ οὐκ εἰμὶ ἱκανὸς κύψας λῦσαι τὸν ἱμάντα τῶν ὑποδημάτων αὐτοῦ· ἐγὼ ἐβάπτισα ὑμᾶς ὕδατι, αὐτὸς δὲ βαπτίσει ὑμᾶς ἐν πνεύματι ἁγίῳ.

'... there comes one who is mightier than me after me, of whom I am not fit to stoop down to loosen the thong of his sandals. I immersed (baptized) you in water, but he will immerse (baptize) you in (the) Holy Spirit.'

Luke 3:16b

...Ἐγὼ μὲν ὕδατι βαπτίζω ὑμᾶς· ἔρχεται δὲ ὁ ἰσχυρότερός μου, οὗ οὐκ εἰμὶ ἱκανὸς λῦσαι τὸν ἱμάντα τῶν ὑποδημάτων αὐτοῦ· αὐτὸς ὑμᾶς βαπτίσει ἐν πνεύματι ἁγίῳ καὶ πυρί·

'... I indeed immerse (baptize) you in water; but one mightier than I is coming, of whom I am not fit to loosen the thong of his sandals: he will immerse (baptize) you in (the) Holy Spirit and fire.'

John 1:26b-27,32b-33

...Ἐγὼ βαπτίζω ἐν ὕδατι· μέσος ὑμῶν ἔστηκεν ὃν ὑμεῖς οὐκ οἴδατε, ὁ ὀπίσω μου ἐρχόμενος, οὗ οὐκ εἰμὶ ἄξιος ἵνα λύσω αὐτοῦ τὸν ἱμάντα τοῦ ὑποδήματος.

'... I immerse (baptize) you in water; among you stands one whom you do not know, who is coming after me, of whom I am not worthy to loosen the thong of his sandal.'

... ὅτι Τεθέαμαι τὸ πνεῦμα καταβαῖνον ὡς περιστερὰν ἐξ οὐρανοῦ, καὶ ἔμεινεν ἐπ' αὐτόν· κἀγὼ οὐκ ᾔδειν αὐτόν, ἀλλ' ὁ πέμψας με βαπτίζειν ἐν ὕδατι ἐκεῖνός μοι εἶπεν· Ἐφ' ὃν ἂν ἴδῃς τὸ πνεῦμα καταβαῖνον καὶ μένον ἐπ' αὐτόν, οὗτός ἐστιν ὁ βαπτίζων ἐν πνεύματι ἁγίῳ·

'... I beheld the Spirit descending like a dove from heaven, and he remained on him. I did not know him, but he who sent me to immerse (baptize) in water said to me, "Upon whom you see the Spirit descending and remaining on him, this is he who immerses (baptizes) in (the) Holy Spirit.'"

John must have said these words many times and obviously there was some variation in the repetition. The Gospel writers then introduced additional variations when they translated John's original Hebrew or Aramaic saying into Greek. The saying is found seven times in all in the New Testament. Below, you will find versions of it on the lips of Jesus and Peter, and from the pen of Paul. We will look more closely at how they used his words in Chapter 9:

Acts 1:5, Jesus speaking, preparing his disciples for Pentecost:
ὅτι Ἰωάννης μὲν ἐβάπτισεν ὕδατι, ὑμεῖς δὲ ἐν πνεύματι βαπτισθήσεσθε ἁγίῳ οὐ μετὰ πολλὰς ταύτας ἡμέρας.

'For John indeed immersed (baptized) in water, but you will be immersed (baptized) in (the) Holy Spirit not many days from now.'

Acts 11:16, Peter speaking:
ἐμνήσθην δὲ τοῦ ῥήματος τοῦ κυρίου ὡς ἔλεγεν· Ἰωάννης μὲν ἐβάπτισεν ὕδατι, ὑμεῖς δὲ βαπτισθήσεσθε ἐν πνεύματι ἁγίῳ.

'I remembered the word of the Lord, how he said, "John indeed immersed (baptized) in water, but you will be immersed (baptized) in (the) Holy Spirit.'"

1 Corinthians 12:13, Paul writing:[7]
καὶ γὰρ ἐν ἑνὶ πνεύματι ἡμεῖς πάντες εἰς ἓν σῶμα ἐβαπτίσθημεν, εἴτε Ἰουδαῖοι εἴτε Ἕλληνες, εἴτε δοῦλοι εἴτε ἐλεύθεροι, καὶ πάντες ἓν πνεῦμα ἐποτίσθημεν.

CHAPTER 4: BAPTISM IN THE HOLY SPIRIT

'For in one Spirit we all into one body were immersed (baptized), whether Jews or Greeks, whether slaves or free, and all one Spirit were given (or made) to drink.'

Immersion in, not baptism with

We looked at the meaning of the Greek verb *baptizō* (βαπτίζω) in Chapter 3, but there is another translation problem with John's saying that revolves round a small preposition. The Greek preposition *en* (ἐν), which is normally followed by a noun in the dative case, is used on each of the seven occasions when 'in the Holy Spirit' is mentioned above. It is used three times for 'in water'. The other times this phrase appears, the noun in the dative case is used but without the preposition. It was not uncommon to do this in first-century Greek and it meant the same thing, although in this case the variation is thought to be a stylistic device.[8]

In the entry for *en* (ἐν) in the latest edition of Walter Bauer's Greek-English Lexicon of the New Testament, we are told that the uses of this preposition are 'many and various'.[9] We are then given twelve different shades of meaning, with twenty further subdivisions of those twelve meanings.[10] We are told that the original hearers and readers would 'readily absorb the context and experience little difficulty' in understanding what was intended. Given that John's words came after he had immersed people in the River Jordan, which provides the context, it should be obvious that he meant, 'I immerse you *in* water' – 'in' being the principal meaning of *en*, category one in Bauer's lectionary. But – and this is a big but – most contemporary English translations have John saying, 'I baptize you *with* water', transliterating rather than translating *baptizō*, and using the causal or instrumental meaning of *en*, which is 'with' (category 5 in Bauer's lectionary).[11]

The early English translations of the bible (Wycliffe, Tyndale, Bishop's Bible, Great Bible) say that John baptized 'in' water, but this was before the effects of the Anabaptist controversy were felt, when attitudes hardened over the amount of water used for baptisms.[12] Subsequent English translations, including the KJV, have almost invariably used 'with'.[13] To say that John baptized people *with* water, rather than *in* water, is a political translation. If we put aside the baggage of sixteenth and seventeenth-century European church politics, as we should, and stop using the transliteration 'baptize' – with all the images it conveys of different baptismal practices – and start using 'immerse' instead, it becomes obvious that the correct translation of *en* in this context is 'in'. There is no contextual reason for using 'with'.

When we look at the second half of John's prophecy, about the Coming One immersing people in the Holy Spirit, we find that most English versions again transliterate *baptizō* and employ the causal or instrumental meaning of *en,* saying that the Coming One will baptize people with the Holy Spirit – a commonly used phrase in the Pentecostal and charismatic traditions. But that is to ignore the main point of John's immersions in water, which was to paint a graphic picture of how the Coming One was to immerse people in the Holy Spirit. As John immerses people in water, so the Coming One will immerse people in the Holy Spirit. Again, this is a political translation as there is no contextual reason for using 'with'. There is no other discernible reason either and, tellingly, in 1 Corinthians 12:13, which is the only time baptism in water is not mentioned alongside baptism in the Spirit (i.e. where there is no political intrusion into the translational process), almost every version uses the preposition 'in'.

The politically driven convention of using the transliteration *baptize* and the preposition *with* is one that should be questioned. And it is not just translators who do this; there are preachers and writers who refer to people being baptized *by* the Holy Spirit, or about a person's baptism *of* the Holy Spirit. We should let Jesus have the last word on this. During the Last Supper, he made a clear distinction between the Spirit being *with* his pre-Pentecost disciples, and how the Spirit was to be *in* his post-Pentecost disciples. He said, 'the Spirit … dwells with [Greek: *para*] you and will be in [Greek: *en*] you.'[14] Let us not obscure the meaning of John's carefully chosen words in their meticulously staged prophetic context.

Immersed in the Spirit

This concentration on the precise translation of John's words is necessary, not only because his expression that the Coming One would immerse people in the Holy Spirit is the unique core prophecy of this great prophet, but also because it is what gave particular meaning to his baptisms. We should take great care to render it in the way he originally meant, so we can climb into his head, as it were, and better think his thoughts after him. We might need to *metanoy*.

As we saw in Chapter 3, people came to hear him preach. His message was that the kingdom of heaven was now at hand and that people should prepare themselves. They should have a *metanoia*. This was followed by a very Jewish act of immersion in water, which was done in a highly symbolic stretch of the River Jordan, where they would have a second *metanoia* to do with the nature of his baptism – his was an immersion of *metanoia* and confession not of ritual cleansing. It was then, when they were coming up from the water, or were back on the riverbank, with a new vision of the kingdom of heaven and with their sins forgiven, that he would preach his third *metanoia*, saying that his immersions contained a visual revelation about what the Coming One would do. As John had immersed them in water, the Coming One would immerse people in the Holy Spirit and fire. Although John evidently drew inspiration from the prophets of old, this message was revolutionary and new. No one had ever prophesied anything like it and it was this, arguably more than anything else, that made his baptisms unique.

To understand more fully what John meant, let us remind ourselves of the role of the Spirit of God throughout the pages of Scripture.

He (the Spirit) is there on page one, when the earth was 'formless and void' and covered in water, when he hovered over it to bring life to the planet.[15]

Then, remembering that in the Hebrew of the Old Testament, as in the Greek of the New Testament, spirit, wind and breath are the same word (*ruach* in Hebrew, *pneuma* in Greek), we encounter God breathing on Adam to infuse him with life.[16]

The Holy Spirit was active from time to time throughout the Old Testament, empowering people for particular tasks,[17] until eventually the prophets began to sense that there would be a greater outpouring.[18] This began to happen at the outset of the New Testament when the Holy Spirit was especially active around the births of Jesus and John.[19]

The next development was when John, through his baptismal symbolism, made a connection between the coming of Jesus and the outpouring of the Spirit. Then, when Jesus was baptized – in that carefully chosen, symbolically perfect setting – the Holy Spirit confirmed Jesus in, and anointed him for, his role in bringing in this age of the Spirit. Thereafter, we see the Holy Spirit at work in and through Jesus in a powerful way.[20] Jesus gave power to his disciples,[21] but promised that the Holy Spirit was still to be poured out on them in a new way. The Spirit was *with* them, but was to be *in* them.[22]

After his resurrection, Jesus breathed the Spirit on the disciples and told them to wait in Jerusalem until they received the promised fullness of the Spirit.[23]

At his ascension, Jesus quoted John the Baptist to his disciples and told them that they would soon be immersed in (the) Holy Spirit. There were no better words or image to prepare them for what they were about to experience than John's carefully crafted expression, which is what makes John the Prophet of Pentecost.[24]

On the day of Pentecost, ten days later, the Holy Spirit began to flow in the way that had been promised, and Peter quoted the prophet Joel to make the connection:

> And in the last days it shall be, God declares, that I will pour out my Spirit on all flesh, and your sons and your daughters shall prophesy, and your young men shall see visions, and your old men shall dream dreams; even on my male servants and female servants in those days I will pour out my Spirit, and they shall prophesy.
> (Joel 2:28-29, quoted by Peter in Acts 2:17-18)

Notice the liquid metaphor of pouring used here by Joel and Peter. Peter, who had been a disciple of John, understood his message and he concluded his Pentecost sermon by using the language and symbolism he had learned from the Prophet of Pentecost:

> And Peter said to them, '[*Metanoy*] and be [immersed] every one of you in the name of Jesus Christ for the forgiveness of your sins, and you will receive the gift of the Holy Spirit. For the promise is for you and for your children and for all who are far off, everyone whom the Lord our God calls to himself.'
> (Acts 2:38-39)[25]

There were many immersion pools (*mikva'ot*) in and around the temple that were put to good use for the 3,000 who responded to Peter's call for a *metanoia* on that remarkable day. As these people were baptized, they would have remembered John's brilliant visual prophecy, that just as he had immersed people in water, there was one to come who would likewise immerse people in the Holy Spirit and fire.

(The) Holy Spirit

You may have noticed that each time John's core prophecy is recorded in the Greek New Testament 'Holy Spirit' (πνεύματι ἁγίῳ[26]) is written without a definite article. For my literal translation into English, I did consider the idea of similarly leaving the article out, but in the end, I followed the convention of adding one in, although I did put it in brackets, like this: (the) Holy Spirit. If I had not done this John's prophecy would read: 'He will immerse you in Holy Spirit and fire,' and one could argue that this is a better translation.[27]

In the Greek Gospels, sometimes a definite article is used for the Holy Spirit and sometimes not, and there does not seem to be a particular pattern to this.[28] It is nevertheless intriguing that when recording and quoting John's words the Gospel writers and others consistently did not use a definite article, and I thought I should point this out.

I mention it because we have a long history in the Church of not using a definite article when calling upon the Holy Spirit – for example, we say, 'Come Holy Spirit' ('*Veni Sancte Spiritus*' in Latin). And some prefer never to use a definite article for the Holy Spirit, believing this to be a more personal way of addressing or referring to the third person of the Trinity. It is not the way that most of us are used to doing things, but it is worth thinking about.

The call to inner purity

The addition of 'and fire' in Matthew's and Luke's Gospels is first of all a reference to the tongues of fire on the Day of Pentecost, prophesied by John.[29] There are some who say it is also to do with judgement because elsewhere John mentions fire in relation to judgement, as we shall see in the next chapter. But fire is also sometimes required for Old Testament ritual cleansing, as we saw in Chapter 2, and for refining. In this context, where John was speaking about immersion in the Holy Spirit and fire, for which immersion in water is the symbol, cleansing is what he most likely had in mind rather than judgement.[30]

It was the Old Testament purity laws and their attendant ritual washings (which John, as an observant Jew, will have practised regularly) that provided an essential context for John and his message. The immersions that John proclaimed, however, were substantially different. John proclaimed an immersion of *metanoia*. For his prophetic purposes what mattered to John was the imagery it provided for his message, not ritual purity. In doing this, John laid the basis for Christians to abandon the practice of washings for ritual purity. Our immersions (baptisms) have a completely new meaning. What Jesus later said about ritual purity radically changed the way Christians view such rituals:

Now when the Pharisees gathered to him, with some of the scribes who had come from Jerusalem, they saw that some of his disciples ate with hands that were defiled, that is, unwashed. (For the Pharisees and all the Jews do not eat unless they wash their hands, holding to the tradition of the elders, and when they come from the market-place, they do not eat unless they wash. And there are many other traditions that they observe, such as the washing of cups and pots and copper vessels and dining couches.) And the Pharisees and the scribes asked him, 'Why do your disciples not walk according to the tradition of the elders, but eat with defiled hands?' ...
And he called the people to him again and said to them, 'Hear me, all of you, and understand: There is nothing outside a person

that by going into him can defile him, but the things that come out of a person are what defile him.' ...

'For from within, out of the heart of man, come evil thoughts, sexual immorality, theft, murder, adultery, coveting, wickedness, deceit, sensuality, envy, slander, pride, foolishness. All these evil things come from within, and they defile a person.'
(Mark 7:1-5,14-15,21-23, cf. Matthew 15:1-20; Luke 11:37ff)

What is important to Jesus and his followers is an inner purity of the heart, not conformity to an external ritual. In the Old Testament cleansing for some forms of uncleanness also required a burnt offering – blood and fire. This has a particular resonance for Christians, because our cleansing is by the blood of Jesus and by the fire of the Holy Spirit in us and all around us – so powerfully symbolised in baptism. Immersion for ritual cleansing is another one of those things from the Old Testament that we no longer do, like sacrificing animals, because such things have been replaced by immersion in the Holy Spirit, and by the blood of the cross and the fire of the Spirit.[31]

It is part of the genius of John to make the link between Jesus and the outpouring of the Holy Spirit in the way that he did, and to do it so powerfully and so graphically. He provided us with the most potent expression to describe the work of the Spirit in a believer's life – to be immersed in the Holy Spirit. Now the Holy Spirit is both in us, as we learn elsewhere, and all around us, as we learn from John.[32] As well as repeating John's expression, Jesus also called it being 'clothed with power from on high'.[33]

A matter of interpretation

How, then, are we to interpret John's phrase? Risking oversimplification, in the Church today, there are broadly three ways.

There is firstly what we will call the traditional (or episcopal, or sacramental) interpretation, which is when someone who has been baptized as an infant (by sprinkling in the West, as a symbol of immersion[34]), later wants to confirm their baptism. A bishop is then called upon to hear their confession of faith and lay hands on them for the gift of the Holy Spirit, which is the connection between baptism and the Holy Spirit in this tradition.[35]

The second is what we will call the evangelical understanding in which the gift of the Holy Spirit is believed to be given when a person comes to a personal faith in Christ. In this school of thought baptism in the Holy Spirit is often equated with being born again.

Thirdly, Pentecostals say that the baptism in the Holy Spirit is a second blessing, subsequent to being born again, often with the expectation that it is to be accompanied by the gift of speaking in tongues.

Bearing in mind that one should always be wary of too narrow an understanding of the Holy Spirit, it is best, I think, to look for truth in all three of these understandings.

It is a good thing for an experienced Christian (a bishop or someone else) to lay hands on people and ask for the blessing of the Holy Spirit, especially on those seeking to make a public confession of their faith in Jesus.

It is a good thing too to acknowledge that the Holy Spirit works powerfully in the life of a believer who comes to Christ, to be aware of the work of the cross (blood) and of the Holy Spirit (fire) in the life of a believer.

And it is also good to emphasise that the Holy Spirit will continue to be active in the life of a believer, causing the fruit of the Spirit to grow in them, and giving them gifts of the Spirit.

It is a good thing for Christians to be open to having a second blessing of the Holy Spirit, and many more beside.[36]

No longer temporary

Some weeks after Jesus' baptism, the fourth Gospel records John calling out, 'Behold, the Lamb of God, who takes away the sin of the world!'[37] He then said that God's sign to him that enabled him prophetically to recognise the Coming One was that he would see the Holy Spirit descend on Jesus and *remain* on him. Famously, he saw the Holy Spirit descend in the form of a dove, and he saw the Spirit remain on Jesus.

This idea of remaining was significantly different from the experience of the Holy Spirit in the Old Testament. There the Spirit would anoint people just for the time it took to do the task they were called to do.

What John was witnessing was the beginning of the age of the Spirit, in which the Spirit remained on Jesus and, since that first Pentecost, also remains on Jesus' disciples.

It might take a *metanoia* to grasp this fully, but the Holy Spirit is always present with us even when we might not sense him, in much the same way that the sun is always there even when we do not feel it. There are occasions when we have a heightened awareness of the Holy Spirit's presence, and times of particular anointing, but the truth is that he is always with us, even when we do not feel it.

There is a spiritual exercise that helps this Johannine *metanoia* take root in us.

Centre yourself on the Lord.

Now place your finger tips on your stomach.

Then, while saying, 'The Holy Spirit is in me and all around me all the time,' move your hands up over your head and round to your side, palms up.

It is helpful to remember and give thanks for the everyday reality of the Holy Spirit living in us and all around us.

Anointed for service

There is no written record of John referring to Jesus by name or using a loaded term like 'Messiah' to describe him, although he witnesses Jesus being anointed by the Holy Spirit and 'messiah' means 'anointed' or 'anointed one'.[38] And on one occasion he is recorded saying to one of his disciples, 'I am not the Christ [Messiah], but I have been sent before him.'[39] He did not refer to Jesus as King either, although he did announce that the kingdom was at hand. He chose to refer to him as 'the Lamb of God, who takes away the sin of the world!'[40] as we have already discussed, and as 'the one who is to come', which is rendered as the Coming One in some translations, and also throughout this book.[41]

We know that Jesus was wary of directly referring to himself as the Messiah in order not to draw too much attention to himself until his time had come,[42] which John will have known, so his carefully coined expression – 'The Coming One' – was perfect, containing, as it does, echoes of John's commissioning text in Malachi, 'Behold, he is coming.'[43] It is another brilliant piece of Johannine phraseology.

In his core utterance, John also told us something else about the Coming One: he was to be powerful. John did not see himself as being worthy to undo the thongs of his sandals or to carry them, seen at the time as a menial task to be performed by a servant who washes the feet of an honoured guest. There is even an ancient rabbinical text that says, 'All works which a slave performs for his master, a disciple should do for his teacher, except undoing shoe straps.'[44] In contrast to this tradition, John said he was not even worthy to perform this work of a slave.

Jesus is certainly powerful, but he is also, like John, full of humility as he demonstrated at the Last Supper when he washed the feet of his own disciples. Jesus and John both demonstrated this essential mark of a godly person: along with true spiritual authority, humility.

Missing the point

There is another first-century source that tells us about the baptism of John. Josephus, a Jewish historian, wrote this in AD 93/94:

> John was a pious man, and he was bidding the Jews who practised virtue and exercised righteousness toward each other and piety toward God, to come together for baptism. For thus, it seemed to him, would baptismal ablution be acceptable, if it were used not to beg off from sins committed, but for the purification of the body when the soul had previously been cleansed by righteous conduct.[45]

In his younger days, Josephus had been involved in a Jewish baptist sect, following a teacher called Banus.[46] This may well have sparked an interest in John, but it also may have coloured his understanding. We need to remember that, although he was an excellent witness to the events of his times, Josephus had a twofold agenda that influenced his work.

Josephus had been born 'Joseph Ben Matthias' and had been a commander of the northern Jewish forces in the rebellion against Rome that broke out in AD 66. However, he saw the way the wind was blowing, changed sides, and gained considerable honours by ingratiating himself with his new masters, even changing his name to 'Titus Flavius Josephus'. Titus Flavius was the commander of the Roman forces fighting against the Jews, appointed after his father, who had commanded the army, was made emperor, founding the Flavian dynasty. Titus succeeded his father to the throne in AD 79.

Josephus wrote extensive historical works, notably *Jewish War* (*Bellum Judaicum*) and *Antiquities of the Jews* (*Antiquitates Judaicae*) in which his twofold agenda was to flatter his new masters, and to be an apologist for the Jews following the debacle of the rebellion, which resulted in the destruction of Jerusalem in AD 70.

It is fair to say that Josephus interpreted John's baptism through Jewish eyes, saying that John's baptisms were about purity. He either failed to grasp the importance of John's Jesus-centred teaching, or possibly he did understand what John was about but deliberately downplayed it, in the same way that he consistently downplayed any hint of messianism within Judaism as part of his agenda to restore the reputation of the Jews in the eyes of the Romans. Attitudes towards Christians among the Jews had hardened during the revolt as the Christians, most of whom were Jews who had converted, had refused to join in, and it is possible that Josephus reflected this too.

Josephus also wrote about Jesus, but in a very curt way.[47] If he did miss the part of John's message that pointed to Jesus he was not the only one to do so. There was a group of John's disciples that Paul encountered at Ephesus who did a similar thing.[48] Disciples do not always grasp all that their teacher is saying!

So many people, from Josephus on, have missed the point of John's baptism and the significance of his prophetic oracle. It was a baptism of *metanoia* that pointed to the Coming One. It told us a great deal about Jesus' nature and about the great work he was to do, ushering in an age in which believers can live in the Holy Spirit, the age of the Spirit. It was a baptism of *metanoia* in that it tells us something very important about our ongoing relationship with the Holy Spirit. We should learn not just to translate it correctly but also to use it in the way that John and Jesus – and Peter and Paul – meant it to be used.

It is fascinating to speculate, as we did in the last chapter, how the idea of baptism could have evolved in his mind, but it took the guidance of the Holy Spirit and John's prophetic genius to pull all the threads together and preach his message so powerfully.

> ... it was so that he might be revealed to Israel that I came immersing (baptizing) in water.
> (John 1:31b)[49]

CHAPTER 5: MAKE STRAIGHT THE WAY OF THE LORD

I am 'The voice of one crying in the wilderness,
"Make straight the way of the LORD,"'
as the prophet Isaiah said.
(John 1:23, NKJV)
John came to you in the way of righteousness.
(Matthew 21:32a)

John's task was to prepare the way of the LORD, and the main event in that process was the baptism of Jesus, which we will look at in the next chapter. In preparation for that, John developed his great prophetic tool of immersion in water with its multilayered message, including the promise of immersion in the Holy Spirit – his core prophetic oracle. Like all true prophets, though, he had an ethical message. He was a preacher of righteousness and of social justice. This is our focus in this chapter.

The Coming One announced by John was the King who was to usher in the kingdom of heaven. John's role was like that of a herald who goes ahead of a king to announce his imminent arrival and help people to get ready for his coming. In Matthew's Gospel, we are introduced to John's ministry with these words: 'In those days John the Baptist came preaching in the wilderness of Judea, and saying, '[*Metanoy* (or Reconsider)], for the kingdom of heaven is at hand', his first recorded words.[1] The kingdom proclaimed by this voice 'crying in the wilderness' had three elements to it:

- It had a king, a Coming One, who would judge the people, but who was also 'the Lamb of God, who takes away the sin of the world'.

- It was a kingdom in which the Coming One will immerse people in the Holy Spirit.
- It was a kingdom in which people will hear the word, have a *metanoia*, turn their lives to God and away from evil, and live justly.

A brood of vipers

Matthew and Luke record John's principal ethical teaching (Matthew 3:1-12 and Luke 3:1-20) and among the first people we hear of who came to listen to his preaching were members of the two main Jewish religious groups, the Pharisees and Sadducees. There were others who came to hear him, as we learn in Luke's Gospel, and John's message is very much the same for them all:

> But when he saw many of the Pharisees and Sadducees coming to his baptism, he said to them, 'You brood of vipers! Who warned you to flee from the wrath to come? Bear fruit in keeping with [*metanoia*]. And do not presume to say to yourselves, "We have Abraham as our father", for I tell you, God is able from these stones to raise up children for Abraham. Even now the axe is laid to the root of the trees. Every tree therefore that does not bear good fruit is cut down and thrown into the fire.'
> (Matthew 3:7-10)

> He said therefore to the crowds that came out to be baptized by him, 'You brood of vipers! Who warned you to flee from the wrath to come? Bear fruits in keeping with [*metanoia*]. And do not begin to say to yourselves, "We have Abraham as our father." For I tell you, God is able from these stones to raise up children for Abraham. Even now the axe is laid to the root of the trees. Every tree therefore that does not bear good fruit is cut down and thrown into the fire.'
> (Luke 3:7-9)

As we can see, John did not have much sympathy with some of those who came to hear him. He was looking for people whose faith bore fruit, who lived a life worthy of the kingdom, who had a faith that went deeper than mere outward conformity. John was particularly hard on those who arrogantly relied on their racial lineage. In his mind, such a view, coupled with a failure to live ethically, had turned people into 'a brood of vipers', as much use as the stones that littered the wilderness landscape. The kingdom of God that John proclaimed and Jesus established has nothing to do with any kind of race-based religion; it is a worldwide covenant of faith that is equally open to everyone of every race, both Jews and Gentiles for whom Abraham is not a father by blood, but by faith.[2] As Paul put it, 'If you are Christ's, then you are Abraham's offspring, heirs according to promise.'[3]

John's use of the word 'viper' is significant. There are two ancient Greek words for snake: *ophis* is the most common, used, for example, in the Septuagint Greek translation of the Old Testament for the serpent in the Garden of Eden. The other is *echidna*, which is the word used here, that refers specifically to a poisonous snake, hence 'viper'. This denotes something that is more than just cunning and slippery, but malign and noxious too. By using this metaphor, John exposed a way of thinking, acting and speaking that was highly toxic. Furthermore, in spite of the difference in vocabulary (*echidna*, not *ophis*), John may also have had Genesis 3:15 in mind, in which God cursed the seed of the serpent of Eden to enmity with the seed of the woman, who is thought to be Jesus.[4]

The refiner's fire

John also used the image of fire, which is in harmony with Malachi's prophecy that the messenger who preceded the LORD would be like a refiner's fire.[5] In this he is in the prophetic tradition of, for example,

Jeremiah who said, 'The LORD once called you "a green olive tree, beautiful with good fruit." But with the roar of a great tempest he will set fire to it, and its branches will be consumed.'[6] In some areas of the wilderness, wood is scarce. Only trees that are worthless because they are dead, or bear no fruit, or offer no shade, are cut down. Having said that, trees grew plentifully beside the River Jordan and tamarisk trees are common there today. The image of the axe cutting down the trees occurs occasionally in icons featuring John. There is an example of this in Chapter 3.

Matthew and Luke go on to record this saying of John's as he continued to describe the Coming One:

> His winnowing fork is in his hand, and he will clear his threshing floor and gather his wheat into the barn, but the chaff he will burn with unquenchable fire.
> (Matthew 3:12, cf. Luke 3:17)

John's picture of judgement is a rural one. The harvested grain would be put on the threshing floor before a threshing sledge was dragged over it, then it would be scooped into the air on a windy day using a winnowing fork. The grain would fall to the floor while the chaff was blown away.[7] This is a picture of separating what was fruitful from what was worthless, and in this case the waste was to be burned. John's image of a fire that did not go out is also found in the last verse of the prophecy of Isaiah.

Exactly what John meant when he used these symbolic images of judgement we cannot tell. Much of what we as Christians understand of judgement in the afterlife comes from the Gospels and other parts of the New Testament that were written after John's ministry. We therefore have no way of knowing whether John understood things the same way. As he will have discussed many things with Jesus, he probably did, but we cannot be certain.

Crowds, tax collectors and soldiers

When he exhorted people to 'Bear fruit in keeping with [*metanoia*]', John made a distinction between mere outward religious conformity and a truly heartfelt, life-changing response to his call for a *metanoia*. He was looking for a response that bore fruit by way of a change of lifestyle and habits, so people asked him for specific examples. Luke records three categories of people:

> And the crowds asked him, 'What then shall we do?' And he answered them, 'Whoever has two tunics is to share with him who has none, and whoever has food is to do likewise.' Tax collectors also came to be baptized and said to him, 'Teacher, what shall we do?' And he said to them, 'Collect no more than you are authorized to do.' Soldiers also asked him, 'And we, what shall we do?' And he said to them, 'Do not extort money from anyone by threats or by false accusation and be content with your wages.'…
> So, with many other exhortations, he preached good news to the people.
> (Luke 3:10-14,18)

It is quite likely that John had the text of his mandate from Isaiah 40 in mind when he was preaching:

> Every valley shall be exalted,
> And every mountain and hill brought low;
> The crooked places shall be made straight
> And the rough places made smooth …[8]

In an exegetical style called *midrash*, familiar to his contemporaries, he appears to apply this text to his audience.[9] For example, in suggesting that those who have clothing and food should share what they have with those who are destitute, he was metaphorically lowering mountains and raising valleys. When teaching corrupt tax collectors to be honest, he was metaphorically making the crooked ways straight. In teaching soldiers not to abuse their authority (in the way of corrupt law enforcement officers), he was metaphorically making the rough places smooth.

The crowds

John was the arch-exemplar of simple living with the most meagre of diets and very basic clothing, so in urging the crowds to live simply and be generous, he practised what he preached. His message has something very challenging to say to the greedy, selfish, materialistic, consumeristic and environmentally irresponsible society that characterises large parts of the world today. His ethical message is to be generous and live simply. He appealed to people's God-given, Holy Spirit-stimulated, loving conscience to share what they had.

Tax collectors

The baptism site is only eight kilometres from Jericho and was a border-crossing point between Perea on the east bank, ruled by the Tetrarch Herod Antipas, and Judea on the west bank, governed by Pontius Pilate. This would explain the presence of soldiers and tax collectors, for taxes in the ancient world were customarily levied at border crossings. These tax collectors called John 'teacher' (Greek Διδάσκαλε), which makes them his pupils or disciples.[10] This would suggest that the tax collectors in this area were particularly open to John's message, which is interesting because Zacchaeus, whose story is told later in in Luke's Gospel, was a chief tax collector in Jericho and likely, therefore, to have been responsible for the Roman customs operation, on the west bank of the river.[11] In other words, it is highly likely that he heard John's preaching. This would explain his response to Jesus' visit to his house when he said he would give away half his possessions ('Whoever has two tunics is to share with him who has none, and whoever has food is to do likewise'), and offered to repay fourfold anyone who could claim that he had defrauded them ('Collect no more than you are authorized to do').[12] This is exactly the sort of fruit that John thought should follow a genuine *metanoia*. Tax raising in the Roman world tended to be a privatised affair with someone contracted to raise a certain sum from a district, while keeping what he managed to get above the agreed sum. Corruption was endemic to this system, yet John was calling for honest accountability. Again, this has a contemporary ring to it; there is still a problem with corruption in public office around the world. John's is an anti-corruption message. As these public officials were tax collectors there is also an implied call to pay one's taxes, to 'render to Caesar what is Caesar's'.[13]

Soldiers

One writer summed up John's message to these border guards as, 'No bullying; no blackmail; make do with your pay!'[14] It is a timeless message to soldiers and law enforcement officers everywhere. But more generally, his call to be 'content with your wages' is very other-worldly and countercultural in the twenty-first century. Unlike the separatist, communal-living Essenes, John expected those who heard his message to return to their everyday lives in the wider community, where they would demonstrate the sincerity of their repentance by ethical kingdom-living. He also parted company with the zealots and other nationalists when he taught tax collectors and soldiers to carry on with their work, even if it meant supporting the occupation status quo.

During Holy Week, in one of his encounters with the religious establishment in Jerusalem, Jesus told this story:

'What do you think? A man had two sons. And he went to the first and said, "Son, go and work in the vineyard today." And he answered, "I will not," but afterward he changed his mind and went. And he went to the other son and said the same. And he answered, "I go, sir," but did not go. Which of the two did the will of his father?' They said, 'The first.' Jesus said to them, 'Truly, I say to you, the tax collectors and the prostitutes go into the kingdom of God before you. For John came to you in the way of righteousness, and you did not believe him, but the tax collectors and the prostitutes believed him. And even when you saw it, you did not afterwards change your minds and believe him.'
(Matthew 21:28-32)

In saying this, Jesus testified about the effectiveness of John's preaching, and in doing so we see that there were some prostitutes among his audience, who evidently heeded his message, turned their lives round and gave up their trade.[15]

At first sight, John's message, in which he called certain misguided and/or hypocritical religious people vipers and spoke of an axe cutting down trees (representing people who did not bear fruit), comes across as a bit harsh. But when we look closely at it we can see that, although he did not mince his words, his argument was very carefully thought out. John was inclusive and loving; he had a big heart and cared deeply for people and he wanted them to live fruitful lives.

The heart of the Father

While we are looking at John's ethical preaching we should consider again Gabriel's annunciation in the temple that John would 'turn the hearts of the fathers to the children', which reflected John's commissioning text from Malachi that 'he will turn the hearts of the fathers to their children and the hearts of the children to their fathers, lest I come and strike the land with a decree of utter destruction'.[16]

The best we can say is that this message is implicit in John's call to *metanoy* because there is nothing explicit about fathers and sons in the record of his life and teaching, unless it is the words of the Father at Jesus' baptism: 'You are my beloved Son; with you I am well pleased.'[17] Jesus and the Father lead by example. Also, we have assumed in Chapter 1 that John's relationship with his own older priestly father as he grew up was a good and fruitful one. What we can say is that utter destruction did come to the land in the way that Malachi had warned. John's prophetic warnings were not heeded. The temple, and indeed much of Jerusalem, was destroyed and a great number of Jews were enslaved after the revolt of AD 66-73.[18] Then there were two more rebellions against Rome that led, in AD 136 under the Emperor Hadrian, to an even greater destruction and enslavement and a ban on Jews ever entering Jerusalem, except for one day each year.

Speaking truth to power

We should also remember John's criticism of the tetrarch Herod Antipas for, among other things, having an affair with his brother's wife and divorcing his own wife in order to marry her.

> But Herod the tetrarch, who had been reproved by him for Herodias, his brother's wife, and for all the evil things that

Herod had done, added this to them all, that he locked up John in prison.
(Luke 3:19-20)

In doing this, John dramatically reflected the life and preaching of Elijah. Elijah came from the wilderness (from Tishbe in Gilead, on the east side of the River Jordan) and, without warning, appeared before King Ahab, who was in thrall to his scheming wife Jezebel, and delivered to him a short, powerful, water-related message. He then withdrew to the Brook Cherith, which, as we have seen, was thought to be close to John's carefully chosen baptism site.[19] Similarly, John appeared in the wilderness by the River Jordan, at a site associated with Elijah, and embarked on a short and dynamic water-related prophetic ministry, during which he challenged the ruler, the tetrarch Herod Antipas, who was in thrall to his scheming wife, Herodias. Herodias – like Jezebel with Elijah – became John's bitter enemy, seeking to kill him. We will look at the details of this in chapters 7 and 8. Speaking out about the sanctity of marriage was to cost John his life.

Apart from some prostitutes, mentioned by Jesus, viper-like religious types and 'the crowds', John's message was directed at abuse of power by public officials: tax collectors, soldiers and the ruler. In this case it was a ruler who abused his power absolutely by his arbitrary arrest of John, followed by his capricious execution. It is a salutary reminder to us of the potential for abuse by those who work for the state. And a reminder that there is no divide between sacred and secular in the kingdom of heaven preached by John. God watches over it all and will judge all.

Preparing the ground

As well as John's encounter with the tetrarch, his preaching and popularity also attracted the attention of the temple authorities in Jerusalem who sent a delegation of priests and Levites to question him and find out what he was up to. Their encounter with John, which took place after Jesus' baptism and just before Jesus returned to see John after his forty-day fast, is recorded in the fourth Gospel. Their exchange elicits from him, among other things, the paraphrase of Isaiah 40:3 that has been used for the title of this chapter:

> This is John's testimony, when the Jews sent priests and Levites from Jerusalem to ask him, 'Who are you?' He declared, and didn't deny, but he declared, 'I am not the Christ.' They asked him, 'What then? Are you Elijah?' He said, 'I am not.' 'Are you the prophet?' He answered, 'No.' They said therefore to him, 'Who are you? Give us an answer to take back to those who sent us. What do you say about yourself?' He said, 'I am the voice of one crying in the wilderness, 'Make straight the way of the Lord,' as Isaiah the prophet said.' The ones who had been sent were from the Pharisees. They asked him, 'Why then do you baptize, if you are not the Christ, or Elijah, or the prophet?' John answered them, 'I baptize [immerse] in water, but among you stands one whom you don't know. He is the one who comes after me, who is preferred before me, whose sandal strap I'm not worthy to loosen.' These things were done in Bethany beyond the Jordan, where John was baptizing.
> (John 1:19-28, WEB)

From a later encounter Jesus had with 'the chief priests and the scribes and the elders' that took place in Holy Week, we discover that the authorities did not endorse John's ministry.[20] Having satisfied themselves, though, that John was not making a claim to be the Messiah, or Elijah or the Prophet,[21] the authorities wanted to know just what the point of his baptism was, so he told them part of his core message, that there was a Coming One who was standing among them, who was very exalted. He did not tell them who this person was, nor did he tell them the second part of his core message about immersion in the Holy Spirit, which he reserved for people who had responded to his first two metanoias. That part of his message came the next day, after the delegation had left.[22]

At first sight it seems strange that, having gone to such lengths to identify himself with Elijah, he should deny being Elijah. However, there are two possible explanations for that denial. The first is that he understood himself not to be Elijah in some kind of reincarnation sense, which is what the question 'Are you Elijah?' may have implied, but to have, as Gabriel had said, the spirit of Elijah, which is something different.[23] In other words, the authorities asked the wrong question; they should have asked him if he had the spirit of Elijah. The second is that he was also a humble man who did not want to detract from his mission to prepare the way of the LORD by inviting attention on himself. As he later said, 'He must increase, but I must decrease.'[24] Jesus later put the record straight when he unequivocally acknowledged that John was Elijah as promised by the prophet Malachi.[25]

We are told in Luke 3:18 'with many other exhortations, he preached good news to the people' but what these other exhortations might have been we are tantalisingly unable to say. What we do know is that in much of his teaching and preaching John anticipated not just Jesus as the Coming One but also a good deal of the spirit of his teaching. He prepared the ground well. Now we will see what happened when Jesus came to see him.

CHAPTER 6: THE BAPTISM OF JESUS

There was a man sent from God, whose name was John.
He came as a witness to testify to the light, so that all might believe
through him. He himself was not the light,
but he came to testify to the light.
(John 1:6-8)

John was a prophet, a great prophet. As such he would have taken note of the circumstances of his life and regarded them as being part of the providence and guidance of God, especially his lifelong relationship with Jesus. But on something as critical as the recognition of the Coming One, who was at the heart of his core prophetic oracle as the one who was to immerse people in the Holy Spirit, he will have wanted direct confirmation. This is why God promised him a special sign known only to him. Here is the sign:

> I did not know him, but he who sent me to immerse (baptize) in water said to me, 'Upon whom you see the Spirit descending and remaining on him, this is he who immerses (baptizes) in the Holy Spirit.'
> (John 1:33)[1]

John had known Jesus as his cousin, and in Matthew's account of the baptism (see below), John plainly did know Jesus, so what did he mean when he said, 'I did not know him'? What he meant was that he had heard others testify that God had spoken to *them* about Jesus, but God had promised John a sign so that *he* would know Jesus prophetically as the Coming One, as well as know him personally. If he had intended to say that he did not know Jesus at all, the Greek verb *ginōskō* would have been used. Instead, the fourth Gospel has

John using the verb *oida*, which suggests complete knowledge. In other words, John was indicating that he did not *fully* know Jesus, that he had not at that time been able to recognise him prophetically. That changed when John saw the Holy Spirit descend on Jesus in a visible way and remain on him.[2]

As the Son of God, Jesus himself would have been looking for a sign that his public ministry was to begin. He would have been waiting for the anointing of the Holy Spirit, which the prophet Isaiah had foreseen in Jesus' commissioning text that begins, 'The Spirit of the Lord GOD is upon me because [he] has anointed me …'[3] This is what is implied in his title Messiah (Hebrew *Mashiach*), and its Greek equivalent *Christos*, which both mean 'anointed one'.

At the time John sensed was right, when 'the word of God came to [him]',[4] he began his dramatic public ministry down by the River Jordan. Crowds made the journey through the wilderness to hear him and to be baptized by him, which is testimony to his charismatic personality, the holiness of his lifestyle, the compelling nature of his message and God's blessing on his ministry. All this time, John will have been looking out for that confirming sign from God. Then, by divine appointment, Jesus arrived by the riverbank and asked John to baptize him:

Then Jesus came from Galilee to the Jordan to John, to be baptized [immersed] by him. John would have prevented him, saying, 'I need to be baptized [immersed] by you, and do you come to me?' But Jesus answered him, 'Let it be so now, for thus it is fitting for us to fulfil all righteousness.' Then he consented. And when Jesus was baptized [immersed], immediately he went up from the water, and behold, the heavens were opened to him, and he saw the Spirit of God descending like a dove and coming

to rest on him; and behold, a voice from heaven said, 'This is my beloved Son, with whom I am well pleased.'
(Matthew 3:13-17)

In those days Jesus came from Nazareth of Galilee and was baptized [immersed] by John in the Jordan. And when he came up out of the water, immediately he saw the heavens being torn open and the Spirit descending on him like a dove. And a voice came from heaven, 'You are my beloved Son; with you I am well pleased.'
(Mark 1:9-11)

Now when all the people were baptized [immersed], and when Jesus also had been baptized [immersed] and was praying, the heavens were opened, and the Holy Spirit descended on him in bodily form, like a dove; and a voice came from heaven, 'You are my beloved Son; with you I am well pleased.'
(Luke 3:21-22)

Revealing the Trinity

What John witnessed at Jesus' baptism, and what we witness in these passages from the Gospels, is the most profound of divine self-revelations – the first, the greatest and the most glorious overt revelation of the Holy Trinity in human recorded history. John prepared the way of Yahweh/Jehovah (יהוה, the LORD of Isaiah 40:3) and the Trinity appeared.

Thanks to the synoptic Gospels we have the details of what John witnessed: the Father spoke audibly from heaven about how he loves his son and is well pleased with him;[5] the righteous and ritually pure incarnate son, now in his thirties, was prayerful and ready to be anointed for his extraordinary mission; and the heavens opened –

such an evocative detail – and the Holy Spirit visibly came down on Jesus, appearing as a gentle dove, and remained on him as John had been promised, anointing him for the task ahead.

John had faithfully set the scene for this unique theophany, this majestic epiphany, this profound self-revelation of Yahweh/Jehovah as the Father, the Son and the Holy Spirit. A colossal shift took place at the baptism, like the moving of tectonic plates, as the world moved away from the simple monotheism of the Old Testament to the complex, sophisticated and beautiful Trinitarian monotheism of the New. It is a sublime and tender revelation, one that allows us a tantalising glimpse of the close inter-relationship of the members of the Trinity, in a dynamic relationship of love and delight.[6] It is entirely typical of the unshowy understated way that God reveals himself.

Jesus' baptism was the pinnacle of John's life, experience and ministry. He had expected Jesus to show up at the baptism site at some point but, despite the prophetic promise he had been given, what he witnessed must have exceeded all his dreams. His dear cousin, with whom he had enjoyed an extraordinary relationship since they were both in the womb, was anointed and recognised from heaven as the much-loved Son of God. There is not another moment like it in the history of the human race.

New beginnings

At Jesus' baptism, there are unmistakable echoes of the creation story from Genesis 1:1-3. When the earth was immersed in water, the Spirit of God hovered (like a bird) over the water and God spoke saying, 'Let there be light.'[7] With this in mind, it is worth re-reading the prologue of the fourth Gospel, with its conscious echoes of the beginning of the book of Genesis, and in which John the Baptist bears witness to Jesus as the light of the world.

In the beginning was the Word, and the Word was with God, and the Word was God. He was in the beginning with God. All things were made through him, and without him was not any thing made that was made. In him was life, and the life was the light of men. The light shines in the darkness, and the darkness has not overcome it.

There was a man sent from God, whose name was John. He came as a witness, to bear witness about the light, that all might believe through him. He was not the light, but came to bear witness about the light.

The true light, which gives light to everyone, was coming into the world. He was in the world, and the world was made through him, yet the world did not know him.

(John 1:1-10)

At this point it is also worth re-reading John's commissioning text in Isaiah 40. As already noted in Chapter 3, the river in Ezekiel's vision was to flow into and fill the Arabah – a large area that includes the Jordan valley where John baptized.[8] We have also noted that *arabah* is the Hebrew word for desert that Isaiah used in verse 3 of chapter 40. John was a Hebrew speaker who studied these texts in great depth, so he cannot have failed to notice this connection. So, bearing this in mind, and remembering John's midrash on the mountains, valleys, crooked paces and rough places, referred to in Chapter 5, and the exquisite revelation of the Trinity that took place at Jesus' baptism, here is the text again:

The voice of one crying in the wilderness:
'Prepare the way of the LORD [Yahweh/Jehovah];
Make straight in the desert [*arabah*]
A highway for our God.

Every valley shall be exalted
And every mountain and hill brought low;
The crooked places shall be made straight
And the rough places smooth;
The glory of the LORD [Yahweh/Jehovah] shall be revealed,
And all flesh shall see *it* together;
For the mouth of the LORD [Yahweh/Jehovah] has spoken.'
(Isaiah 40:3-5, NKJV)

Given that God spoke audibly when Jesus was revealed at his baptism, the last phrase of this prophecy of Isaiah's is also worth noting: 'the mouth of the LORD has spoken.'[9]

It is extraordinary how completely this prophecy came to life at Jesus' baptism. It brings to mind another prophecy from Isaiah:

Behold my servant, whom I uphold, my chosen, in whom my soul delights; I have put my Spirit upon him ...
(Isaiah 42:1a, quoted in Matthew 12:18)

The testimony of the fourth Gospel

The fourth Gospel has its own way of doing things and it treats the baptism of Jesus in the same way that it treats the Last Supper: it records neither of them. It mentions the Last Supper simply as a context for the following five chapters that are devoted to describing events that happened later that evening.[10] Similarly, there is only a hint of the baptism having happened in chapter 1 verses 14 and 15 (see below). The first sentence contains a phrase reminiscent of what the Father said when he spoke from heaven about his son, and in the second sentence we hear of John bearing witness to Jesus, as he was able to do at the baptism and subsequently. John is here described as having 'cried out' his witness, which reminds us of his commissioning text in Isaiah 40 verses 3 and 6 where the voice in the wilderness cries out.

> And the Word became flesh and dwelt among us, and we beheld His glory, the glory as of the only begotten of the Father, full of grace and truth. John bore witness of Him and cried out, saying, 'This was He of whom I said, 'He who comes after me is preferred before me, for He was before me.'
> (John 1:14-15, NKJV)

In another way that reminds us of the creation story, the fourth Gospel then carefully describes seven consecutive days at the start of Jesus' ministry, starting in chapter 1 verse 19 and ending at the wedding in Cana in chapter 2 verses 1 to 11.[11]

On the second of those seven days, some six weeks after the event,[12] John bears witness to what he had seen when Jesus was baptized:

> And John bore witness: 'I saw the Spirit descend from heaven like a dove, and it remained on him. I did not know him, but he who sent me to immerse (baptize) in water said to me, 'Upon whom you see the Spirit descending and remaining on him, this is he who immerses (baptizes) in the Holy Spirit.' And I have seen and have borne witness that this is the Son of God.'
> (John 1:32-34)[13]

Fulfilling all righteousness

The only bit of dialogue between Jesus and John that has been recorded for us was at Jesus' baptism. When he saw Jesus, John said, 'I need to be baptized by you, and do you come to me?' Which was an acknowledgement that John saw Jesus as the rabbi, the teacher, the master. Jesus, however, knew he should be baptized, so, using the phrase, 'it is proper for us in this way to fulfill all righteousness'[14] – his first recorded words since the temple incident as a boy – he acknowledged that it was God's will that he should be baptized and, of course, fulfilling God's will was all that Jesus and John ever wanted to do.[15] Jesus' baptism was not a baptism of *metanoia*, unlike all John's other baptisms it was a baptism of revelation and anointing. Others confessed their sins as they were baptized by John, Jesus had no need.

The way Jesus approached ritual purity is also a sign of his desire to 'fulfill all righteousness', for he was ritually pure at the time of his anointing. As we have noted in previous chapters, Jesus and John transformed notions of ritual purity, which for New Testament Christians is given by immersion in the Holy Spirit and by the blood of the cross and the fire of that Pentecostal Spirit. However, Jesus was being very careful at this point to fulfil all the requirements of the Old Testament.[16]

After his baptism Jesus and John were both given the sign they sought: the heavens were opened, and the Holy Spirit gently descended on Jesus 'in bodily form, like a dove' according to Luke, or simply 'like a dove' in Matthew and Mark. In Matthew's and Mark's Gospels it is recorded that Jesus saw the dove; in the fourth Gospel it is recorded that John saw it. In this way, both Jesus and John were given their sign and Jesus received his anointing.

The fourth Gospel also records that the Spirit was to remain on Jesus, which, as we have noted, is in contrast to the Old Testament experience when the Spirit came on people for particular reasons. This is an important part of the New Testament promise and experience, a foretaste of Pentecost.[17] Much of what is symbolised in water baptism for us happened to Jesus.

This personal prophetic sign of seeing the Spirit descend on Jesus and remain on him was foundational to John's witness of Jesus as the light of the world. It is hard to overstate its importance to him.

Given the significance of this moment and its unique and dramatic nature, it is not surprising that it is a popular subject for artists and filmmakers, who like to portray Jesus in the river being immersed (or sprinkled) by John in some way, and a white dove, or a bright light to symbolise the dove, descending on him.[18] However, remembering that John probably did not physically immerse Jesus, that it was probably a self-immersion in accordance with standard Jewish practice, we should now note, as Matthew and Mark tell us, that the Holy Spirit anointed Jesus after his baptism when he had come up from the water. 'Come up' is a verb in the active voice, which means that it was something that Jesus did for himself. No one helped him up.[19] This could mean that Jesus was then standing in the river, having come up from being immersed under the water, or it could equally mean that he had come all the way out of the river and was standing on the riverbank. It is impossible at this distance to tell which is correct. Luke adds the detail that the Spirit descended on Jesus while he was praying, which is what one would expect.

There was another reason for Jesus to choose to be baptized like everyone else, apart from the need to 'fulfill all righteousness': it was so that he could perfectly identify with fallen humanity, with all baptized Christians and with John.

John's baptism was, after all, the precursor of one of the rites instituted by God as a sign for the salvation of the world, and by being baptized in this way Jesus gave his full endorsement to John and to baptism.

The divinity of Jesus

After his baptism Jesus fasted for forty days in the wilderness and then, according to the fourth Gospel (which doesn't record the fast), he returned to the baptismal site for three days.[20] There John transferred to him some of his disciples. The text of that reunion is found below, but before reading it pause to picture the scene in context. John's life's work had been leading up to the theophany of Jesus' baptism. Then, following his baptism, the Spirit drove Jesus into the wilderness, where he spent forty days fasting, praying and being tempted by the devil in an environment that John, the man of the wilderness, knew very well. For the best part of six weeks therefore, John continued with his preaching and baptisms, all the while carrying inside him the knowledge of what he had witnessed. Toward the end of this waiting period he had that visit from an inquisitive deputation from the religious authorities in Jerusalem. Now, with this context in mind, read what happened the next day when Jesus showed up:

The next day he saw Jesus coming towards him, and said, 'Behold, the Lamb of God, who takes away the sin of the world! This is he of whom I said, "After me comes a man who ranks before me, because he was before me." I did not know him; but in order that he should be revealed to Israel, this is why I came immersing (baptizing) in water.' And John bore witness: 'I saw the Spirit descend from heaven like a dove, and it remained on him. I did not know him, but he who sent me to immerse (baptize) in water said to me, "Upon whom you see the Spirit descending and remaining on him, this is he who immerses (baptizes) in the Holy Spirit." And I have seen and have borne witness that this is the Son of God.'
(John 1:29-34[21])

When we read that in context, the joy of John's exclamation is almost tangible as he cried out, 'Behold, the Lamb of God, who takes away the sin of the world!' As John had leaped for joy in the womb at the recognition of Jesus this was the verbal equivalent – an expression of pure joy. In verse 9 of Isaiah chapter 40, part of John's commissioning text, Zion and Jerusalem are urged not to be afraid but to lift up their voice to the cities of Judah and call out, 'Behold your God!' John was that voice. He was not afraid, but he was wise enough to know that to have said, 'Behold your God!' about a person in that first-century Jewish environment would have led to their deaths. However, his carefully chosen form of words – 'Behold the Lamb of God' – which he repeated the following day, is obviously derived from it. It is a brilliantly conceived euphemism to describe Jesus – pure oracular prophecy at its very best.

In using this phrase John was also making a link between Jesus and the paschal lamb, who is not just the lamb of Passover but became the glorified lamb of the Apocalypse.[22] As he covertly proclaimed Jesus' divinity in this way, John would also have had in mind Isaiah 40:3 – 'Prepare the way of the LORD' (Yahweh/Jehovah), God's exhortation through Malachi to 'prepare the way before me', and Zechariah's Benedictus in which he predicted that his son was to 'go before the Lord to prepare his ways'.[23]

Furthermore, John's statement about Jesus being *before him* (John 1:15,30) has nothing to do with being older, as Jesus was five months younger. It is to do with Jesus' pre-existence. Add to this the observation we have already made in Chapter 5 that John expected the Coming One to judge the whole world and we can see how John had a very real awareness of the human/divine nature of Jesus right from the outset of his ministry. 'I have seen and borne witness', he said, 'that this is the Son of God.'[24]

The sentiment contained in John's saying, 'After me comes a man who ranks before me' (John 1:15,30) occurs in various forms seven times in the New Testament, as does John's saying about immersion in the Holy Spirit, as we saw in Chapter 4.[25] Both these sayings reveal the heart of John's ministry. John wanted to reveal the Coming One, which happened supremely at his baptism. He also wanted to say something about the nature of the Coming One and what he would do: he is exalted, indeed divine, and will inaugurate the age of the Spirit. The Church calendar in the Eastern Orthodox Church recognises that a core function of baptism is to reveal Jesus as it celebrates the baptism of Jesus at the feast of Epiphany (which means manifestation or revelation), a custom that is becoming more common in the West with the advent of the Common Lectionary.[26]

Disciples of John, disciples of Jesus

> The next day again John was standing with two of his disciples, and he looked at Jesus as he walked by and said, 'Behold, the Lamb of God!' The two disciples heard him say this, and they followed Jesus.
> (John 1:35-37)

John had disciples and there were some who went home and some who stayed close to him, learning from him and, presumably, helping him with his ministry. Andrew, Simon, Philip, Nathanael and a fifth unnamed disciple – commonly thought to be John the Evangelist – were some of John's disciples mentioned in the fourth Gospel.[27] These men came from Galilee, although John was a Judean and lived and worked there.[28]

John saw it as part of his work to hand followers over to Jesus. This was in accordance with Gabriel's declaration at his annunciation that he would 'make ready for the Lord a people prepared'. So, on day two of Jesus' sojourn at Bethany beyond the Jordan, John recommended Jesus to two of his disciples. Andrew, who was one of them, immediately fetched his brother Simon, whom Jesus called Cephas (Peter).[29] The next day Jesus called Philip who went and told his friend Nathanael and it was these disciples, including the unnamed disciple – four of whom became apostles – who set off with Jesus the following day for the three-day walk to the family wedding in Cana, Nathanael's home town, where Jesus performed his first miracle – turning water used for purification into wine.[30]

In chapter 3 of the fourth Gospel, we encounter Jesus' disciples baptizing people back in Judea, not far from John, and this, we are told, happened before John was put in prison.[31] In the other Gospels, events appear to happen in a different order. There we hear that John was imprisoned before Jesus called his disciples – including some of those John had earlier introduced to him.[32] There are some who say that this is a contradiction, but it seems more likely that Jesus called these disciples in stages – that they were introduced to him in Bethany, after which they did a few things together, but he delayed his final call for them to follow him until after John was arrested.

Three encounters

Jesus and John had known each other all their lives, but the New Testament only records three encounters between them. Each one of them is perfectly exquisite:

- While both of them were still in the womb John became the first unprompted person to recognise Jesus, at the meeting of the mothers. This was what prompted Elizabeth's beautiful prophecy and was hugely comforting to Mary, who responded with the Magnificat.

- John set the scene for the baptism of Jesus, where we have a record of a conversation between them – the only such record. This is where Jesus received his anointing, and where the first and greatest overt revelation of the Trinity in recorded history took place.

- When Jesus returned to the baptism site after his forty days of fasting in the wilderness he was welcomed by John crying out, 'Behold, the Lamb of God, who takes away the sin of the world!' He repeated this the next day to some of his disciples, who sought out Jesus and later became apostles.

Taking time to meditate on these encounters is a rewarding spiritual experience. Read the texts again, then prayerfully close your eyes and imagine yourself at the scene as an observer. Experience the moment.[33]

'He must increase, but I must decrease'

John's public ministry was almost over at this point, his job was nearly done and there was just one more episode in his relationship with Jesus before his arrest. The next events after the wedding in Cana, according to the Gospel of John, were a lakeside holiday, followed by Jesus' visit to Jerusalem for the Passover when he turned over the tables of the money-changers and animal-vendors for the first time and had his famous talk with Nicodemus. This is what followed:

After this Jesus and his disciples went into the Judean countryside, and he remained there with them and was baptizing. John also was baptizing at Aenon near Salim, because water was plentiful there, and people were coming and being baptized (for John had not yet been put in prison).

Now a discussion arose between some of John's disciples and a Jew over purification. And they came to John and said to him, 'Rabbi, he who was with you across the Jordan, to whom you bore witness – look, he is baptizing, and all are going to him.' John answered, 'A person cannot receive even one thing unless it is given him from heaven. You yourselves bear me witness, that I said, 'I am not the Christ, but I have been sent before him.' The one who has the bride is the bridegroom. The friend of the bridegroom, who stands and hears him, rejoices greatly at the bridegroom's voice. Therefore, this joy of mine is now complete. He must increase, but I must decrease.'

He who comes from above is above all. He who is of the earth belongs to the earth and speaks in an earthly way. He who comes from heaven is above all. He bears witness to what he has seen and heard, yet no one receives his testimony. Whoever receives his testimony sets his seal to this, that God is true. For he whom God has sent utters the words of God, for he gives the Spirit without measure. The Father loves the Son and has given all things into his hand. Whoever believes in the Son has eternal life; whoever does not obey the Son shall not see life, but the wrath of God remains on him.

Now when Jesus learned that the Pharisees had heard that Jesus was making and baptizing more disciples than John (although Jesus himself did not baptize, but only his disciples), he left Judea and departed again for Galilee.
(John 3:22-4:3)

Refuting the sceptics

There are some translations that do not put inverted commas at the end of the second paragraph above (at the end of v. 30), but at the end of the following paragraph (at the end of v. 36), making out that John spoke verses 31 to 36 as well (there is no punctuation in the original Greek to guide us). It is these translations that inspire critics who maintain that there was a conspiracy in the early Church to alter the record and put words into John's mouth that he did not utter but which give extra credence to Jesus. The response to such claims is to point out that verses 31 to 36 are more like editorial comments made by the gospel writer, that they are written in the style of the fourth Gospel, and that we were never meant to think that the Baptist spoke them. There is nothing in that paragraph that is not implicit in the teaching of John, but it nevertheless appears to be a summary of what had gone before, written by John the Evangelist, who had been a disciple of John the Baptist and who 'got him'. It is the right place for a summary, following, as it does, John saying, 'He must increase, but I must decrease.'

In response to this sort of critique, we should question the premise that the Church, after years of reflection, put words into John's mouth rather than concluding that the opposite is true and that the great prophet Rabbi John[34] significantly influenced the theology of the early Church. The early Christians admired John immensely and took him very seriously, as we shall see in Chapter 9.

We have just seen an example of the way John's story is treated in the *Sceptic John* process described in the Introduction. This is a good time to pause and look at some of the tools used in that process.

Redaction criticism
One of the academic tools used to analyse the Gospels is redaction criticism, which involves asking how each Gospel writer influences the story he tells. For example, it is usually understood that Mark's is the earliest Gospel, then Matthew's (although some say Matthew's was first), which makes the additional detail in Luke's account of Jesus' baptism – that Jesus was praying when the heavens opened – interesting. Sceptics say that Luke had an agenda to emphasise prayer, so he invented this detail, adding it to his narrative, which is a suggestion that casts doubt on Luke's integrity.[35] But the assertion that each Gospel writer invented stories to further his agenda is far from being the only way that such differences can be accounted for. For example, the fact that the Gospels only recount a fraction of the

events of Jesus' life, which is acknowledged in John 21:25, allowed the evangelists to pick and choose which details they included, without the need to invent new ones. Likewise, redaction or editing is to be expected in any writing process, and it is a travesty to suggest that this infers that the Gospel writers made things up. It is also quite natural for different witnesses of an event to remember different details and for the Gospel authors to differ in the details that they selected from the different witness accounts they will have had to hand.[36] It is a good thing that different writers emphasise different aspects of the story; it should be celebrated as it provides a fuller, more rounded picture of what happened. It is sad when people feel the need to invent notions about improper redactor interference to explain these differences. Redaction criticism is a useful tool, used numerous times in the writing of this book, but it can be overapplied, which is what has happened in the *Sceptic John* process.[37]

The embarrassment hypothesis
In the later stages of the sceptical quest for the historical John, a hypothesis emerged that it was an embarrassment to the early Christians that John had baptized Jesus because, so it is asserted, this made John superior to Jesus. For that reason, it is maintained, the Gospel writers felt the need to invent stories about John (particularly the infancy narrative) and ascribe sayings to John to make him inferior to Jesus, 'to make John safe'.[38]

This is a hypothesis that demonstrates a real lack of understanding of John, his immersions, his message and his role as the forerunner of Jesus. It ignores the profound relationship that Jesus had with his relative, lifelong friend and closest collaborator. And it reveals a regrettable disrespect for the integrity of the Gospel writers, who loved and admired John, as did all the early Christians, who looked to John as a prophetic guide through those momentous early years, as we shall see in chapters 9 and 10. They were happy for his story to be told. The embarrassment hypothesis completely misses the point. Far from being an embarrassment, John was a much-admired hero to the Church.

I feel genuinely sad that it has been necessary to be so forthright about the methods used in the *Sceptic John* process. *Sceptic John* is a severely diminished John, leaving us blind to the brilliant revelations about Jesus and the Holy Spirit, indeed about the Trinity as a whole, that shine through his prophetic life.

Jesus and his disciples baptizing

The Judean countryside was an obvious place for Jesus to go because of the preparatory work that John had done there. In fact, this is another way in which John kick-started Jesus' ministry. Jesus stayed there with his disciples, apparently close to where John was baptizing, and organised them to baptize those who came to him. It was Jesus' disciples who did the baptizing, not Jesus himself, because the baptizing that he does is in the Holy Spirit, as John prophesied. There may be implied differences in baptismal practices between John and Jesus' disciples and these might have led to the discussion between a Jew and John's disciples about purification (which was, of course, the goal of Jewish immersions). We cannot tell if there were differences in administration, but if that were so, all we can do is observe that John and Jesus' disciples, while they both had the job of pointing people to Jesus, were participating in different phases of Jesus' ministry.

Later baptisms performed by the post-Pentecost Church are conducted in yet another phase and are different again because the full significance of the Pentecostal symbolism of baptism can now be seen.

Where is Aenon?

The synoptic Gospels do not tell us the name of the site of John's baptizing, but the fourth Gospel is more specific, mentioning Bethany beyond the Jordan, and then Aenon (Αἰνών in Greek, which means 'many waters' or 'many springs' – the plural of *ain*, which means 'spring'), which was near Salim (Σαλείμ in Greek, which means 'peace').[39] No one knows for sure the locations of Aenon or Salim, except that they were in Judea. All the Gospel tells us is that at Aenon there was 'plenty of water'.[40] There are three possible sites that have been proposed, which are shown on the map in the Introduction:

1. There has long been a tradition that a site about twelve kilometres south-south-east of Scythopolis (modern Beth Shean), beside the west bank of the River Jordan is where Aenon was. There is plenty of water at this place, which seems to be its chief merit in its claim to be the correct location.
2. Another site is about ten kilometres north-east of Shechem (modern Nablus), in the Wadi Far'ah, in the heart of Samaritan country, where there are springs. A village called Salim is eleven kilometres away. But why is Aenon described as being near Salim, when it is an obscure place eleven kilometres away, while the better known Shechem is closer? Nevertheless, this second site is the most recent suggestion and is the one preferred by those who think that John ministered near here to prepare the way for Jesus' work among the Samaritans that immediately follows this incident.[41]
3. The third site is close to Bethany beyond the Jordan, where Jesus was baptized, up the Wadi al-Kharrar which is traditionally thought to be the Brook Cherith, where Elijah stayed during the drought that he had proclaimed and was fed by there by ravens.[42]

Madaba mosaic map. The inscription reads:
ΑΙΝΩΝ ΕΝΘΑ ΝΥΝ Ο ΣΑΠΣΑΦΑΣ
(Ainōn, where now is Sapsaphas)
Sapsaphas = Place of willows[43]

The first and third of these sites are shown on the famous sixth-century mosaic map at Madaba, a town on the east side of the River Jordan not far from the baptismal site. It is a fascinating guide to the traditions of that time, but it is notoriously inaccurate. Each of these three possible locations has its advocates, and any one of them may prove to be correct, but it is the third of these sites that is preferred in this book, shown above on the Madaba map. Here are the reasons why:

1. The next recorded incident in John's life was his arrest by Herod Antipas and this is the only one of these three sites that

was in territory that he ruled, in Perea. It is also the closest to Machaerus, also in Perea, where John was incarcerated and beheaded.[44]

2. It stays true to John's careful symbolic positioning east of Jerusalem, described in Chapter 3.

3. It has a strong connection with Elijah.

4. The Madaba map says that in the sixth century, Aenon was called Sapsaphas (also known as Sapsas), which has been identified close to Wadi al-Kharrar.[45]

5. A reasonable explanation for the change of location is because of the spring floods. The River Jordan swells dramatically when the snows of Mount Hermon melt in the spring. It makes sense for John to stay as close as possible to his carefully chosen location at Bethany beyond the Jordan during these floods, and this wadi is ideally located for just that purpose and has several springs in it (remember, Aenon means 'many springs').[46]

6. One of the possible etymological roots of 'Bethany' is 'Beth Ainon', which means 'House of Springs', which suggests a possible close connection between Aenon and Bethany.[47]

7. Although it is John's baptizing that is being described, the context seems to suggest that it was probably not far from where Jesus was ministering and Jesus, according to John 3:22 and 4:3, was in Judea at the time. None of these three sites was politically part of Judea in those days, although this one was certainly the closest of these three – on the opposite bank of the River Jordan and only a stone's throw away. Having said that, in those days of fluctuating boundary lines, this area was referred to as 'Judea beyond the Jordan' in Matthew 19:1 and Mark 10:1.[48]

One potential problem with this location is that, while in Aenon, John's disciples refer to Jesus as 'he who was with you across the

Jordan.'[49] This is a reference to John's main baptism site, which at first sight makes it look as if Aenon was on the other side of the river to that main site. However, the phrase rendered here as 'across the Jordan' in the ESV, *peran tou Iordanou* in Greek, is rendered 'beyond the Jordan' or 'east of the Jordan' in a number of other versions of John 3:26, which is in keeping with the way the phrase is generally translated when it occurs elsewhere in the New Testament, including its use in 'Bethany beyond the Jordan' (*Bethania peran tou Iordanou*).[50] *Peran tou Iordanou* appears to be a first-century equivalent to 'Transjordan' today and is generally used to describe land to the east of the river. This means that John's disciples were talking about a time when Jesus was with John in the area known as 'beyond the Jordan', or 'Transjordan', and not about a time when he was on the other side of the river.

The exact location of Aenon is at present, as with so many biblical sites, one of those problems that defies a definite solution, but there is good reason to think that it was in the Wadi al-Kharrar close to John's usual baptism site at Bethany beyond the Jordan.

John as witness

John had finished what he set out to do. In a dynamic and relatively short ministry, this charismatic and faithful man had drawn crowds from all around Judea, including Jerusalem, and made a great impact on their lives. He had brilliantly prepared the way of the LORD and now he was decreasing while Jesus was increasing. There was not a shred of jealousy in his nature; he was like the friend of the bridegroom who rejoiced at the growing recognition of the one he loved.[51] As Jesus had been a friend to the bride and groom at the wedding in Cana, helping them to celebrate, so John, Jesus' very good friend, rejoiced to see the first dawning of the Church, the bride of Christ. It made his joy complete.

As the fourth Gospel moves on to chapter 5, by which time John had been arrested, we see the healing of the blind man at the Pool of Bethesda, after which there was a dispute with some of the Jewish establishment about Jesus' authority. During this dispute Jesus invoked John as a witness to him, and then put their relationship in perspective:

> There is another who bears witness about me, and I know that the testimony that he bears about me is true. You sent to John, and he has borne witness to the truth. Not that the testimony that I receive is from man, but I say these things so that you may be saved. He was a burning and shining lamp, and you were willing to rejoice for a while in his light. But the testimony that I have is greater than that of John. For the works that the Father has given me to accomplish, the very works that I am doing, bear witness about me that the Father has sent me.
> (John 5:32-36)

John was not 'the Light', as is made clear in the prologue to the fourth Gospel, but he was a burning and shining lamp. Jesus and John came together in public ministry for only a short while, but in that time, they changed the world. For those with eyes to see, John had not only introduced the Messiah, he had also understood his divine/human nature and had set the scene for and was present at Jesus' anointing at the first and greatest overt revelation of the Trinity in recorded history, of which he was a faithful witness. He had also prophesied about the outpouring of the Holy Spirit that took place at Pentecost, passed on some disciples to Jesus – a quarter of his apostles – and provided Jesus with a rite, an embryonic sacrament, that has touched the lives of every Christian who has ever lived.

The lamp had burned brightly for a season.

But now that light was about to be extinguished.

Part 3: MARTYRDOM

CHAPTER 7: BOUND AND IN PRISON

> But Herod the tetrarch, who had been reproved by him for
> Herodias, his brother's wife, and for all the evil things that Herod
> had done, added this to them all, that he locked up John in prison.
> (Luke 3:19-20)

The Herod that most people know about is the Herod of the Christmas story, Herod the Great, patriarch of the influential but troubled Herod dynasty and one of the most tyrannical rulers in history, who even put to death several of his own children and his favourite wife.[1] The Emperor Augustus once said of him that it would be better to be Herod's pig than his son, which, given the Jewish aversion to pigs, does not bode well for his sons![2]

The Herod who imprisoned John was Herod Antipas, one of these sons. On his death in 4 BC, Herod the Great's extensive domain was divided among three of his surviving sons and his sister, as shown on the map in the Introduction: Archelaus (whose mother was Malthace) was appointed ethnarch of Idumea, Judea and Samaria – the bulk of the kingdom; Herod Antipas (also a son of Malthace) was made tetrarch of two non-contiguous territories, Galilee and Perea; Herod Philip (whose mother was Cleopatra of Jerusalem) was made tetrarch of Batanea, Trachonitis and Auranitis; and a small portion was bequeathed to Herod the Great's sister Salome.[3] By the time of John's ministry, Salome had died, Archelaus had been exiled, and a Roman procurator ruled their territories, which were renamed Provincia Judaea. Pontius Pilate, who was appointed to the post in AD26, was the fifth of these procurators.

Herod the Great's mother was a Nabatean and Herod Antipas had married the daughter of Aretas IV, also known as Hareth, king of Nabatea, which was a flourishing Arab nation with an extensive territory to the south and east.[4] The Nabateans made their money chiefly by exploiting the trade routes that passed through their land, the King's Highway being the principal one, and they built a Hellenistic style capital at Petra.[5] They surrounded the southern end of Herod Antipas' Perea, which was populated by a mixture of Jews and Arabs potentially loyal to Nabatea. His marriage was therefore politically and strategically important.

Things began to go wrong when, on a visit to Rome, Antipas stayed with one of his half-brothers (who was the son of Herod the Great's third wife, Mariamme[6]). There is a gap in our knowledge about the name of this half-brother that causes some confusion. He is called Herod by Josephus, who appears simply to be using the family name, and he is referred to as Philip in the New Testament.[7] We shall call him Philip/Herod to distinguish him from the earlier mentioned Herod Philip.[8]

This son had originally been highly favoured in Herod the Great's will but was disinherited during the tumultuous last years of his reign, in which his mother was implicated in a palace plot.[9] Philip/Herod had married Herodias, whose father was Aristobulus, another half-brother of Antipas and Philip/Herod, who was executed by Herod the Great in one of the palace intrigues. Her mother was Berenice, daughter of Herod the Great's sister, Salome.[10]

Herodias' soaring ambition is one of the subplots of this story. She must have been bitterly disappointed with the final terms of the will. Philip/Herod and Herodias had a daughter named after Herodias' grandmother, Salome.[11] In Rome, Antipas and Herodias had an adulterous affair that led to her divorce from Philip/Herod and marriage to Antipas, an arrangement that Herodias only agreed to on the condition that Antipas divorce his wife, the Nabatean princess, which he agreed to do. She, however, got wind of this arrangement and travelled to Machaerus, a fortress near Antipas' southern border, from which her father's soldiers whisked her away to Petra, not very far away down the King's Highway, before she could be shamed. Her father, King Aretas, was furious at the way his daughter had been treated and thereafter Antipas had good reason to feel nervous about the security of Perea with its ethnically mixed population.[12] His anxiety was justified, as we shall see in the next chapter.

Herod's family tree

On the next page there is a select family tree showing all the members of the Herod family who are mentioned in this book. Out of interest, Drusilla is also listed, as she is mentioned in the New Testament too, which brings to eleven the number of Herod family members mentioned in the Bible:

Herod the Great: of the Christmas story in Matthew's Gospel.
Archelaus: Matthew 2:22.
Herod Antipas: imprisoned and executed John. Tried Jesus.
Philip/Herod: mentioned by John as a cuckold.
Herodias: criticised by John, later engineered his execution.
Salome: the dancing girl.
Herod Philip: Luke 3:1. Later became Salome's first husband.
Herod Agrippa (a.k.a. Agrippa I): Acts 12 records his unpleasant death.
Agrippa (a.k.a. Agrippa II): sat in judgement over Paul in Acts 25 and 26.
Bernice: Acts 25:13; 26:30. Joined her brother Agrippa II in judging Paul.[13]
Drusilla: Acts 24:24. Wife of the procurator Felix.

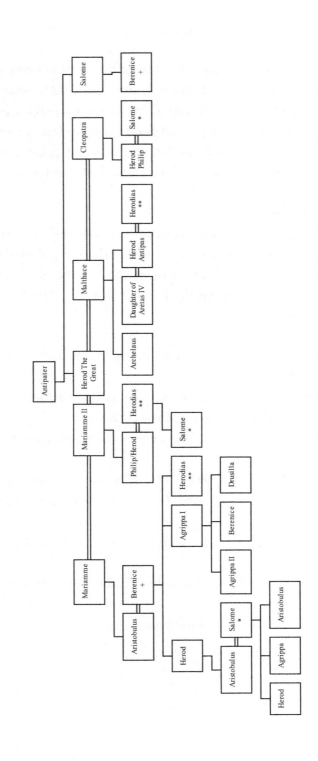

In Old Testament law it is permitted for a man to marry his brother's wife if his brother has died. It is even a duty for him to do so if his brother has had no children. But it is against the Law and considered impure to do so if the brother is still alive, especially if he already has a child.[14] Not surprisingly, John the Baptist was critical of Antipas for his marital arrangements, and for other unspecified indiscretions.[15] He will not have been the only one to criticise an arrangement that was so contrary to the Torah.

Hilltop fortress

John preached close to a crossing point for people passing from Judea to Perea. Antipas and his new wife would very likely have passed there on their journeys between the two non-contiguous parts of his tetrarchy, especially if they travelled via Jerusalem. John could easily have spoken to them. In response, partly on account of the sensibilities of his new wife, according to Matthew 14:3-4 and Mark 6:17-19, and partly because of fears about this popular preacher drawing away the loyalty of the Jewish section of his already vulnerable Perean territory, according to Matthew 14:5 and Josephus, Antipas decided to arrest John and take him to his southern hilltop fortress of Machaerus, from where his Nabatean wife had recently fled.[16]

Machaerus is a dramatic site overlooking the Dead Sea from the east, about thirty kilometres as the crow flies from the place where John baptized Jesus. On a clear day, the view from Machaerus includes the Judean wilderness, Qumran, Jerusalem (although not quite as far as Ein Kerem) and almost Bethany beyond the Jordan. From this high vantage point, John would almost have been able to see where he had lived and worked all his life.[17] It is the right sort of place for him to end his days – a place in the wild wilderness on a dramatic hilltop not far from Mount Nebo where Moses died, and Elijah's Hill where Elijah was carried off with a flaming chariot. As Moses had led the Israelites to the Moabite plain and was taken from there by God up the nearby Mount Nebo to see the Promised Land before his death, so John was arrested on the Moabite plain and taken away to a nearby hilltop fortress, where he was to die – after he had glimpsed the promised kingdom of God at the theophany of Jesus' baptism.

For Herod had seized John and bound him and put him in prison for the sake of Herodias, his brother Philip's wife, because John had been saying to him, 'It is not lawful for you to have her.' And though he wanted to put him to death, he feared the people, because they held him to be a prophet.
(Matthew 14:3-5)

For it was Herod who had sent and seized John and bound him in prison for the sake of Herodias, his brother Philip's wife, because he had married her. For John had been saying to Herod, 'It is not lawful for you to have your brother's wife.'
(Mark 6:17-18)

But Herod the tetrarch, who had been reproved by him for Herodias, his brother's wife, and for all the evil things that Herod had done, added this to them all, that he locked up John in prison.
(Luke 3:19-20)

The hilltop fortress of Machaerus.[18]

Three-dimensional computer model of Herod's fortress at
Machaerus, viewed from the east.[19]

Theoretical cutaway view of the fortress at Machaerus, viewed from the south. The dining rooms (*triclinium*) were in the upstairs of the rectangular building shown with a pitched-roof.[20]

One burning question

The New Testament narrative suggests that John had a more open custody than the subterranean dungeon in which filmmakers sometimes like to portray him, possibly a kind of house arrest in the lower, northern part of the fortress.[21] It was in such a setting that John's disciples were able to have access to him and brought him eagerly awaited news of Jesus' work. What he heard prompted him to send a message to his cousin in the form of a question that at first sight is quite unexpected. Here are the two Gospel texts, side by side, as there are some differences in presentation:

Matthew 11:2-19

Now when John heard in prison about the deeds of the Christ, he sent word by his disciples and said to him, 'Are you the one who is to come, or shall we look for another?'[22]

And Jesus answered them, 'Go and tell John what you hear and see: the blind receive their sight and the lame walk, lepers are cleansed and the deaf hear, and the dead are raised up, and the poor have good news preached to them. And blessed is the one who is not offended [or caused to stumble[23]] by me.'

Luke 7:18-35

The disciples of John reported all these things to him. And John, calling two of his disciples to him, sent them to the Lord, saying, 'Are you the one who is to come, or shall we look for another?' And when the men had come to him, they said, 'John the Baptist has sent us to you, saying, "Are you the one who is to come, or shall we look for another?"'

In that hour he healed many people of diseases and plagues and evil spirits, and on many who were blind he bestowed sight. And he answered them, 'Go and tell John what you have seen and heard: the blind receive their sight, the lame walk, lepers are cleansed, and the deaf hear, the dead are raised up, the poor have good news preached to them. And blessed is the one who is not offended [or caused to stumble[24]] by me.'

As they went away, Jesus began to speak to the crowds concerning John: 'What did you go out into the wilderness to see? A reed shaken by the wind? What then did you go out to see? A man dressed in soft clothing? Behold, those who wear soft clothing are in kings' houses. What then did you go out to see? A prophet? Yes, I tell you, and more than a prophet. This is he of whom it is written, "Behold, I send my messenger before your face, who will prepare your way before you." Truly, I say to you,[25] among those born of women there has arisen no one greater than John the Baptist. Yet the one who is least in the kingdom of heaven is greater than he.

When John's messengers had gone, Jesus began to speak to the crowds concerning John: 'What did you go out into the wilderness to see? A reed shaken by the wind? What then did you go out to see? A man dressed in soft clothing? Behold, those who are dressed in splendid clothing and live in luxury are in kings' courts. What then did you go out to see? A prophet? Yes, I tell you, and more than a prophet. This is he of whom it is written, "Behold, I send my messenger before your face, who will prepare your way before you." I tell you, among those born of women none is greater [or, 'There is not a greater prophet'[26]] than John. Yet the one who is least in the kingdom of God is greater than he.'

From the days of John the Baptist until now the kingdom of heaven has suffered violence, and the violent take it by force. For all the Prophets and the Law prophesied until John, and if you are willing to accept it, he is Elijah who is to come. He who has ears to hear, let him hear.

But to what shall I compare this generation? It is like children sitting in the market-places and calling to their playmates, "We played the flute for you, and you did not dance; we sang a dirge, and you did not mourn." For John came neither eating nor drinking, and they say, "He has a demon." The Son of Man came eating and drinking, and they say, "Look at him! A glutton and a drunkard, a friend of tax collectors and sinners!" Yet wisdom is justified by her deeds.'

(When all the people heard this, and the tax collectors too, they declared God just, having been baptized with the baptism of John, but the Pharisees and the lawyers rejected the purpose of God for themselves, not having been baptized by him.)

'To what then shall I compare the people of this generation, and what are they like? They are like children sitting in the marketplace and calling to one another, "We played the flute for you, and you did not dance; we sang a dirge, and you did not weep." For John the Baptist has come eating no bread and drinking no wine, and you say, "He has a demon." The Son of Man has come eating and drinking, and you say, "Look at him! A glutton and a drunkard, a friend of tax collectors and sinners!" Yet wisdom is justified by all her children.'

Because it is such a surprising question there are several quite different explanations given for it: here are four.

The first is that John sent his disciples to Jesus so that *they* could be reassured about him. Those putting this idea forward point to John 3:25f which, they say, is evidence of dissension between some of John's disciples and Jesus and that it is these disciples that John sent with the question. There is no doubt that their visit to Jesus will have made a great impression on them, but there is some doubt that the incident in John 3 amounted to dissension. And there is more in John's question and in Jesus' reply than this hypothesis allows.

The second is that John had a moment of doubt about his identification of Jesus, despite the extraordinary sign that he was given. While this idea is a comforting reminder of John's humanity it does not seem to be the way that Jesus understood the question, judging by his reply and by him then saying to the crowd that John was not going to be shaken like a reed blowing in the wind, and that there is no greater person who has ever lived.

Thirdly, some say that it is possible that John had a different expectation of Jesus' ministry – possibly of the kind of rule of God that would see him released from prison. Those advocating this view suggest that John might have had a single-stage view of God's kingdom, as did many of his contemporaries (as we can see in the Benedictus), whereas Jesus has a two-stage view – the first stage being what we experience now, the second being the age to come.[27] There is no external evidence for this hypothesis, but it has nevertheless been suggested that this could provide an explanation for John's concern and his question might have been designed to nudge Jesus into more action.

It is the fourth explanation that seems to fit the facts best, however: that John realised his time preparing the way of the LORD had come to an end and he was asking Jesus to testify himself that he was the

Coming One. In his reply Jesus did not directly say that he was the Messiah, as the time for this kind of overt self-identification had not yet come. Jesus, in any case, had to be careful what he said because these messengers were about to return to Herod's fortress where they might be interrogated. However, he did respond positively in two ways. Firstly, he demonstrated that he was doing the works expected of the Messiah, alluding directly to his mandate in a passage from Isaiah, the same prophet who had meant so much to John. He alluded to the texts he had earlier read out in the synagogue in Nazareth in the early stages of his ministry. We should note that in his reply to John, Jesus does not refer to proclaiming liberty to the captives, which appears to be a coded message to John, who will have noticed the omission. John was not going to be freed from prison.

'The Spirit of the Lord is upon me, because he has anointed me to proclaim good news to the poor. He has sent me to proclaim liberty to the captives and recovering of sight to the blind, to set at liberty those who are oppressed, to proclaim the year of the Lord's favour.'
And he rolled up the scroll and gave it back to the attendant and sat down. And the eyes of all in the synagogue were fixed on him. And he began to say to them, 'Today this Scripture has been fulfilled in your hearing.'
Luke 4:18-21 (Jesus reading Isaiah in the synagogue in Nazareth[28])

The second indirect way that Jesus acknowledged that he was John's Coming One came as John's disciples were taking their leave. Jesus spoke to the crowd about John in glowing terms, saying, as we have already noted in Chapter 4, that there has never been a greater man, or a greater prophet. This was a way of letting John know how much he was valued by Jesus, and it was a way of testifying that what John had said about Jesus was true. He also said that John was Elijah, with all the messianic expectations that implies, and he referred to himself as the Son of Man, which was the title of the messiah in Daniel's prophecy.[29]

By his question John had asked Jesus to concur that he was the Coming One. In these indirect yet unmistakeable ways, Jesus clearly replied affirmatively.

Jesus gave his blessing to John, who was in no way offended by his cousin or caused to stumble by him. Some think of this blessing as a general beatitude, the beatitude of the unoffended. It is a good beatitude: if life is hard, as John's was at the time, and God does not step in miraculously to relieve the problem, do not become offended by God or let this shake your faith. It is a blessing not to get upset or angry with God when life becomes turbulent and confusing.

The reed that would not bend

It is a curious fact about Jesus and John that they were both reluctant to testify about themselves, preferring rather to testify about each other. Testimony about Jesus came from his works, the Father, the Holy Spirit, Scripture and from John. Here Jesus gave testimony to his audience about what he thought about his cousin: he was among the greatest people who had have ever lived, an unshakeable prophet, Elijah himself. He also acknowledged that not everyone was going to grasp this, which is still true today.

It was commonly accepted then, as is still often the case among Jews today, that the gift of prophecy had ceased after Malachi had died and was not expected to resurface until Elijah reappeared. We saw earlier how John equivocated about being Elijah, but here (recorded by Matthew), Jesus confirmed it. John was, as Gabriel had said at his annunciation, the one prophesied by Malachi who had the 'spirit and power of Elijah'.[30] The long drought of prophecy had come to an end.

John is often thought of as an Old Testament prophet in the sense that he was the herald of Jesus and the kingdom, but he did not live to see the kingdom come in the way that Jesus ushered it in on the Day of Pentecost, when the disciples were immersed in the Holy Spirit and fire. This is why Jesus said, 'the one who is least in the kingdom of heaven is greater than he'. This was not a comment on John because Jesus had just said that John was up there with the greatest people who have ever lived. It was a comment on the nature of the kingdom. John was the Prophet of Pentecost, but he did not live to see it and did not, therefore, enjoy its full benefits, as we do. At the same time, he was more than an Old Testament prophet; he was the transforming prophetic link between the Old Testament and the New.

In the Jordan valley there is a vigorous variety of reed that grows tall, waving about and rustling whenever the wind blows, and there is a photograph at the end of Chapter 3 that shows them. This forms the basis for Jesus' analogy. In contrast to reeds blowing about in whatever direction the wind blew, John would bend his principles for no man.[31]

Similarly, Jesus spoke about John's ascetic dress sense. This again was a vivid picture. The contrast between the hardy John, dressed in clothes made of camel hair, and Antipas and his court, in their rich finery, was all too obvious to his listeners.[32] The irony, of course, is that John was then imprisoned in one of those palaces.

Where eagles soar

According to Matthew, Jesus spoke about John suffering violence. At its core, Christianity has a doctrine of suffering. Christianity is not a triumphalistic religion, but one of servanthood and suffering, in which it can be said that 'the blood of the martyrs is the seed of the Church.[33] Indeed, the central act of Christian worship is the remembrance of the brutal death of its founder. The greatest blessings (beatitudes) Jesus' followers can enjoy are meekness, mourning, hungering, thirsting, suffering, persecution and the like. As Jesus said to John's messengers, the challenge is not to be offended or caused to stumble by these things.[34] It has always been true that genuine prophetic people have suffered violence, as Jesus pointed out in Matthew 23:31-35.[35] They always will.

In the same way that Jesus referred to his commissioning text from Isaiah, if John meditated in captivity on his own commissioning text from Isaiah 40 he may have remembered other passages from the chapter:

- Verse 3 reads, 'The voice of one crying in the wilderness: 'Prepare the way of the LORD, Make straight in the desert A highway for our God' (NKJV). The ways of Herod Antipas were anything but straight so, although we hear that Herod 'liked to listen to him' (NRSV), we also hear that 'he was greatly perplexed' by what he heard and that he 'wanted to put him to death'.[36]

- Verses 15-17 may have kept his situation in perspective: 'Behold, the nations are like a drop from a bucket, and are accounted as the dust on the scales ... All the nations are as nothing before him, they are accounted by him as less than nothing and emptiness.' And verse 23 adds, '[God] brings princes to nothing, and makes the rulers of the earth as emptiness.'

- Machaerus is a place where eagles circle above, so John may have recalled the last few verses of Isaiah 40, 'He gives power to the faint, and to him who has no might he increases strength. Even youths shall faint and be weary, and young men shall fall exhausted: but they who wait for the LORD shall renew their strength; they shall mount up with wings like eagles; they shall run and not be weary; they shall walk and not faint.' In his inner self, despite the outward circumstances, John was in a much stronger position than his captor. He knew that the liberty of the kingdom of God is first and foremost an inner liberty.

There are some who point out that Jesus expects his disciples to visit people in prison, but that he did not visit John in prison.[37] The truth is, though, that if Jesus had visited John there was a very real risk that he would have been incarcerated too, which was not part of his plan and would not have suited his purpose. He was, though, assured that others were visiting him and doing what they could for him.

CHAPTER 8: HEAD ON A PLATE

When Herod's birthday came, the daughter of Herodias danced
before the company and pleased Herod, so that he promised with
an oath to give her whatever she might ask.
(Matthew 14:6-7)

Jesus called Herod Antipas a fox, which was not in any way a term
of admiration, as it can be in our culture, even if that admiration
might be grudging. It was a term of disrespect, referring to someone
of weak morals.[1] Notorious also is the proverbial fox in the henhouse
so it is perhaps ironic that, two verses on from calling Antipas a fox,
Jesus refers to himself as a hen.[2] This sums up the character of this
scion of a troubled family, in thrall to his scheming and manipulative
new wife, Herodias, who proved ultimately to be his downfall.

The Herod she had married had not ultimately been so highly
favoured in his father's will, having fallen foul of a court conspiracy
and been disinherited, so when a half-brother came to stay who
had been bequeathed a territory he ruled as a tetrarch, she beguiled
him into marriage and divorced her first husband. Vengeful towards
anyone who criticised her, she wanted to kill John and, despite the
measure of protection that Antipas provided for him,[3] she finally
succeeded in plotting his death. When Antipas eventually had to
face the Nabateans in battle in AD 36-37, the conflict was partly due
to the way he had treated the Nabatean king's daughter at Herodias'
bidding a few years earlier. Antipas' army was defeated and the local
Jewish population attributed the defeat to God's justice for the way
he had treated John, also at Herodias' bidding.[4] The capture and
destruction of Machaerus during this conflict will have encouraged
this way of thinking.[5]

Herodias' final miscalculation in AD 38-39, fuelled by her consuming ambition and her jealous nature, was to persuade Antipas to go to Rome to ask that he be given royal status in the way that the new emperor Caligula had made her brother, Agrippa I, king of the territory that Herod Philip had ruled.[6] Rome's response was to banish Antipas to exile either in Lyons in Gaul, or in Spain (just as his brother Archelaus had earlier been banished).[7] Herodias went with him, although she was given the option of keeping her property and not going. Josephus' comment on this episode reads, 'And thus did God punish Herodias for her envy at her brother, and Herod also for giving ear to the vain discourses of a woman.'[8]

One of the parallels between John and Elijah, as we noted in Chapter 5, is that Elijah criticised the king and queen of his day, Ahab and Jezebel, which resulted in Jezebel trying to kill him, just as Herodias plotted John's death.[9] Herodias and Jezebel are well-matched.

A birthday party

It is hard to work out how Antipas felt about John; he appears to have been conflicted. He seems to have been justifiably afraid of John's political potential, for many Jews regarded him as a prophet, and Antipas had already upset the Arab half of his Perean population by divorcing his Nabatean wife.[10] Nevertheless, he was annoyed at the criticism of his marriage and would have preferred it if John was silenced.[11] At the same time, he seemed intrigued by John and spent time talking with him while he was in custody, although he was 'perplexed' by what he heard. He did, though, try to protect him from the worst of his wife's vengefulness and, no doubt for political reasons, let this be commonly known.[12] Later, after John's execution, he betrayed a measure of Macbeth-like doubt as he was haunted by the memory of John's death, fearing that Jesus was John come back to life again.[13] Having said that, these doubts did not trouble him quite enough; he later took part in the travesty that was Jesus' trial.[14]

There were others at the time of John who fomented rebellion – sometimes citing prophecies that the time of Gentile rule was ending – and these were brutally dealt with by the Romans. John, though, was a preacher of righteousness, not rebellion, and the Romans left him alone. It was Antipas who had him arrested and taken off to Machaerus, and his motives were more mixed.

If John was baptizing at or near Bethany beyond the Jordan, then Machaerus was the logical place to take him. If Antipas was worried about the political situation in Perea after his divorce, then again Machaerus was the logical place for him to be. Herod the Great had fortified it for exactly this purpose, according to Josephus.[15]

Machaerus was the only palace we know of that Antipas had inherited from his father, which also makes it a natural place to hold a 'royal' birthday party, even if it was remote. Josephus described it as 'breath-taking in the size and beauty of the various rooms' but it was no Versailles and numbers will have been limited, even if some of the guests were accommodated in the lower city, where their retainers will have been housed.[16] Naturally, the local Perean aristocracy were there, and the New Testament also adds that that some Galilean nobility were there too, together with his senior military men.[17]

As it was a birthday party, Antipas' family was present, although he had no children and his immediate family consisted only of his new wife and her daughter. We have no knowledge of any others from his extended family who may have attended. It is very likely that at some time during their stay Antipas and his senior nobles and military men will have met together to discuss the security situation in Perea.

Just a little girl

Before we look at that fateful birthday party, we should try to work out when it happened.

John's public ministry, as we have seen, started in AD 29 and the best date we have for the crucifixion of Jesus is in the spring of AD 33, which narrows down the possibilities, as John predeceased Jesus.[18] If Jesus had a three-year ministry, then his baptism took place in AD 30, the year after John started baptizing people. There followed a period when Jesus' and John's ministries overlapped, so John's arrest and beheading may have happened in AD 31, two years before the crucifixion.[19] This would mean that John's ministry lasted about two years.

The dates provided in Josephus' writings are sometimes tantalisingly beyond our reach, despite the considerable information he supplies about the Herod family.[20] Having said that, the approximate birth date for Herodias is thought to be c.15 BC, and for Antipas c.20 BC. However, it is the date of Salome's birth, and hence her age at John's execution, that concerns us most.

There is no external evidence concerning Salome's birth date. Estimates have varied because of differing views about the date of John's execution and assumptions about how old she must have been for her to have danced erotically, as is often assumed. There are, however, two bits of incidental evidence in Matthew's and Mark's Gospels that help us to pinpoint her age with some accuracy. In Matthew 14:11 and in Mark 6:22 and 28 (see below), Salome is referred to as 'the girl', which is a translation of the Greek word *korasion*, a diminutive of *korē*, which means literally 'a pupil' or 'apple of the eye', but was used colloquially and affectionately for 'girl'.

In the previous chapter of Mark, we find the story of Jairus' daughter, whom he introduced to Jesus as 'my little daughter'.[21] Jesus is reported by Mark to have said to her in Aramaic, '*Talitha cumi*', which means (as Mark tells us), 'Little girl, I say to you, arise'. *Talitha* is the feminine form of the word meaning 'young', related to the Aramaic word for lamb, and the Greek translation we are given for it by Mark is *korasion* – the same word used to describe Salome – and which is rendered 'little girl' in English. In the next verse, we are told that she was twelve years old.[22]

Matthew's version of the story of Jairus' daughter gives less detail, but also uses *korasion* to describe her.[23] The point is that *korasion* is the word for younger, pre-pubescent girls, and that is the way that both Matthew and Mark used it. In the New Testament *korasion* is used only in these two stories of Salome and Jairus' daughter – two young pre-pubescent girls. In those days a girl became a woman at puberty and the appropriate Greek word for her thereafter became *gynē*, which was not used of Salome.[24]

Then there is the question of whether Salome was married or not at the time. We know from Josephus that her first husband was another half-brother of her father and stepfather, Herod Philip, mentioned in Chapter 7 as the tetrarch of Batanea, Trachonitis and Auranitis.[25] However, her behaviour at the party, at which she went to her mother for advice and not a husband, and did what her mother told her, would suggest that she was still single. As women were generally married at an early age in those times, this would also suggest that she was pre-pubescent. The likelihood is that Herod Philip, who was probably in his fifties, married his young half-niece, Salome, shortly after these events when she had reached puberty, although the marriage did not last long as he died childless shortly afterwards, in AD 34.

In the popular imagination Salome is often seen as a seductive temptress dancing with seven veils, hence in her late teens or early twenties. The actual evidence points to her being a young girl on the cusp of puberty, aged about eleven or twelve at the time of these tragic events. If Salome was this age at the time of John's execution she was born in AD 19 or 20.

> But when Herod's birthday came, the daughter of Herodias danced before the company and pleased Herod, so that he promised with an oath to give her whatever she might ask. Prompted by her mother, she said, 'Give me the head of John the Baptist here on a platter.' And the king was sorry, but because of his oaths and his guests he commanded it to be given. He sent and had John beheaded in the prison, and his head was brought on a platter and given to the girl, and she brought it to her mother.
> (Matthew 14:6-11)

> But an opportunity came when Herod on his birthday gave a banquet for his nobles and military commanders and the leading men of Galilee. For when Herodias's daughter came in and danced, she pleased Herod and his guests. And the king said to the girl, 'Ask me for whatever you wish, and I will give it to you.' And he vowed to her, 'Whatever you ask me, I will give you, up to half of my kingdom.' And she went out and said to her mother, 'For what should I ask?' And she said, 'The head of John the Baptist.' And she came in immediately with haste to the king and asked, saying, 'I want you to give me at once the head of John the Baptist on a platter.' And the king was exceedingly sorry, but because of his oaths and his guests he did not want to break his word to her. And immediately the king sent an executioner with orders to bring John's head. He went and beheaded him in the prison and brought his head on a platter and gave it to the girl, and the girl gave it to her mother.
> (Mark 6:21-28)

A fateful dance

Antipas had not been married long so he will have been pleased that his new wife's daughter wanted to do a turn before his guests at his birthday party and was delighted when it went well (there were probably the usual anxieties about how a stepchild might behave). Dancing was quite normal at such parties; in fact, Orientals delighted in it. The norm would be for people to dance on their own, or in groups of men or women, and it would have been perfectly natural for Salome to have danced before the guests with no loss of dignity. That was when, perhaps having imbibed a little too much, Antipas made his fateful promise to reward her with anything up to half his kingdom, which, although it was in two halves, was not a kingdom and was not his to give.[26] He was showing off.

From the biblical text in which Salome 'came in' to dance, then 'went out' to consult her mother and 'came in' again to reply to Antipas, it appears that the women and the men were being entertained separately, as would be normal at these occasions, and there were two sizeable dining rooms (*triclinium*) for that purpose at Machaerus, as we can see from the plan below.[27]

Győző Vörös, who has led the recent archaeological work at Machaerus, has imagined this scene differently. He has suggested that the fateful dance happened as Antipas and his guests dined *al fresco* in the larger peristyle courtyard, with the men and women dining together.[28] For this to fit the biblical account, Salome will have had to go out *with* her mother rather than *to* her mother for a consultation and then returned to the courtyard with her request.

Prompted by her vengeful mother, and to Antipas' dismay, Salome famously replied that she would like John's head on a plate (or a tray). Antipas, against his better judgement, ordered that John should be beheaded, which was not a common form of execution at this time in Palestine, but would, of course, have been necessary to separate the head from the body in order to present it on a plate.[29]

It has been pointed out that this would have resulted in a much quicker death than might otherwise have been the case, if it was done efficiently, which is a small mercy for John. Nevertheless, John's violent end has made its mark in history, where it still ranks with the most capricious of executions, and has left its mark on the English language where vengeful people still want their victim's 'head on a plate'.

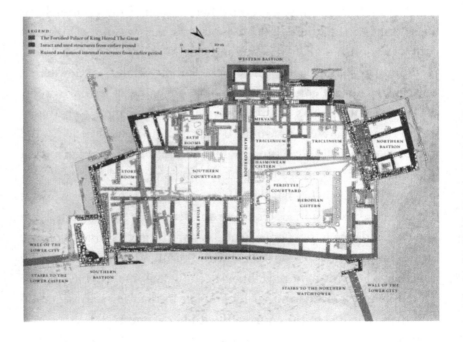

Ground plan of Machaerus.[30]

When discussing this story, one man said his reply would have been that John's head belonged to the half of his kingdom he had not promised, but Antipas did not possess this nimbleness of mind. He felt obliged in front of his nobles to keep his foolish promise, instead of being a man of wisdom who knew how to defuse a difficult situation, or a man of principle who recognised an injustice when it was being done. He no doubt wanted to please his new wife and her daughter and perhaps thought he could impress his important guests by showing off his arbitrary power over life and death. He was a weak man, easily manipulated by his wife, who wanted to appear strong.[31] All he succeeded in doing was to show off the level of his personal corruption and enter the hall of infamy.

There was no Magna Carta to keep this 'king' in check and no *habeas corpus* to protect John, so in this tragic way he lost his life and became the first martyr of the New Testament – a death that is remembered on 29 August, the Feast Day of the Beheading, or Decollation, of John the Baptist.[32] Even in his violent and treacherous death he was anticipating Jesus' end. He died a prophet's death.

From the days of John the Baptist until now the kingdom of heaven has suffered violence, and the violent take it by force. (Matthew 11:12)

The myth of Salome

Antipas and Herodias come out of this story badly, but what about Salome, the famous dancing girl? There is a long tradition in the Church of perceiving her as an icon of seductiveness. Oscar Wilde elaborated on this with his 1894 play about her, *Salome*, which takes some serious liberties with the facts. In his play, Antipas murdered Salome's father, Salome tried to seduce John who rejected her, which was why she wanted revenge, and Herod later had Salome executed. In 1905 Richard Strauss composed an opera based on the play and in 1988 Ken Russell directed a bizarre film, *Salome's Last Dance*, which depicted Wilde using prostitutes to perform the play in a brothel. There are other films and television programmes too, and plays, ballets, poems, books, songs and computer games portraying John's macabre end. In 2002 a book was published advocating erotic dancing called *Sisters of Salome*, in which Salome was compared to the likes of Mata Hari.[33] By then, the story of Salome was being dismissed as a misogynist castration fantasy.[34]

Unfortunately, it is this sort of distortion of the story that now informs the popular image of Salome and her dance, but it is no more than a figment of the imagination, sheer hokum.[35] So, what was going on? The Herod family was notorious for its excesses, but despite all we know about them there is no record of this sort of thing at all. In fact, there is no record at all from the ancient world of a princess behaving this way.[36]

Given Salome's age at the time, such a dance would not have happened. Furthermore, she was also shortly going to be marrying a tetrarch and would therefore have had to be very careful about her reputation, as would her parents, which would certainly not have been enhanced by dancing seductively in front of the whole court. The Herods were nothing if not politically shrewd. As we shall see below, she managed to maintain a good reputation for the rest of her days. The most likely scenario is that her dance was a home entertainment turn by a young girl that brought delight to her proud, indulgent – and perhaps slightly drunk – stepfather, who was in thrall to his new bride, her mother. Having said that, the idea of it being an erotic dance for a lecherous 'king' will no doubt remain a popular idea, and it makes no difference to the outcome.

There is a further footnote to Salome's affairs. After her husband Herod Philip's death, she married another relative, Aristobulus, who was made king of Armenia minor by Nero in AD 54-55.[37] Amazingly, some coins have survived from this time with Aristobulus' likeness on them and an image of Salome on the reverse.[38]

Salome and Aristobulus had three children, all of whom were given family names: Herod, Agrippa and Aristobulus. She was evidently a woman who was capable of attracting men of importance and, unlike her scheming mother, she succeeded in becoming a queen.

Coin of Salome as queen of Armenia Minor (right). Minted in AD 66-67, when she would have been forty-six to forty-eight years old, it bears the legend BACIΛIC ΣΑΛΩΜΗ (BASILIS SALŌMĒ = Queen Salome). The obverse of the coin (left) has the head of her husband with the legend BACIΛEWC ΑΡΙΣΤΟΒΥΛΟΥ (BASILEŌS ARISTOBULOU = King Aristobulus).[39]

Mourning for John

After losing his life in this extraordinary way, John was buried by his disciples.[40] The first thing they then did was take the news to Jesus.

And his disciples came and took the body and buried it, and they went and told Jesus.

Now when Jesus heard this, he withdrew from there in a boat to a desolate place by himself.'
(Matthew 14:12-13a)

When his disciples heard of it, they came and took his body and laid it in a tomb.'
(Mark 6:29)

In Greek the word translated 'desolate' (above) is *eremos*, the same word used in the last verse of Luke chapter 1 to describe John going to live in the 'wilderness'.[41] When Jesus heard about John's death, he went into the wilderness to be alone; it was the appropriate place for him to go to mourn for his cousin. John's death will have had a profound effect on him. Jesus respected John, whom he had known all his life: he imitated him, quoted him, acclaimed him as a man and a prophet, and now he mourned him deeply.

John was dead and buried, but whatever hopes Herodias and Antipas may have entertained, this was far from being the end of him.

In the next chapter, we look at John's legacy.

Part 4: LEGACY

CHAPTER 9: POSTMORTEM

John did no sign, but everything that John said
about this man was true.
(John 10:41)

It is Matthew and Mark who record John's death and Matthew who tells us that Jesus went alone into the wilderness to mourn. Jesus was not on his own for long; the next thing we hear from both these Gospel writers is that a crowd of 5,000 men, plus their families, gathered around him. They were no doubt shocked to hear the news, for people had expected great things of John. Immediately, though, we are shown the difference between the two of them: John had performed no miracles, but Jesus healed all who were sick; John had taught people to share their food, Jesus shared with 5,000 plus; John had immersed people in water, but Jesus walked on it.[1]

Having said that, John's memory was to have an impact on his illustrious cousin, and his prophetic legacy was to help guide the early Church. His head may have been given to Herodias on a plate, and his body buried by some of his disciples, but John's influence certainly did not die with him. They may have killed the messenger, but they could not silence his message. John was much too well-liked and respected for his capricious death to pass unnoticed by his disciples, by Jesus' disciples, by what remained of Antipas' conscience, by the religious authorities and by a sizeable swathe of the population at large – so much so, in fact, that when the Nabatean King Aretas, the father of Antipas' scorned first wife, successfully waged war on Perea five or six years later, Antipas' defeat was widely believed by his Jewish population to be God's retribution for the death of John. This is how Josephus summed it up:

And when everybody turned to John – for they were profoundly stirred by what he said – Herod feared that John's so extensive influence over the people might lead to an uprising (for the people seemed likely to do everything he might counsel). He thought it much better, under the circumstances, to get John out of the way in advance, before any insurrection might develop, than for himself to get into trouble and be sorry not to have acted, once an insurrection had begun. So, because of Herod's suspicion, John was sent as a prisoner to Machaerus, the fortress already mentioned, and there put to death. But the Jews believed that the destruction which overtook the army came as a punishment for Herod, God wishing to do him harm.[2]

As we saw in Chapter 8, it was not just Antipas' Jewish subjects who had doubts about John's execution, for it appears to have unsettled the tetrarch's mind too. The memory of what he had done seems to have haunted him, for when he heard about Jesus' ministry he feared that John had returned from the dead. Of course, it was Jesus who rose from the dead, but it is interesting to see how Antipas and others thought it could happen to John.

At that time Herod the tetrarch heard about the fame of Jesus, and he said to his servants, 'This is John the Baptist. He has been raised from the dead; that is why these miraculous powers are at work in him.'
(Matthew 14:1-2)

King Herod heard of it, for Jesus' name had become known. Some said, 'John the Baptist has been raised from the dead. That is why these miraculous powers are at work in him.' But others said, 'He is Elijah.' And others said, 'He is a prophet, like one of

the prophets of old.' But when Herod heard of it, he said, 'John, whom I beheaded, has been raised.'
(Mark 6:14-16)

Now Herod the tetrarch heard about all that was happening, and he was perplexed, because it was said by some that John had been raised from the dead, by some that Elijah had appeared, and by others that one of the prophets of old had risen. Herod said, 'John I beheaded, but who is this about whom I hear such things?' And he sought to see him.
(Luke 9:7-9)

It is pure speculation to say so, but it could even be that the abuse meted out by Antipas and his men on Jesus, when he finally encountered him at his trial, was prompted in part by relief that he turned out not to have been John.[3] Despite the ill-treatment, at least Antipas did not directly condemn Jesus at his trial, as he had summarily condemned John, although he did not release him either and returned him to the Romans.

John's reputation spread far and wide and, to their frustration, his influence was unstoppable by any of his opponents. What would have pleased John much more was that people, friends as well as enemies, were making connections between him and Jesus and that his reputation was helping Jesus in his work. In the passage below, the disciples' report mirrors what Antipas had been told. We can see that Antipas was not the only one to wonder whether Jesus was John come back to life:[4]

Now when Jesus came into the district of Caesarea Philippi, he asked his disciples, 'Who do people say that the Son of Man is?' And they said, 'Some say John the Baptist, others say Elijah, and

others Jeremiah or one of the prophets.' He said to them, 'But who do you say that I am?' Simon Peter replied, 'You are the Christ, the Son of the living God.'
(Matthew 16:13-16, cf. Mark 8:27-29; Luke 9:18-20)

Not long after this incident, Jesus went up a mountain with a small group of disciples and was transfigured before them with Moses and Elijah. On their way down, the disciples not unnaturally asked Jesus about the expectation of Elijah's return. This was when Jesus unequivocally confirmed that John was Elijah:[5]

He answered, 'Elijah does come, and he will restore all things. But I tell you that Elijah has already come, and they did not recognize him, but did to him whatever they pleased. So also the Son of Man will certainly suffer at their hands.' Then the disciples understood that he was speaking to them of John the Baptist.
(Matthew 17:11-13, cf. Mark 9:12-13)

Here we can also see that Jesus began to prepare his disciples for his own impending death by comparing himself to John.

The legacy of prayer

A little while later, John's name appeared in Jesus' ministry in connection with his teaching on prayer. John had taught people how to pray, which led one of Jesus' disciples to ask him that he might also teach them how to pray. The result, according to Luke's account, was that Jesus taught them what we know as the Lord's Prayer. Jesus also taught this prayer on other occasions, as it is also recorded in Matthew's Gospel during the Sermon on the Mount,[6] but we owe this version of it in part to John the Baptist.

Now Jesus was praying in a certain place, and when he finished, one of his disciples said to him, 'Lord, teach us to pray, as John taught his disciples.' And he said to them, 'When you pray, say: 'Father, hallowed be your name.
Your kingdom come.
Give us each day our daily bread,
and forgive us our sins,
for we ourselves forgive everyone who is indebted to us.
And lead us not into temptation.'
(Luke 11:1-4)

Jesus fully understood John and he knew that his core prophetic message was that he, the promised Coming One, would immerse people in the Holy Spirit, so, when he was asked about prayer as John had taught about prayer, he also talked about praying to receive the Holy Spirit. The following parable, which is unique to this context, is often quoted in relation to lessons on prayer in general, but its context is more specific; it is prayer for the gift of the Holy Spirit that Jesus was talking about. The second part of this passage, the ask/seek/knock part of Jesus' teaching, is also found in the Sermon on the Mount, where it does refer to prayer in general, not just prayer for the Holy Spirit.[7]

And he said to them, 'Which of you who has a friend will go to him at midnight and say to him, 'Friend, lend me three loaves, for a friend of mine has arrived on a journey, and I have nothing to set before him'; and he will answer from within, 'Do not bother me; the door is now shut, and my children are with me in bed. I cannot get up and give you anything'? I tell you, though he will not get up and give him anything because he is his friend, yet because of his impudence he will rise and give him whatever he needs.

And I tell you, ask, and it will be given to you; seek, and you will find; knock, and it will be opened to you. For everyone who asks receives, and the one who seeks finds, and to the one who knocks it will be opened. What father among you, if his son asks for a fish, will instead of a fish give him a serpent; or if he asks for an egg, will give him a scorpion? If you then, who are evil, know how to give good gifts to your children, how much more will the heavenly Father give the Holy Spirit to those who ask him!'
(Luke 11:5-13)

There are three important lessons that we learn here. The first is that, although John prophesied that Jesus would immerse people in the Holy Spirit, Jesus says that we should pray to the Father for this gift. This has been a controversial topic in the past: when the Western Church added to the Nicene Creed the assertion that the Holy Spirit proceeds from the Father 'and the Son' (the *filioque* clause), it became one of the contentious issues that led to the Great Schism of 1054. John said that we are immersed in the Spirit by the Son. The Son said we should pray to the Father for the gift. Praying for the gift of the Holy Spirit is a profoundly Trinitarian experience.

Ezekiel's visionary river, discussed earlier, provides us here with a good visual aid. The river represents the Holy Spirit who flows from the Holy of Holies, which represents the Father, via the altar, which represents the Son. As with prayer in general, we pray to the Father through the Son for the gift of the Holy Spirit.

But when the Helper comes, whom I will send to you from the Father, the Spirit of truth, who proceeds from the Father, he will bear witness about me.'
(John 15:26. Cf. Acts 2:33)

The second truth is that, unlike the grudging neighbour of the parable, the Father is eager and willing to give the gift of the Holy Spirit to those who ask. The inference is that it is not an inconvenience to him at all, but a delight.

The third lesson is for those who are anxious about the Holy Spirit, an anxiety that Jesus understands and addresses in a gentle pastoral way. In verses 9 to 10, Jesus seems to be speaking to those who think that they are in some way unworthy of the Holy Spirit, so that God would not give the gift to them. Jesus reassures them no fewer than six times that we can have real confidence that our prayer for the Holy Spirit will be answered. A second concern, addressed in verses 11 to 13, is about those who fear that if they ask for the Holy Spirit they are going to open themselves up to something horrible – the snake or the scorpion of Jesus' parable. His response is gently to mock this idea and he ends up by saying, 'how much more will the heavenly Father give the Holy Spirit [i.e. not something horrible] to those who ask him!'

Immersion in the Spirit

In an earlier episode, while Jesus was in Jerusalem for the Feast of Tabernacles (the seven-day Jewish festival that followed the harvest, a few days after the Day of Atonement), Jesus made another connection with John's teaching that he would be the one to immerse people in the Holy Spirit.[8]

On the last day of the festival, there was a grand procession, involving everyone from the high priest down, that began in the centre of the temple. A golden bowl was carried to the Pool of Siloam, filled with water, and carried with much singing of hallels and waving of lulabs back to the altar, around which they would march seven times, splashing the water onto it with great ceremony.

In part, this was a prayer for good rains during the coming rainy season after the long dry season, and in part it was a prayer that the river in Ezekiel's vision, representing the outpouring of the Holy Spirit, would start to flow.

As we have seen, this vision seems to have influenced John's message and his choice of baptism site – a second great watery prophecy about the Holy Spirit. This is what happened at that Feast of Tabernacles:

> On the last day of the feast, the great day, Jesus stood up and cried out, 'If anyone thirsts, let him come to me and drink. Whoever believes in me, as the Scripture has said, 'Out of his heart will flow rivers of living water.' Now this he said about the Spirit, whom those who believed in him were to receive, for as yet the Spirit had not been given, because Jesus was not yet glorified.
> (John 7:37-39)

The temple authorities were not best pleased by this interruption, and they tried to arrest Jesus, but failed. The point is that Jesus and John appear to be united in their understanding of Ezekiel's vision and its application, although neither of them is recorded mentioning it directly.

John's impact on Jesus

There are, not surprisingly, occasions when John's teaching paralleled Jesus' teaching. We have already noted that, according to Matthew's Gospel, Jesus began his preaching with the same words that John had earlier begun his preaching: '[Metanoy], for the kingdom of heaven is at hand.'[9] Also, John's expression, 'the axe is laid to the root of the trees'[10] is mirrored by Jesus in Matthew 7:19. Both Jesus and John talk of the need to bear fruit,[11] and they both use the term 'offspring of vipers'.[12] They both also dismiss the idea that blood descent from

Abraham is sufficient for salvation,[13] and John's use of the wheat and chaff image is not unlike Jesus' parable of the wheat and the tares.[14] Because of these similarities there are those who argue that a good deal of teaching attributed to Jesus actually originated with John, but was put into the mouth of Jesus by the Gospel writers. The evidence for this is speculative and unconvincing.[15] Quite the opposite is true, for we saw earlier that they very likely spent a good deal of time together in their formative years, so it is to be expected that they had similarities in their messages.

It is not unnatural for Jesus to be compared to John; these two charismatic preachers were similar in many ways. Indeed, by visiting the same place that John had made his own, which he did on several occasions, Jesus deliberately invited comparison. The principal difference, of course, was that Jesus, as the incarnate Son of God, performed many miraculous signs of the kingdom, as the fourth Gospel notes when it records the verdict of those who had listened to John's message and sought out Jesus:

He went away again across the Jordan to the place where John had been baptizing at first, and there he remained. And many came to him. And they said, 'John did no sign, but everything that John said about this man was true.' And many believed in him there.
(John 10:40-42)

John would have been delighted at this response, for it was everything he had worked for: 'He must increase, but I must decrease' was how he had expressed it.[16] John was a humble man with a mission that he put before all other considerations, and as the way up in the kingdom of God is down, John, who put himself last, is honoured with the most pre-eminent.

What is also significant about this lingering stay at the place where John baptized is its timing, towards the end of Jesus' ministry and after a difficult time in Jerusalem. Jesus used it as a place of retreat. After this, Jesus made one more journey up north and then began his final journey to Jerusalem, down the east side of the river, which he crossed one last time at the baptism site on his way via Jericho to Jerusalem, probably lingering at Bethany beyond the Jordan once more.

It is not surprising that Jesus went 'again' to this place of regular retreat, the place he chose to be in to draw strength for his coming ordeal.[17] It was the place where he had been anointed for his mission by the Holy Spirit in the form of a dove, and where he had audibly heard the voice of the Father blessing him – the greatest of all Trinitarian sites. This auspicious spot was the best place for him to gain strength before his final journey for a host of other powerful symbolic reasons too. Here are some:

Jesus had been baptized there and baptism was on his mind, for as his death approached he referred to it as a baptism, which we have come to call his baptism of blood.[18]

It was where the first Christian sacrament began its life, and he was shortly to initiate the other great sacrament of the Church at the Last Supper.

Jesus had been joined here by his first disciples – the seed of the kingdom.

It was where John had called him 'the Lamb of God, who takes away the sin of the world!' and where he had prophesied about the Coming One who was to immerse people in the Holy Spirit – prophecies he was going to need ringing in his ears during the coming ordeal.

It was a place that symbolised entry into the kingdom – the kingdom he was about to fulfil at that first Easter and Pentecost.

It was a place with strong associations with great men of faith such as Moses, Joshua, Elijah, Elisha and, of course, John. As he faced his own death at the hands of unjust authorities, Jesus will have drawn strength from the courage that John showed when facing his own end. It is no accident that he was at the baptism site at that stage in his ministry; there was no better place in the world for him to be, and he owed it to John.

From Bethany beyond the Jordan on the way to Jerusalem, Jesus passed through Jericho, and from there on, right up to Calvary itself, Jesus could see Machaerus, for it is visible along the whole route. Even as he hung on the cross, on the reasonable assumption that the Romans placed it facing the city, if he looked to his right, Jesus could see the site of John's martyrdom in the far distance, before the darkness descended.[19] In this way, he could draw strength from John's courage in the face of injustice, as he too died for the sake of the kingdom of God. He could be comforted by the thought of seeing John again soon. Jesus and John were united in death.

A photograph taken from the Notre Dame hotel in Jerusalem with the domes of the Holy Sepulchre – the traditional site of the crucifixion – in the foreground and Machaerus, forty-four kilometres in the distance, marked with an arrow.[20]

From the very beginning to the very end of Jesus' life, John was his forerunner and, by paying the ultimate price for being faithful to his calling, John prepared the way for Jesus one last time.

'I tell you that Elijah has already come, and they did not recognize him, but did to him whatever they pleased. So also the Son of Man will certainly suffer at their hands.' Then the disciples understood that he was speaking to them of John the Baptist.
(Matthew 17:12-13)

It was when Jesus passed through Jericho that last time that he encountered Zacchaeus. We saw in Chapter 5 how John's teaching appears to have affected Zacchaeus' response to Jesus' presence in his house. It would not be a surprise to learn that Jesus and John had talked together about Zacchaeus at some point.

John's memory and Jesus' death

When Jesus reached Jerusalem for his last turbulent week, we find that the memory of John still troubled the temple authorities, for they had been conspicuously less than supportive of John, as we learn from an earlier incident that took place while John was in prison:

(When all the people heard this, and the tax collectors too, they declared God just, having been baptized with the baptism of John, but the Pharisees and the lawyers rejected the purpose of God for themselves, not having been baptized by him.)
(Luke 7:29-30)

The authorities were wary of the adulation of John, still common among the people, even though by this time it was two years or so after his death. When they challenged Jesus' authority, he was able to invoke John's reputation to demonstrate the duplicity of his opponents. They, in turn, were aware of the standing that John still had with the people and were unable to maintain their argument.

And when he entered the temple, the chief priests and the elders of the people came up to him as he was teaching, and said, 'By what authority are you doing these things, and who gave you this authority?' Jesus answered them, 'I also will ask you one question, and if you tell me the answer, then I also will tell you by what authority I do these things. The baptism of John, from where did it come? From heaven or from man?' And they discussed it among themselves, saying, 'If we say, "From heaven", he will say to us, "Why then did you not believe him?" But if we say, "From man", we are afraid of the crowd, for they all hold that John was a prophet.' So they answered Jesus, 'We do not know.' And he said to them, 'Neither will I tell you by what authority I do these things.'
(Matthew 21:23-27, cf. Mark 11:27-33; Luke 20:1-8)

Jesus was sparring with them, but he made his point very clearly; the authority of the temple hierarchy was very different from Jesus' and John's prophetic authority. The baptism of John was from heaven. Such was the hypocrisy of the temple authorities that Jesus pressed his point even further in the ensuing verses. In doing so, it is fair to say, he played his part in increasing the tension between them and he used John's memory to do it:

'What do you think? A man had two sons. And he went to the first and said, 'Son, go and work in the vineyard today.' And he answered, 'I will not', but afterwards he changed his mind and went. And he went to the other son and said the same. And he answered, 'I go, sir', but did not go. Which of the two did the will of his father?' They said, 'The first.' Jesus said to them, 'Truly, I say to you, the tax collectors and the prostitutes go into the kingdom of God before you. For John came to you in the

way of righteousness, and you did not believe him, but the tax collectors and the prostitutes believed him. And even when you saw it, you did not afterwards change your minds and believe him.'
(Matthew 21:28-32)

These two episodes are usually reckoned to have taken place on the Tuesday of holy week, three days before the crucifixion. In this way, the memory of John was with Jesus right up to the end of his ministry and, as we have seen, the site of John's violent death could be seen by Jesus as he hung on the cross – giving him moral support through his own baptism of blood.

Baptism in water and the Spirit

After Jesus' crucifixion and resurrection, John's baptism morphed in a fascinating way into Christian baptism. Jesus told his followers to make disciples all round the world, to teach them all his commandments and baptize them with a full Trinitarian baptism.

Yahweh/Jehovah (יהוה) had been revealed at Jesus' baptism as the Father, the Son and the Holy Spirit, and this is to be recalled symbolically in Christian baptism. Just as at Jesus' baptism, where we witness the Father's love for the Son, the Son incarnate and identifying with humanity, and the Holy Spirit anointing Jesus, so at Christian baptism we identify with the Father and his love, with the Son who lived, died and rose again for us, and the Holy Spirit who is in us and all around us.

> Go therefore and make disciples of all nations, baptizing them in the name of the Father and of the Son and of the Holy Spirit, teaching them to observe all that I have commanded you.
> (Matthew 28:19-20a, cf. Mark 16:16)

As well as preparing the way of Yahweh/Jehovah (יהוה), which is symbolised in Christian Trinitarian baptism, John also told people that the Coming One, who was mighty, would immerse people in the Holy Spirit in the same way that he had just immersed them in water. As his ascension drew near, Jesus was about to use this powerful visual prophecy of John's to prepare his disciples for the approaching Day of Pentecost. These are Jesus' parting words to his disciples as recorded at the end of Luke's Gospel and in the opening chapter of Acts:

> And behold, I am sending the promise of my Father upon you. But stay in the city until you are clothed with power from on high. (Luke 24:49)

> ... he ordered them not to depart from Jerusalem, but to wait for the promise of the Father, which, he said, 'you heard from me; for John indeed immersed (baptized) in water, but you will be immersed (baptized) in (the) Holy Spirit not many days from now.'

> ... you will receive power when the Holy Spirit has come upon you; and you will be witnesses in Jerusalem and in all Judea and Samaria, and to the end of the earth.
> (Acts 1:4b-5,8)[21]

After this saying he ascended into the clouds. As we can see, Jesus' concern at his ascension was that his disciples should stay in Jerusalem to receive the power and presence of the Holy Spirit. And the words Jesus chose to prepare his disciples for Pentecost were the words of John's carefully crafted prophecy, with all the well-known imagery that went with it. There were no better words than these to use before that momentous event.

John's words were well-known to the apostles, four of whom had been disciples of John, and the others evidently knew him in some way, as did Matthias, who was chosen to take the place of Judas.[22] For some reason, Jesus used John's image of being immersed in the Spirit but not his image of being immersed in fire, which is surprising, given the events of Pentecost, although he had previously used that image in Luke 12:49, when he said, 'I came to cast fire on the earth'. In this way, Jesus' final message on earth included a quote from John – just as the first words of his ministry were borrowed from John – and what he said was that the Prophet of Pentecost's core prophecy was about to be fulfilled. Ten days later the Church was born, and the age of the Spirit began.

The evolution of Baptism

Christian baptism is the sacrament of entry into the Church. Jesus told us to baptize disciples 'in the name of the Father and of the Son and of the Holy Spirit', which contains, as we have seen, a symbolic reminder of the great Trinitarian theophany of Jesus' own baptism. And, as John prophesied, baptism symbolises the overwhelming of the Holy Spirit in a believer's life. We are immersed in the Spirit in the same way that we are immersed in the water of baptism.[23] That much we get from the Gospels,[24] but the epistles point us in the direction of even more symbolism:

- Baptism is an identification with the burial and resurrection of Jesus (Romans 6:3-5. Cf. 2 Timothy 2:11).
- Baptism contains an acknowledgement that we have died to our old life and have begun a new life in Christ; we have put on Christ (Romans 6:1-4; Colossians 2:11-14; Galatians 3:27).
- Baptism contains a parallel with the Exodus, in which the Israelites passed under the sea and the cloud. It is thus a symbol

of deliverance from bondage (1 Corinthians 10:1-2).

- Baptism contains a parallel with the flood, through which people were saved in the ark. The ark is likened to Christ and the good conscience we can have because of his death and resurrection (1 Peter 3:18-21).

The washing away of sins is a commonly mentioned symbol for baptism. I have deliberately left this to last because even though it is commonly used it is questionable. Firstly, because ritual washing for ritual cleansing is what John did not do and, as has been noted earlier, his baptisms were not the means of cleansing from sin, repentance was. In other words, it is not an appropriate symbol to use for John's baptisms. The second reason is that the Bible texts used to justify the use of washing from sin as a symbol for Christian baptism are not altogether convincing. Here are the texts:

Rise and be baptized, and wash away your sins, calling on his name.
(Acts 22:16b, RSV. Ananias speaking to Paul after his Damascus Road experience.)

It is calling on the name of the Lord that washed Paul's sins away, not his baptism. Ananias did not say, 'Be baptized *to* wash away your sins.'[25]

He saved us, not because of works done by us in righteousness, but according to his own mercy, by the washing of regeneration and renewal of the Holy Spirit, whom he poured out on us richly through Jesus Christ our Saviour ...
(Titus 3:5-6)

This is a beautiful description of baptism in the Holy Spirit, not baptism in water.

For Christ also suffered once for sins, the righteous for the unrighteous, that he might bring us to God, being put to death in the flesh but made alive in the spirit, in which he went and proclaimed to the spirits in prison, because they formerly did not obey, when God's patience waited in the days of Noah, while the ark was being prepared, in which a few, that is, eight persons, were brought safely through water. Baptism, which corresponds to this, now saves you, not as a removal of dirt from the body but as an appeal to God for a good conscience, through the resurrection of Jesus Christ ...
(1 Peter 3:18-21)

This text is referred to in the fourth bullet point above. The washing that Peter refers to in this passage is the washing of a good conscience through the work of Christ. There must have been some whom Peter addressed who mistakenly thought of baptism as a washing of the body. It will always be the case that people will misunderstand this amazing sacrament, and it will always be the job of the Church to explain it clearly, as Peter tried to do.

Washing is such an obvious symbol for baptism that it is not surprising that it is commonly used. It does not appear to be a biblical one, though, so we should be cautious. This is possibly because it can cause confusion, in that it could cause people to think that their baptism washes them from sin, which is not the case.

There is no shortage of powerful symbolism in Christian baptism. The challenge to the Church is to conduct baptisms in such a way that the symbolism is understood and communicated. As John said, 'I came baptizing in water that he might be revealed' and our baptisms should do the same.[26]

John's prophecy fulfilled

John continued to play a part in the life and ministry of Jesus right up to the end. Thereafter, John went on being a major influence in the early Church, and not just because of continuing baptisms. His name was mentioned during the ten days that the disciples remained in Jerusalem praying for the Holy Spirit to come, during which they looked for a successor to Judas and decided he should be someone who had been with them 'from the baptism of John'.[27] This was said by Peter, who had been one of John's disciples, and who had followed Jesus from the very beginning.

Peter understood John's message and its significance and when the Day of Pentecost arrived, he urged those there, as John had done, to '*Metanoy* and be immersed.'[28] Now, for the first time, they were to be baptized with a Christian baptism. John's baptism had pointed to this day. Peter also promised that those who have a *metanoia* and are baptized would have their sins forgiven and would be filled with the Spirit – as John had foretold – and that this promise applied not just to those present, but also to everyone in the future who follows Christ.

As the 3,000 who responded to Peter's message were baptized (immersed), they very likely had John's message on their minds: 'I immerse you in water; the Coming One will immerse you in the Holy Spirit and fire.'[29]

And Peter said to them, 'Repent [*Metanoy*] and be baptized [immersed] every one of you in the name of Jesus Christ for the forgiveness of your sins, and you will receive the gift of the Holy Spirit. For the promise is for you and for your children and for all who are far off, everyone whom the Lord our God calls to himself.'
(Acts 2:38-39)

On the day that John's prophesied immersion in the Holy Spirit and fire first occurred, Peter – a one-time disciple of John – set the agenda for the Church throughout history. Maybe John's teaching about sharing food and possessions also influenced the behaviour of the early Church in Jerusalem, where they set about doing just that.[30]

Some while later Peter found himself preaching in the home of the Roman centurion Cornelius in Caesarea. This proved to be another watershed moment for the Church, as it led to the inclusion of Gentiles within it, and again John played a key role.

From what Peter said it is clear that his Gentile audience already knew about Jesus, and they also knew about the baptisms of John. Part way through his sermon he was interrupted when the Holy Spirit fell on his listeners – just as John had prophesied, and just as had happened to them on the Day of Pentecost. They also began to speak in tongues. Peter and those with him then baptized Cornelius' whole household with a Christian baptism in recognition of what had just happened, just one of the many examples of baptism in the Acts of the Apostles.[31]

[']… you yourselves know what happened throughout all Judea, beginning from Galilee after the baptism that John proclaimed … [']

While Peter was still saying these things, the Holy Spirit fell on all who heard the word. And the believers from among the circumcised who had come with Peter were amazed, because the gift of the Holy Spirit was poured out even on the Gentiles. For they were hearing them speaking in tongues and extolling God. Then Peter declared, 'Can anyone withhold water for baptizing these people, who have received the Holy Spirit just as we have?' And he commanded them to be baptized in the name of Jesus Christ.

(Acts 10:37,44-48a)

However, when those in the Church back in Jerusalem heard about this incident, it proved to be somewhat controversial so they asked Peter to give an account of what had happened. Peter responded by telling them the story of what took place and how God had poured out the Holy Spirit on the assembled Gentiles as he had on them at Pentecost. In telling the story he recalled how Jesus had used John's words to describe this prophesied outpouring.

> And I remembered the word of the Lord, how he said, 'John indeed immersed (baptized) in water, but you will be immersed (baptized) in (the) Holy Spirit.' If then God gave the same gift to them as he gave to us when we believed in the Lord Jesus Christ, who was I that I could stand in God's way?
> (Acts 11:16-17, referring to Acts 1:5)[32]

Two chapters further on the writer of Acts recounts Paul's first recorded synagogue sermon, in Pisidian Antioch, on his first missionary journey. This sermon is thought to be typical of what he normally said in such circumstances, and he introduced Jesus to the congregation in this way:[33]

> ... God has brought to Israel a Saviour, Jesus, as he promised. Before his coming, John had proclaimed a baptism of repentance [*metanoia*] to all the people of Israel. And as John was finishing his course, he said, 'What do you suppose that I am? I am not he. No, but behold, after me one is coming, the sandals of whose feet I am not worthy to untie.'
> (Acts 13:23b-25)

This was in AD 47-48,[34] so seventeen years after his execution John's reputation lived on among the Jewish diaspora, as did familiarity with his baptisms of *metanoia* and his prophetic message about the Coming One. John was still the herald of Jesus.

Coming full circle

There is further proof of the importance of John in the early Church in the way that Acts records three occasions when the reception of the Holy Spirit was accompanied by the concurrent sign of the recipients speaking in tongues.[35] One of these was the dawning of the age of the Spirit, the birth of the Church itself on the Day of Pentecost (Acts 2). Another was at the home of Cornelius, the first Gentile to receive the Spirit (Acts 10). Both these events are of substantial historic significance. The third occasion was when some disciples of John in Ephesus received the Holy Spirit. The importance of this was by no means lost on those who witnessed it. The ministry of John had gone full circle. All that John had set out to do had now come to pass. In the mind of the author of Acts, namely Luke, who is also the one who gave us the details of John's beginnings, this completion of John's ministry was seen to be important enough to be signified in the same way as the birth of the Church itself and the inclusion of the Gentiles within it.

> And it happened that while Apollos was at Corinth, Paul passed through the inland country and came to Ephesus. There he found some disciples. And he said to them, 'Did you receive the Holy Spirit when you believed?' And they said, 'No, we have not even heard that there is a Holy Spirit.' And he said, 'Into what then were you baptized [immersed]?' They said, 'Into John's baptism [immersion].' And Paul said, 'John baptized [immersed] with the baptism [immersion] of repentance [*metanoia*], telling the people to believe in the one who was to come after him, that is, Jesus.' On hearing this, they were baptized [immersed] in the

name of the Lord Jesus. And when Paul had laid his hands on them, the Holy Spirit came on them, and they began speaking in tongues and prophesying. There were about twelve men in all. (Acts 19:1-7)

From what they said it appears that these disciples had not heard John properly, or had not heard his full message, or not understood it, or had forgotten it. Disciples cannot always be relied upon properly to represent their teacher! Nevertheless, they were still able to recognise the truth of what Paul told them as the fulfilment of John's preaching and they embraced Jesus as their Saviour, receiving as they did the Holy Spirit in the way that is prefigured in baptism and in John's prophecy that the Coming One would immerse people in the Holy Spirit. And they spoke in tongues. This kind of episode very likely happened many times with disciples of John the Baptist. Apollos, for example, had only experienced the baptism of John until Priscilla and Aquila showed him a better way.[36]

At first sight, it does not seem proportionate that John's ministry coming full circle should be signified in the same way as the birth of the Church and the inclusion of Gentiles, but that is to underestimate the importance of John to early Christians. He was a hero to them, second only to Jesus. This was not just because he was Jesus' cousin, miraculously conceived. It was because he was revered as a martyr. He was the originator of the rite of baptism. They honoured his teaching, his role as forerunner, his exemplary life and his close partnership with Jesus. He was the subject of prophecy himself and the prophet who introduced the world both to Jesus, the second person of the Trinity, and to a new understanding and experience of the Holy Spirit, the third person of the Trinity. Indeed, it was John who had set the scene for the introduction of the Trinity to the world.

Paul later took up this theme, saying that John was the one who began the process of preaching the kingdom of God, something that Jesus had earlier acknowledged, as did Peter in Acts 1:22, as we have just seen.[37] In fact, because John began his preaching at Bethany beyond the Jordan, and because Jesus was anointed there, the site of the baptism is one of the places where people contend that Christianity began.

Drinking the Spirit

This brief survey of John's influence on the early Church is not complete without looking at the seventh and final time that his prophecy about immersion in the Holy Spirit is quoted in the New Testament. The wording is slightly different and uniquely among those seven occasions, immersion in water is not mentioned here by Paul, probably because his audience was formed mainly of Gentiles who did not have a background of Jewish immersions in water.

The quotation is found, fittingly, in Paul's great discourse on spiritual matters in 1 Corinthians chapters 12 to 14 that was penned, it seems, in response to a question from the Church in Corinth. It is not surprising that in it he should refer to the two great watery images of the Holy Spirit that come from Jesus and John, saying that we should both *drink* the Spirit and be *immersed* in the Spirit.

> For in one Spirit we all into one body were immersed (baptized), whether Jews or Greeks, whether slaves or free, and all one Spirit were given to drink.
> (1 Corinthians 12:13)[38]

What Paul wrote here is that all Christians are immersed (baptized) in the Spirit into the body of Christ, which is made up of people of all nations ('Jews or Greeks'[39]) and is very egalitarian (slaves and free people). This is a significant saying because what he was telling the Corinthians is that entry into the Church is by immersion (baptism) in the Holy Spirit.

In Chapter 4 we noted that there are (risking oversimplification) broadly three schools of thought when it comes to interpreting John's prophecy about immersion in the Holy Spirit: the evangelical, the traditional and the Pentecostal, although the boundaries between them are often blurred.

- Generally, the evangelical approach to this verse is that entry into the Church is a spiritual event, equivalent to being immersed in the Holy Spirit (often equated with being born again), of which the church-administered sacrament of baptism in water is an outward sign.[40]
- In general, traditionalists say that what Paul is referring to here is confirmation of a person's baptism in water during which the Spirit is passed on to the person being confirmed through the laying on of the bishop's hands.
- Belief that baptism in the Spirit is a second blessing means that Pentecostals generally think either that 'all' the members of the Church in Corinth had received the second blessing, or contend that Paul is referring here to conversion and water baptism *not* to John's prophecy.

After writing about all Christians being immersed in the Spirit, Paul wrote about all Christians *drinking* the Spirit. This is a phrase that is unique to this passage, although it reminds us of Jesus' offer of living water to the woman at the well and his invitation to people at the Feast of Tabernacles to come to him and drink, which would result in rivers of living water – the Holy Spirit – flowing from them.[41]

There are some who follow Luther, Calvin and others here and say that drinking the Spirit refers in some way to Paul's teaching on the communion meal in the previous chapter of 1 Corinthians, but it is more likely that it is an expression used by Jesus and Paul to make us think about the abundance of the Spirit in us as well as all around us. [42] We both drink the Spirit and are immersed in the Spirit.

1 Corinthians chapters 12, 13 and 14 provide the perfect context for ending our look at how John's great prophecy was used by the first-century Church. For in this passage, Paul reminds us that every church member's God-given spiritual gifts are to be used lovingly and effectively for building up the Church, the body of Christ.

The gift of immersion in God's Spirit, and the spiritual gifts that flow from it, are to be used in loving, practical ways for the good of the whole Church.

CHAPTER 10: POSTSCRIPT

One Lord, one faith, one baptism ...
(Ephesians 4:5)

Mary, Peter and Paul have caught the imagination of Christians down the ages, and a great deal of attention has also been paid to the four Gospel writers, and others, which is all very understandable, but in their day, all of these giants of the early Church held John in the highest esteem as a 'man sent from God', second only to Jesus.[1] John was crucial to the early Christians as a guide to help them through their formative years as they grappled with the big issues of the day, giving them, among other things, a framework for understanding what happened on the Day of Pentecost, and for the inclusion of Gentiles converts in the Church.

And they were not the only ones to hold him in such high regard for, although John's role was to be a witness to Jesus and to give testimony about the bridegroom, on several occasions Jesus returned the favour and gave testimony about John, including this: '... among those born of women there has arisen no one greater than John the Baptist'.[2]

As we conclude our look at the life and message of John, we should ask ourselves whether we think that he lived up to this greatest of accolades, and there are two reasons why we should.

Firstly, Christianity in its many branches is the most numerous religion in the world, the majority religion on five of the world's six inhabited continents,[3] and all baptized Christians across the globe have in some way felt John's influence. He is the initiator of the religious rite practised on more people in history than any other.

In the following centuries, a multitude of different baptismal traditions emerged, the principal ones being:

- The Eastern Church, where the tradition is one of baptizing babies and adult converts by immersion.
- The Western Church, where baptismal practice has evolved so that babies and adult converts are baptized by sprinkling.
- The Baptist and Pentecostal traditions, in which it is adult believers who are baptized by immersion.

Whatever our tradition might be, the challenge to us all is to help those present at a baptismal service, or at any other service for that matter, to understand and embrace all that baptism 'in the name of the Father and of the Son and of the Holy Spirit' symbolises.[4]

From John we learn that disciples of Jesus are immersed in the Holy Spirit, of which immersion in water is a potent symbol: the Holy Spirit is in us, as we learn elsewhere, and all around us, as we learn from John. And from Jesus we learn that whoever asks their loving heavenly Father for the gift of the Holy Spirit will receive it.[5] This is a great and powerful message for us to proclaim.

His legacy of baptism and its symbolism might on its own be enough to place John up there among the greatest people who have ever lived.

There is nevertheless a second reason for concurring with Jesus' accolade that lies, perhaps even more compellingly, in the brilliant way he fulfilled his unique calling as the one who prepared the way of the LORD. He was the herald of Jesus. He was the one who set the scene for the introduction of the Trinity to the world, and he was the Prophet of Pentecost. This makes John's divine commission one of the most significant in history.

Who can deny that he fulfilled his calling with a genius, with a level of dedication, and a clear-eyed singleness of purpose that is truly inspirational and unsurpassed?

John 'was not the light',[6] but he was, as Jesus so eloquently put it,

a burning and shining lamp
(John 5:35)

APPENDIX: BIRTH AND ANNUNCIATION DATES

The date of John's birth: 6 BC

Since John was born between five and six months before Jesus, the calculation of his date of birth is dependent on our understanding of the date of Jesus' nativity. Dionysius, who worked out our BC/AD dating system, calculated the date of the nativity as 25 December in the year 1 BC and began the new era on 1 January AD 1, with no year zero in between. However, the information on which Dionysius based his calculations was flawed, as the Herod of the Christmas story is generally thought to have died in the spring of 4 BC. The table on the next page is based on an article by C.J. Humphreys, published in 1992, which concluded that Jesus was born between 9 March and 4 May in 5 BC, possibly between 13 and 27 April, which was Passover time.[1] Working from the hypothesis that Jesus was born in April in the year 5 BC, the other dates in the table on the next page are estimates that work back from then, using the information available to us from the Gospels. It seems likely that John the Baptist was born around November in the year 6 BC and that the first event in the New Testament, John's annunciation, took place in or around February of the same year.

Month

0   February 6 BC   John's annunciation.

1   March 6 BC

2   April 6 BC

3   May 6 BC

4   June 6 BC

5   July 6 BC   Elizabeth told no one for five months.[2]
                           Jesus' annunciation in Elizabeth's sixth
                           month.[3]

6   August 6 BC

7   September 6 BC   Mary stayed with Elizabeth and
                           Zechariah for 'about three months'.[4]

8   October 6 BC

9   November 6 BC   John born.

10   December 6 BC

11   January 5 BC

12   February 5 BC

13   March 5 BC

14   April 5 BC   Jesus born.

The date of the start of John's ministry: AD 29

Working out the date of the start of John's ministry should be the most straightforward dating exercise in the entire Bible, given the very precise information that Luke provides.

> In the fifteenth year of the reign of Tiberius Caesar, Pontius Pilate being governor of Judea, and Herod being tetrarch of Galilee, and his brother Philip tetrarch of the region of Ituraea and Trachonitis, and Lysanias tetrarch of Abilene, during the high priesthood of Annas and Caiaphas, the word of God came to John the son of Zechariah in the wilderness.
> (Luke 3:1-2)

There are, though, still some disputes about the date, the main one being a question about what year Luke was measuring his fifteen years from. Octavian, also known as Augustus, came to power following the assassination of Julius Caesar in 44 BC and became the first ruler of the Roman Empire to be declared *Imperator*, in 27 BC. He reigned as such until his death in AD 14 at the age of seventy-five. As he was the first emperor, there was no direct precedent for his succession. He was anxious that the office should remain in his family and that the succession should be peaceful because he had had to fight a series of civil wars to consolidate his power after the assassination of Julius Caesar. His plans were complicated by the deaths of his direct heirs, so he eventually chose his wife's son from a previous marriage, Tiberius, and adopted him in the Roman fashion. In AD 12 Octavian's trusted and powerful lieutenant Agrippa, Tiberius' father-in-law, died, so Octavian took the opportunity to pass on some significant powers to Tiberius. This was later called the co-princeps of Tiberius and, although it was not a term that was used at the time, it has tended to stick. Tiberius did not become emperor until Octavian's death two years later.

Josephus and first-century Roman historians counted Tiberius' years from his accession as emperor, and they followed the convention of counting his first year from 1 January of the year following the accession, i.e. year one for Tiberius was AD 15, making AD 29 the fifteenth year.[5] This is backed up by evidence from coins and inscriptions. There are, however, some scholars who say that Luke was referring to the fifteenth year after Tiberius' appointment as 'co-princeps' in AD 12.[6] The scholars who argue for the earlier date do so because of a desire to fit in with a chronology that dates Jesus' crucifixion in the spring of AD 30, because, if Jesus was crucified in AD 30, the start of John's ministry cannot have been in AD 29. If, however, one begins counting from AD 12, following the convention of counting from 1 January in the following year, John's ministry would have started in AD 27, which could just fit in with a date of AD 30 for the Passion, although it does not give a long enough time for John to have had an independent ministry before the baptism of Jesus.

To answer this problem, some ignore the standard convention and assume year one of Tiberius was AD 12 and that John's ministry started in AD 26.[7] The principal argument used to support this chronology is that Luke uses the word *hēgemonia* (ἡγεμονία) for 'reign', which can mean imperial rule or it can mean the rule of someone lesser, such as a governor or, it is argued, a co-princeps.[8] They argue that Luke would have used the word *basileia* (βασιλεια) if he had meant us to think he was referring to Tiberius' accession as emperor. Basilea can mean royal rule, although not necessarily imperial rule (it was used, for example, for King Herod [9]). There are four weaknesses to this argument, the first of which is that it is not linguistically convincing.[10] Secondly, at this stage of imperial rule, Roman emperors studiously avoided royal titles in order to maintain a semblance of a republic, and *basileia* would not have been as appropriate as *hēgemonia*.

Thirdly, Luke referred to Tiberius as Tiberius Caesar, which was his adopted family name but was also an imperial title at that time and was used as such by Jesus, recorded by Luke.[11] Lastly, Luke's Gospel was addressed to Theophilus, who had a Romanised Greek name and is widely thought to have been a Roman official, and Luke claimed to be writing an 'orderly account' to him. It is very unlikely that he would have used an obscure dating method to do this.[12]

There is no doubt that Luke's intention was to provide a precise date and it is perfectly reasonable to assume that he would have used the convention of his day to do so. To maintain that he would do otherwise is to make this competent, intelligent man look amateurish and uninformed. It makes more sense to conclude that Luke was referring to the fifteenth year from the calendar year following Tiberius' accession as Emperor in AD 14, i.e. that Luke was meaning the year AD 29.

The need to make the less than convincing argument that Luke followed an obscure dating convention is removed if one accepts a later date for Jesus' crucifixion. This is where advances in astronomy and the availability of greater computing power come to our rescue. Using these tools, C.J. Humphreys and W.G. Waddington have for the first time accurately recreated ancient Jewish lunar calendars to calculate the date of first-century Passovers, by which method they provide us with a reliable date for Jesus' crucifixion on 3 April AD 33, when he was thirty-seven years old.[13] This would mean that he started his ministry in AD 30 when he was thirty-four years old, which accords with Luke's statement in verse 23 of chapter 3 that states he was 'about thirty years of age' (ὡσεὶ ἐτῶν τριάκοντα) when he began his ministry, an imprecise round figure that could mean any age ranging from twenty-five to thirty-four.[14]

There can be little doubt that John's ministry started in AD 29. There is little doubt either that Luke was using the Roman Julian calendar that, like ours, started each year on 1 January and ended on 31 December.

In the unlikely event that he was using one of the Jewish lunar calendars of the day, which is the other dispute surrounding the date, AD 29 was a year that might have started as early as the autumn of AD 28, or that might have ended as late as the spring of AD 30.[15]

This makes 2029 the bimillennial year of John's declaration of the kingdom of God.

ENDNOTES

Preface

[1] Verse 5 is taken from the literal translation in Chapter 4.

[2] John 3:1-8.

[3] Matthew 11:2-19.

[4] Isaiah 40:3, NKJV.

Introduction

[1] Matthew 11:9; Luke 7:26. In Luke 7:28 in the NKJV you will see Jesus saying that there has never been a greater prophet than John (more about this in Chapter 4).

[2] Public domain. (By Anonymous – http://www.svyatayarus.ru/data/icons/54_deisusniy_chin/index.php, Public Domain, https://commons.wikimedia.org/w/index.php?curid=15840450 [accessed 1.5.19]).

[3] Anabaptist means re-baptizer and is, strictly speaking, a misnomer, a pejorative nickname given to them by their critics, as anabaptists did not re-baptize. What they did was dispute the validity of infant baptism and baptize people by immersion when they were older, which, according to their doctrine, was not a re-baptism but a true once-only baptism.

[4] J.P. Meier, *A Marginal Jew: Rethinking the Historical Jesus*, vol. 2, Part One: Mentor (New York: Doubleday, 1994, pp. 19-233), p. 23 (J.E. Taylor concurs in *The Immerser: John the Baptist within Second Temple Judaism* [Grand Rapids, MI: Eerdmans, 1997], p. 9).

[5] See www.lynnetruss.com/journalism/sisters-of-salome (accessed 17.4.19).

Chapter 1: Miraculous Birth

[1] Solomon's temple, the first temple, had been destroyed long ago, and the second temple, built by Zerubbabel and the returnees from exile in Babylon was replaced by this one built by Herod. It is generally known by historians as the second temple, although it is sometimes known as the late second temple or Herod's temple. Herod was later called 'the Great' mainly to distinguish him from the other members of his family also called Herod, several of whom feature in the story of John, but also because of his extraordinary building achievements, the temple being one of them. It was not, in fact, finally completed until AD 63, just before the outbreak of the Jewish revolt in AD 66 and the destruction of the temple in AD 70, which was prophesied by Jesus.

[2] Josephus wrote that there were twenty-four courses or divisions (*ephēmeria* in Greek) of priests (*Life of Flavius Josephus* 1.2 [1.1]). *Against Apion* 2.108 (2.8), also written by Josephus, says that there were only four courses, which is a scribal error according to his translator W. Whiston, but it adds the detail that each course numbered 5,000.

[3] There is a description of this process in Exodus 30. Verses 1-10 describe the ritual and verses 34-38 describe the kind of incense that was to be used (Cf. Psalm 141:2). Exodus 37:25-28 describes the making of the altar of incense and Maccabees 4:49-50 describes the reinstatement of the ritual after the defilement by Antiochus Epiphanes. The decoration of the curtain is described in Exodus 26:31. Cherubim (singular: cherub) are symbolic angel-like winged beings. The Holy of Holies is also known as the Most Holy Place. The central building of the temple was a rectangle three times as long as it was broad and the Holy of Holies was in the end third of the building, i.e. it was built as a square. In fact, it was constructed with a lowered ceiling so that it was a perfect cube, which is also the

shape of the New Jerusalem in Revelation 21:6. It was entered only by the high priest and only once a year on the Day of Atonement (*Yom Kippur*). God's glory was often symbolised in the Old Testament by smoke. Cf. Revelation 8:3-4; 15:8.

⁴ Luke's Gospel begins with this story in the temple and ends with the apostles 'in the temple blessing God'. This incident is similar to Daniel 9:21. Hebrews chapters 8 to 10, written just after the destruction of the temple by the Romans in AD 70, takes up the theme that Jesus rendered the sacrifices and the whole cultic paraphernalia of the temple redundant, which makes this setting for the opening scene of the New Testament all the more poignant. The veil before which Zechariah stood was torn in two at Jesus' crucifixion (Matthew 27:51). Having started in the heart of the temple, the New Testament ends with a vision of the New Jerusalem in which the seer 'saw no temple ... for its temple is the Lord God Almighty and the Lamb' (Revelation 21:22). Jews of the day had a heightened apocalyptic expectation that God would return to the temple, and he did (e.g. Ben Sirach 28).

⁵ Public domain. From the collection of the Metropolitan Museum of Art. The details may not be perfect but it is a very striking representation.

⁶ Messenger is *malak* in Hebrew and *angelos* in the Greek of the Septuagint. Both words also mean angel. In the Orthodox tradition John is regarded as an angel. 'My messenger' is *malachi* in Hebrew – the name of the prophet in 1:1.

⁷ Something is lost when names are transliterated from one language to another. This book uses Zechariah, like the prophet, along with many commentators and Bible translators. This was his name when written in Hebrew, although Zacharias, used by other Bible translators, is the closest transliteration into English of his name as written in the Greek Septuagint translation of the Old Testament

and in the Greek of the New Testament. Zechariah was from the priestly division of Abijah (Luke 1:5), which was the eighth division of the Zadokite priesthood (1 Chronicles 24:10). His name means 'God has remembered' and there is a theme of God remembering in both Mary's Magnificat and Zechariah's Benedictus (Luke 1:54,72).

8 Genesis 15:6.

9 Drawn by D. McNeill.

10 Josephus, *Against Apion* 2.103 (2.8). There may be a little gender equality subtext in the annunciation stories. John's annunciation took place in a part of the temple forbidden to women, but afterwards Zechariah was silenced, and the story focuses on Elizabeth and her baby. Similarly, in Nazareth Mary believed straight away but Joseph hesitated, and after that the story focuses on Mary and her baby. Then the two women came together and, with their children, became the focus of both stories.

11 There is an echo of Elijah here. In 1 Kings 17:1 he says, 'As the LORD, the God of Israel, lives, before whom I stand ...' In Luke 1:19 Gabriel says, 'I am Gabriel. I stand in the presence of God ...'

12 Luke 1:5. Her name in Hebrew is *Elisheba*, which means 'Who swears by God', or 'God is my vow'. The Greek rendering is *Elisabet*.

13 Luke 1:39-40. Ein Kerem (which is sometimes spelt differently) is an Arabic name that means 'The spring of the vineyard' and it is generally identified with Beth Haccerem, which means 'Place of the vineyard' (Nehemiah 3:14; Jeremiah 6:1). Today it is a popular village in its own right, filled with artists and sculptors.

14 These are not the only churches in the village, which is also home to a recently refurbished gold-clad onion-domed Russian Orthodox monastery, a couple of convents and an orphanage.

15 Luke 1:56. John was born, therefore, when Mary was about four months pregnant, i.e. about five months before the birth of Jesus. In the Church calendar, Jesus' annunciation is remembered on 25

March and the visitation sixty-seven days later on 31 May, which, like so many such dates, is not precise.

[16] *Syn* means 'with', 'in company with', and *genes* comes from *genea*, which means 'family'.

[17] Women were generally married soon after puberty in those days, and for Elizabeth to have been too old to bear children she will have been at least in her mid-forties, which makes the age gap thirty years or more. Mary, or *Myriam* in Hebrew, was the name of Aaron's sister (Exodus 15:20), and Elizabeth was the name of Aaron's wife (Exodus 6:23), so the original Mary and Elizabeth were sisters-in-law.

[18] Luke 1:5. There is a tradition found in Nicephorus 2:3 that Elizabeth was the sister of Mary's mother, i.e. Mary's aunt, but this would not make her 'from the daughters of Aaron'.

[19] Matthew 1:18-25; Deuteronomy 22:20-21.

[20] Matthew 1:24; Luke 2:5.

[21] In Latin the text begins *Magnificat anima mea Dominum*, hence its name.

[22] Public domain. (By Fallaner – Own work, CC BY-SA 4.0, https://commons.wikimedia.org/w/index.php?curid=72592808 [accessed 1.5.19]).

[23] John's birth is remembered on 24 June. See Chapter 8, note 32.

[24] Yohanan is sometimes written Johanan, occurring this way twenty-two times in the Old Testament. Yohanan is also the name of one of the Maccabees – the leading family in the intertestamental revolt against Greek rule. In Hebrew, the first letter of John's name is *yod* or *jot*, which is the smallest letter in the Hebrew alphabet. The pronunciation of *yod/jot* differs, with most contemporary Western scholars, and Israelis, preferring the former. This variation in the pronunciation of *yod/jot* would explain why the Hebrew version of John's name is sometimes transcribed as Yohanan and sometimes

as Johanan. In English, and some other languages, the 'h' of John has become silent, but not so elsewhere, where the name is written Johan but pronounced Yohan. English is not the only language that mangles John's name: other versions from around the world include Ivan, Sean, Ian, Hans, Vanya, Jean, Juan, João and Giovanni. In Arabic his name is Yuhanna, although he is called Yahya in the Quran.

[25] Luke 1:63.

[26] Sometimes translated 'Yahweh is gracious', or 'graced by Yahweh'.

[27] *Prodromos* is the Greek word for forerunner (*pro* = before and *dromos* = way) and remains one of John's titles, especially in the Eastern Church. The Latin is *Precursor*.

[28] Luke 3:20 says John was imprisoned. Luke 3:21ff records Jesus' baptism.

[29] From the Chapel of Saint John the Baptist at Siena cathedral. Elizabeth is in bed and the pregnant Mary is seated with a towel while a nurse or midwife washes John. Pinturicchio is the nickname of Bernardino di Betto (1454–1513).

Photograph in the public domain (Creative Commons Attribution 4.0 International [CC BY 4.0]) from the Wellcome Collection (https://wellcomecollection.org/works/mgtx59dc#licenseInformation [accessed 10.5.19]).

[30] E.g. *The Book of Common Prayer*.

[31] In Latin the text begins *Benedictus Dominus*, hence its name. The Magnificat and the Benedictus are the most Semitic parts of Luke's Gospel. According to C.H. Scobie, they are easy to translate into Hebrew and when this is done their poetic character becomes apparent (C.H. Scobie, *John the Baptist* [London: SCM, 1964] p.51).

[32] Isaiah 40:3 is quoted (loosely) in Luke 1:76. It looks as if Zechariah had also been reading Malachi, another of the key texts for John, in his nine months of silence as there is a strong echo of Malachi

4:2 ('the sun of righteousness will rise with healing in its wings') in Luke 1:78f ('the sunrise shall visit us from on high', etc.). There is also an echo of the prologue to the fourth Gospel (John 1:1-9) where Jesus is the Light and John is his witness.

[33] Jeremiah 31:31 (cf. Matthew 26:28; Mark 14:24; Luke 22:20).

[34] In the textual tradition followed by the Authorised (King James) Version, both boys 'grew and became strong in spirit', the last two words being omitted for Jesus (Luke 2:40) in the textual tradition followed by more recent versions.

[35] Genesis 17-18; Judges 13; 1 Samuel 1; John 1:6.

[36] Matthew 11:11.

[37] This is quoted in Matthew 11:10 and Mark 1:2 in relation to John. The 'Me' in this passage is God. See Chapter 5, note 5 about the textual variant in Mark.

[38] There was some confusion during the intertestamental period about this Elijah figure, whether he was to be the forerunner of a messiah or of God, and at the time of Jesus both views were held. Of course, both were true as Jesus was the Messiah and God. These are the last words of the Old Testament (although the Jewish Bible has the books in a different order). In John's annunciation by Gabriel, in Luke 1:16-17, there is an echo of Malachi 4:6.

[39] Translators vary in the use of punctuation in verse 3 of Isaiah 40 above (there being no punctuation in the original to guide us). For reasons that are explained in the next chapter when discussing Qumran, it makes more sense of John's story if we follow here the tradition of the Authorised (King James) Version and others, which is the way it is translated in all four Gospels (Matthew 3:3; Mark 1:3; Luke 3:4; John 1:23), rather than the versions that render it, 'A voice cries: 'In the wilderness prepare the way of the LORD...''

[40] The differences between the first and second parts of Isaiah are such that scholars will often maintain that there were two (or even

three) different authors involved. It seems to me, however, that these differences are perfectly well accounted for by the change in subject matter that led the author to write in a different style. In the same way, the Gospel of John and the book of Revelation were both written by the same person but have a very different subject matter and style. Similarly, C.S. Lewis sometimes wrote for children, sometimes for adults and also penned donnish academic works, employing different styles as he did so.

41 Isaiah 40:3 NKJV; John 1:1.

42 Isaiah 40:8.

Chapter 2: The Wilderness Years

1 Also known as the Infancy Gospel of James, the Book of James and the Protevangelium (or Proto-gospel) of James. The text is easily accessible online and this story can be found in chapters 22–24. M.R. James did not think this section is part of the original (M.R. James, *The Apocryphal New Testament* [Oxford: OUP, 1924] p. 38). See also R.F. Hock, *The Infancy Gospels of James and Thomas* (Santa Rosa, CA: Polebridge Press, 1995). It is almost certainly mythical.

2 The Monastery of St John of the Wilderness. In the garden of this monastery there is a spring that flows into a baptismal pool beside the cave, which is occasionally used today by Ethiopian and Russian Orthodox Christians for the renewal of baptismal vows. The monastery is found at grid reference 31° 46' 04'N 35° 07' 58'E.

3 Josephus writes about the Essenes, 'Marriage they disdain, but they adopt other men's children, while yet pliable and docile, and regard them as their kin and mould them in accordance with their own principles', *Jewish War* 2.119-121 (2.8.2).

4 Luke 1:58.

5 Luke 1:7.

6 Luke 1:14 (NIV UK 2011).

⁷ The Quran was written in the seventh century. In it the pronunciation of John's name is Yahya (Arabic-speaking Christians call him Yuhanna). This version of his story focuses on his miraculous birth (some of the details are different), which is seen to elevate him as one of the twenty-five prophets of Islam, along with his father, Zechariah whose faith is seen as instrumental in his miraculous conception. Apart from the nature of his birth, the Quran briefly states that he was tender, pure, pious, wise, cherishing toward his parents and never insolent or rebellious (Sura 19:1-15, 3:38-41 and 21:89-90. The list of the prophets that includes John and Zechariah is found in Sura 6:84-85). Beyond that, the Quran says nothing about John's life, teaching, mission, or baptisms. There are subsequent Muslim traditions about John (see *Muslim World* 45, 1955, pp. 334-345). The first pope to enter a mosque, John Paul II, visited the Omayyad mosque in Damascus dedicated to John the Baptist, which was built over a pre-existing church. It contains a coffin-shaped white marble shrine surrounded by an iron cage and is one of several sites that purport to contain the head of John the Baptist.

The Mandeans are a syncretistic Gnostic religious sect of uncertain origins based mainly in southern Iraq until the recent troubles when most of them fled persecution. They currently number around 60-70,000 in a worldwide diaspora. Mandeans use baptism as a sacrament of salvation, have John as one of their prophets and a scripture that contains stories about him. The date of their scripture is disputed. Some of it may originate as early as the second century but some of it was written as late as the eighth century, with the stories about John in the later sections. They have sometimes wrongly been called 'St John's Christians'.

Unless one is a convinced Muslim or Mandean it is unlikely that one will find these sources historically convincing. It is akin to someone writing today about a well-documented person from the fourteenth or fifteenth century, putting forward a new piece of contradictory information about them for which there is no available independent verification. No serious historian would give it credence.

8   There is more information about Josephus, including the relevant texts, on my website: johnthebaptistbook.com.

9   See C.H. Scobie, op. cit., pp. 19-22 and R.L. Webb, *John the Baptizer and Prophet* (Eugene, OR: Wipf & Stock, 1991), pp. 43-44 for more detail.

10 Legion of Honor Museum, San Francisco. Public domain. (By El Greco – Web Gallery of Art: Image Info about artwork, Public Domain, https://commons.wikimedia.org/w/index.php?curid=15461960 [accessed 1.5.19]).
   Michael York's portrayal of John the Baptist in the film *Jesus of Nazareth* (1977) is a typical example of this misrepresentation of John.

11 Elijah: 1 Kings 17. Melchizedek: Genesis 14:18-20; Hebrews 7:1-3. The Greek word that is translated 'appeared publicly' (*anadeixis*) in Luke 1:80 only occurs here in the New Testament. Some translators, following the Authorised (King James) Version, use 'shewing', but this is less likely as a translation.

12 Deuteronomy 16. There is an example of one of these visits in Luke 2:41-50.

13 Luke 1:17; Luke 1:76, cf. Isaiah 40:3.

14 He neither took his father's name nor followed his profession.

15 Josephus, *Antiquities* 20.224-251 (20.10).

16 Malachi 2:1-9. Chapters 3 and 4 of Malachi contain prophetic oracles that guided John the Baptist.

17 Luke 1:15.

18 Nazirites were not to cut their hair, and John is often shown with long hair.

[19] Exodus 29:4; 30:17-21; 40:12; Leviticus 8:6; 16:4, 24; Numbers 8:6,7,21; 2 Chronicles 4:2-6. See the plan of the temple in Chapter 1 for the location of the laver.

[20] Sometimes spelt *mikveh* or *miqvah*. The plural is *mikva'ot*. It means 'a gathering of the waters'. There are several *mikva'ot* to be found in the Jerusalem Archaeological Park (aka Ophel Garden) to the south of the Temple Mount, which people would have used during a visit to the temple. It would have been these that many of the 3,000 who were baptized on the Day of Pentecost would have used (Acts 2:41). There are others in private houses in the Wohl Museum in the Jewish Quarter of Jerusalem and others outside the present Old City walls to the West of the Dung Gate. Two have been found at Massadah, five at Machaerus, including one with its roof still intact (G. Vörös, *Machaerus 1* [Milan: Edizioni Terra Santa, 2013], pp. 254f; G. Vörös, *Machaerus 3* [Milan: Edizioni Terra Santa, 2019], pp. 156ff) and many others around the country. Some are smaller individual affairs and others are larger communal ones.

[21] The Mishnah, a late second/early third-century written record of oral Jewish teaching, says that there were six levels of purity for *mikvah* water (*Mishnah*, Seder Tohorot, Tractate Mikva'ot). The idea of running water seems to have lived on in early Christian baptismal practice as it is described in the Didache (Didache 7), which dates to c. AD 100.

[22] See note 2.

[23] Josephus, *Jewish War* 2.160-161 (2.8.13).

[24] Photograph from www.wildolive.co.uk (accessed 15.9.14). Used with permission.

[25] For Orthodox Jews it is so important that when a new community establishes itself the first thing they are required to build is not a synagogue but a *mikvah*.

[26] Mark 7:4. Today there are three principal reasons why Jewish

people undertake ritual cleansing: (1) after menstruation, sexual intercourse, being in contact with blood, touching a dead body and the like. (2) As part of a conversion to Judaism (This would normally take place after circumcision for males. Converts are led by two or three witnesses into the *mikvah* where they listen again to their main duties as a Jew and then immerse themselves. The object of the immersion is not to make them a Jew, but to ritually cleanse them and thereafter they will need further cleansings. There is no record of ritual immersion being part of a conversion ritual until the early part of the second century AD, decades after the destruction of the temple in AD 70 and long after the New Testament had been completed.). And (3) to cleanse pots and pans to make them suitable for kosher cooking, which is deemed necessary when the pots and pans have been made by Gentiles and are therefore seen to be contaminated (see A. Kaplan, *Waters of Eden* [New York: NCSY, 1999], p. 6.). To get married by a rabbi in Israel today requires a certificate to prove that the bride and groom have both been through a *mikvah*.

[27] Leviticus 16:16. While ritual impurity was not sinful it was seen as sinful to enter the temple while impure, hence all the *mikva'ot* nearby. Cf. Leviticus 15:31; 20:3; Numbers 19:13, 20 and Josephus, *Jewish War* 5.227 (5.5.6). Immersion before *Yom Kippur* is still a common custom for Jewish people.

[28] Childbirth: Leviticus chapter 12; cf. Luke 2:22-24. Leprosy: Leviticus chapter 14; cf. Mark 1:40-45.

[29] Cf. Luke 5:33-35; Matthew 9:14-17; Mark 2:18-20.

[30] E.g. *Didache* 8. J.E. Taylor discusses this in her book *The Immerser: John the Baptist within Second Temple Judaism* (op. cit.), pp. 204f.

[31] E.g. Matthew 6:16-18. The context of this passage is Jesus' teaching on prayer: Matthew 6:5-15.

[32] Josephus, *Antiquities* 15.373 (15.10.5).

³³ In the New Testament Isaiah 40:3 is quoted in all four Gospels in relation to John and all the versions are punctuated like this: 'a voice crying in the wilderness, "Prepare the way of the LORD ..."' Unfortunately, unduly influenced by an interpretation preferred by this Jewish sect, as demonstrated by their cache of literature found at Qumran, and ignoring John the Baptist's interpretation as demonstrated by Matthew, Mark, Luke and John, the punctuation of Isaiah 40:3 in some more recent versions (such as NIV, NRSV) has been changed to 'A voice cries out: "In the wilderness prepare the way of the LORD ..."'

³⁴ J. Steinmann (tr. M. Boyes), *Saint John the Baptist in the Desert Tradition* (London: Longmans, 1958), p. 60.

³⁵ Josephus, *Jewish War* 2.143-144 (2.8.8) contains a description of the hardships of an Essene who was cast out of the community.

³⁶ Qumran document 1QS 6:4-6; Luke 7:33-34 (Cf. Luke 1:15).

³⁷ Cf. Matthew 19:12; 1 Corinthians 7:1-9. As we shall see, John was later to die for speaking out about the sanctity of marriage.

³⁸ S. Gibson, *The Cave of John the Baptist* (London: Century, 2004), p. 148. In contrast J. Steinmann, writing in the days when there was a fashion for this sort of thing, advocates a strong connection between John and Qumran (*Saint John the Baptist and the Desert Tradition*, op. cit.).

³⁹ J. Thomas, *Le Mouvement Baptiste en Palestine et Syrie* (Gembloux: Duculot, 1935). Although written before the Qumran discoveries, Thomas describes these baptist groups in detail. Banus is sometimes spelt Bannus.

⁴⁰ Mark 6:14,24. Josephus refers to him as 'John called the Baptist' in *Antiquities* 18.116 (18.5.2). The text can be found on my website johnthebaptistbook.com.

⁴¹ Matthew 11:9 and Luke 7:26; Luke 7:28 (in the textual tradition of the Authorised Version. This is discussed in Chapter 4); Luke 1:76;

Luke 1:17.

As he mainly prophesied before Jesus began his ministry he is sometimes thought of as the last of the Old Testament prophets, although he also prophesied after Jesus' baptism, e.g., 'Behold, the Lamb of God, who takes away the sin of the world' (John 1:29). In truth, he is the prophetic link between the Old Testament and the New.

[42] Matthew 11:7; Luke 7:24.

[43] Matthew 3:4; Mark 1:6.

[44] NKJV. Robe of coarse hair is also translated as 'hairy mantle' (ASV), 'hairy cloak' (ESV) or 'hairy robe' (NASB): Zechariah 13:4. Elijah's mantle is described in 1 Kings 19:13,19; 2 Kings 1:8; 2:8,13,14. In 2 Kings 2:12-14 Elijah's mantle became a badge of office for Elisha and we can think of John's coat like that.

[45] James Neil, *Palestine Explored* (London: Nisbet & Co., 1907), p. 255. In Arabic the word for this kind of garment is 'abāyah. This sort of coat fell into disuse under the British mandate of Palestine when alternative cheaper and smoother clothing began to be imported.

[46] The photograph on the left comes from the Library of Congress and was taken in Ramallah c.1890, 'No known restrictions on publication'. See http://www.loc.gov/pictures/resource/cph.3b16513/ (accessed 3.4.19). The photograph on the right is from the Israel Museum, Jerusalem (used with permission). Wool was sometimes spun in with the camel hair of these garments.

[47] There is an article about the way John the Baptist is portrayed in Art on my website johnthebaptistbook.com.

[48] Luke 7:25 (cf. Matthew 11:8). See Chapter 7, note 32.

[49] 2 Kings 1:8; 1 Kings 18:46. There is one commentator who says that John's leather belt may have been a kind of leather underpants, but it is not very likely: leather is not improved by frequent

immersions in water (J.E. Taylor, op. cit., pp. 34-37). There was once a convention that artistic representations of the infant John portrayed him in a leather loincloth, but this is artistic symbolism, not reality. There is an article on John the Baptist in art on my website, johnthebaptistbook.com.

[50] Jeremiah 49:19; Judges 14:8-9; 1 Samuel 14:25ff; Psalm 81:16; Deuteronomy 32:13.

[51] Josephus, *Jewish War* 4.468 (4.8.3), Damascus Document, Of Food 12:11-15, *Philo, Hypothetica* 2. 11. 5-9. In the same paragraph Josephus records the practice in Jericho of refining a syrup from figs that he calls 'honey', and there are those who point out that the term 'honey' in the ancient world was sometimes (rarely) used of such sticky sweet substances derived from dates, figs and tree gum. They suggest that this is what John ate rather than honey from bees. The arguments are not at all compelling. In the Damascus Document the reference is actually to a prohibition about eating bee larvae that some think refers to properly straining honey before eating it.

[52] Leviticus 11:20-24, especially verse 22; Qumran, Damascus Document, Of Food 12:11-15. The *Mishnah* (*Chullin* 3:7) says, 'Among locusts [these are clean]: all that have four legs, four wings, and jointed legs, and whose wings cover the greater part of their bodies' are permitted for eating. Today locusts are fashionable in exotic restaurants and a quick online search will reveal plenty of recipes, including a recipe book from Australia called *Cooking with Sky Prawns*. See http://news.bbc.co.uk/1/hi/world/asia-pacific/4032143.stm (accessed 3.4.19). It is commonly said that John ate the seeds of carob trees and not locusts, but this is merely pandering to the squeamish and to those who are under the misapprehension that eating locusts contravenes Old Testament dietary laws.

[53] Luke 3:11.

[54] For those who want to investigate the question of John's diet further there is a very thorough book by James A. Kelhoffer called *The Diet of John the Baptist* (Tübingen: Mohr Siebeck, 2005). Its 256 pages should satisfy any level of curiosity.

[55] Isaiah 40:3, NKJV.

[56] Hosea 2:14ff.

[57] Others point to the similarity between *mid'var* and the Hebrew for 'word', which is *davar*, which may indicate that it is a place to hear God's word – a place to *shema* (*shema* is the Hebrew word for 'hear', e.g. in Deuteronomy 6:4).

[58] Leviticus 16:21-22; Matthew 12:43.

[59] Look at all the powerful and important people in their palaces and temples mentioned in the first two verses of Luke chapter 3, yet it was to John in the wilderness that the word of God came.

[60] John 1:6.

Chapter 3: Baptism in Water

[1] Isaiah 40:3.

[2] 'Tetragrammaton' is Greek for 'four letters'.

[3] Hebrew vowels are a series of dots and dashes called pointing and sometimes the vowels for *Elohim* (אֱלֹהִים), meaning God, or *Adonai* (אֲדֹנָי), meaning Lord are written with יהוה and the reader might read one of these words instead.

[4] Matthew 3:3; Mark 1:3; Luke 3:4; John 1:23. Some versions, e.g. NKJV, say LORD.

[5] 1 Kings 17–19. Mount Horeb is also known as Mount Sinai. Luke 1:80 says that John was in the wilderness in preparation for his ministry, but what does not come across in English is that, as noted in Chapter 2, Luke uses the plural of wilderness here in the Greek, i.e. wildernesses (*tais erēmois*), which suggests that he

travelled around. Luke 3:3 says he went into 'all the region around the Jordan'.

6 2 Kings 2:8-14. Malachi 4:5 talks of Elijah's return. Elisha later sent Naaman to be healed by immersion in the River Jordan, but this was not thought to have happened at the same place (2 Kings 5).

7 1 Kings 17:3-6. Today it is called Wadi al-Kharrar and there is a similarity in the sound of the two names Kharrar and Cherith. Wadi in this instance means a river that is mostly dry in the summer, flowing fully in the rainy season. Wadi al-Kharrar has year-round springs. It is not the only place associated with the Brook Cherith, but what matters is whether people believed it to be the place because that is where one can meditate on the event. In the rainy season it flows for two kilometres.

8 The grid reference for Elijah's Hill is 31° 50' 18'N 35° 34'E. It is more like a hillock or a mound than a hill and before it was recently excavated by archaeologists it had been almost covered over by silt and the debris of millennia.

9 When Dionysius worked out the modern calendar he did it at a time when the use of zero had not been established, which means that there is no year zero in the calendar, so twenty years from 6 BC is AD 15 and not AD 14 as one might at first think.

10 The contrast in this verse is wonderful: all those important and powerful men in their palaces and temples, but the word of God went to John in the wilderness.

11 It is common for people to think that Jesus was thirty years old when he began his ministry, but this is based on a misreading of Luke 3:23, which says that Jesus was *about* thirty years of age' (emphasis mine) an imprecise round figure that can mean anything between twenty-five and thirty-four years old. For the details of how these dates are worked out see the Appendix.

12 Psalm 137:1.

[13] Staatliche Museen, Berlin. This is a very gaunt and slightly depressed-looking John in a somewhat European setting. His gauntness is a common motif in paintings of John and is meant to indicate his austere diet. Note the lamb, which is also a common feature in paintings of John who said, 'Behold, the Lamb of God' (John 1:29,36). There is an article about John the Baptist in Art on my website johnthebaptistbook.com.

Photograph in the public domain (By Geertgen tot Sint Jans. The Yorck Project (2002) 10.000 Meisterwerke der Malerei (DVD-ROM), distributed by DIRECTMEDIA Publishing GmbH. ISBN: 3936122202., Public Domain, https://commons.wikimedia.org/w/index.php?curid=151436 [accessed 10.5.19])

[14] Malachi is not the last book of the Jewish Bible, which puts 'The Prophets' before 'The Writings'. It is the last book of 'The Prophets'.

[15] Moses in Exodus 19 and Elijah in 1 Kings 19.

[16] Matthew 17:1-13; Mark 9:2-13.

[17] Written *Yehoshua* in the earlier part of the Old Testament and *Yeshua* in later sections (Nehemiah 8:17) and in Jewish writings at the time of the New Testament. It means Yahweh [or Jehovah] saves.

[18] While the kingdom of heaven is not understood to be exactly identical with the Church, it is worth remembering here that the sacrament of entry into the Church is, of course, baptism that originated here.

[19] In 1 Corinthians 10:1-2 Paul likens baptism to Moses taking the people through the Red Sea and 'under the cloud' – this parallel can be extended to the River Jordan as well. There is a parable in the River Jordan itself. It begins life as snow melt from Mount Hermon that flows through underground streams until it emerges as pure spring water around Banias and then flows into the Sea of Galilee, the same waters that Jesus walked on and calmed. It then flows ever lower and lower, getting muddier and more polluted until it dies in

the Dead Sea in the lowest spot on earth. It is a picture of the fall of humankind, but there is a way out before our inevitable death: John baptized just before the river terminates in the Dead Sea. The image is of salvation offered to all mankind, no matter how low we fall.

[20] Ezekiel 47. Cf. Isaiah 35:6-7; 41:18-20; 51:3; Revelation 22:1-2.

[21] In Joshua 3:16 the Dead Sea is called 'the Sea of Arabah, the Salt Sea'. See the map in the Introduction.

[22] There are two Bethanys mentioned in the Gospel of John: this Bethany, which is known as 'Bethany beyond the Jordan' (John 1:28, RSV) and the better known Bethany that is referred to as being near Jerusalem or the home of Lazarus, Mary and Martha (John 11:1, 18; 12:1). There are a number of Greek manuscripts of John 1:28, used for the translation of the Authorised Version (KJV), that read Bethabara (which means House of the Ford or The Place of Crossing) rather than Bethany and a good deal of ink has been used up on articles arguing for one or the other: we will use Bethany. Bethabara is shown on the sixth-century mosaic map at Madaba on the west bank of the River Jordan, while Bethany is shown on the east bank – they appear to be on opposite sides of this river crossing point. For centuries Bethany beyond the Jordan was a site of pilgrimage, with churches, monasteries and hermitages, but this stopped because of Muslim hostility and, latterly, because it became a militarised zone on the border between Jordan and Israel. Since the Israel-Jordan peace treaty in 1994 archaeological work became possible and the site has since been opened up with a much-visited Baptism Archaeological Park. A dozen new churches are being built there. The story of the archaeological work is told in *The Great Discovery: Jesus Baptism Site*, ed. Dr M. Waheeb (Amman: 2009).

[23] Mark 14:61. Jesus used both 'kingdom of heaven' and 'kingdom of

God' (e.g. Matthew 19:23,24), but he had no need to fear the third commandment.

[24] Matthew 4:17. When Jesus later sent out the Twelve he told them also to preach, saying, 'The kingdom of heaven is at hand' (Matthew 10:7).

[25] The powers of the kingdom break through into the here and now, although, of course, the kingdom is still ultimately to be fulfilled in the future.

[26] 2 Chronicles 7:14 is a classic example of this. This same message is still preached among Jews today. Among first-century Jews there was a heightened apocalyptic expectation and they will have taken particular note of his message.

[27] Returning to God is more of an Old Testament idea, calling Israelites to return to God from whom they had strayed. The New Testament, which has more of a missionary emphasis, tends to focus more on turning (D. Guthrie, *New Testament Theology* [Leicester: IVP, 1981], p. 574).

[28] James 2:20, NKJV; Matthew 3:7-8; Luke 3:7-8.

[29] The Hebrew noun for turning is *teshuvah* (תְּשׁוּבָה) [or shuvah (שׁוּבָה)]. The Aramaic verb is *tuv* (תּוּב).

[30] Sometimes the verb *strephō* (στρέφω) is used.

[31] Acts chapters 9 and 10.

[32] While John urged people to take the realisation (*metanoia*) route to turning, this is, of course, not always the case in the New Testament. For example, in 2 Corinthians 7 Paul notes that an earlier stern letter that he had written to them had caused them to feel remorse (or 'grieved' as it is sometimes translated; the Greek is *lupeō*), but that their remorse was good because it had led to *metanoia* (usually translated 'repentance'), and that led to a change of behaviour, i.e. a turning. Sometimes the order is realisation/reorientation, as it was for John; sometimes the order is remorse/realisation/reorientation, as it was for

the Corinthians. The order can vary, and there can be other factors, such as a revelation. What matters is that people have a restored relationship with God, that they turn to God and away from sin.

Repentance is a bigger concept in the New Testament than is implied by the simple way the process of reorientation/remorse/realisation is usually translated by using just one word: repentance. For sure, these ideas may overlap, but nevertheless greater subtlety is called for in the way they are translated. This is especially so as the word 'repentance' carries with it overtones of remorse that are not always appropriate. For example, when Paul wrote to the Romans saying that God's kindness is meant to lead a person to *metanoia* (usually translated 'repentance') he meant that the realisation that God is kind changes the way a person thinks and acts, not that God's kindness should make them feel sorrowful, which can be implied by the word 'repentance' (Romans 2:4). In the way that these ideas blend into one another, a change of mind may lead to later regrets, but that is not what Paul wrote in the first instance.

[33] *Metanoeite* (μετανοεῖτε), second person plural present active imperative.

[34] A word may have a range of meanings, meaning different things in different situations, which is why words must always be translated in context. There are other contexts in the New Testament that require a different translation for *metanoeō/metanoia*, but this is the meaning in John's preaching.

[35] *Nous* (mind) was sometimes used to translate the Hebrew word for heart in the Greek Septuagint version of the Old Testament, for the heart is what one thinks with in Old Testament Hebrew. An example of this is found in Mary's Magnificat, usually recognised as a very Hebrew part of the New Testament, in which Mary's words in Luke 1:51b are sometimes translated, 'He has scattered the proud in the imagination of their hearts' (NKJV), and sometimes ' ... in

the thoughts of their hearts' (ESV).

Having said that, Jesus made a distinction between heart and mind when he said, our whole heart and soul and strength and mind are involved in loving God (Luke 10:27. Cf. Matthew 22:37; Mark 12:30; Deuteronomy 6:5).

[36] Luke 3:8 (Cf. Matthew 3:8). There are examples of what he meant by this in Chapter 5. The idea of bearing fruit is reminiscent of Ezekiel's visionary river which has trees bearing fruit each month by its banks (Ezekiel 47:12. Cf. Revelation 22:2). It is also reminiscent of the Sermon on the Mount in which Jesus said, 'by their fruits you will know them' (Matthew 7:15-20, NKJV), and of the idea of fruit of the Spirit (Galatians 5:22-23). Isaiah 55:8-9 helps us understand why we need to change the way we think and the way we live.

[37] *Theological Dictionary of the New Testament*, tr. by G.W. Bromily from G. Kittel, *Theologisches Wörterbuch zum Neuen Testament* (Grand Rapids, MI: Eerdmans, 1967. Reprinted 1981), vol. 4, p. 1008. See also 1 Clement 57:1; Tertullian, De Paenitentia 9.

[38] R.L. Webb (op. cit., pp. 184-189) and J.E. Taylor (op. cit., pp. 106-111) both make this assertion. These are books in the *Sceptic John* tradition described in the Introduction.

[39] Luke 1:16,17; Malachi 4:5-6.

[40] *Theological Dictionary of the New Testament*, op. cit., vol. 4, pp. 993-995.

[41] Because *shuv* is translated *metanoeō* in certain contexts in the Septuagint that does not mean that the reverse should be done in all contexts in the New Testament.

[42] Acts 3:19. Like Paul in Acts 21:40, Peter will have been speaking Hebrew in the temple. The Voice translates this as 'rethink everything and turn to God'. The KJV translates this with a very Latin influence as 'repent … and be converted' (the Vulgate reads *paenitemini igitur et convertimini*).

[43] Acts 26:20. In the same vein Paul wrote to the Romans saying, 'Be transformed by the renewing of your mind [*nous*]' (Romans 12:2).

[44] In translations of the Greek New Testament into Hebrew it is common for translators to use *shuv* (turn) to translate *metanoeō* in Matthew 3:2 and *teshuvah* to translate *metanoia* in Mark 1:4 and Luke 3:3. But, in Acts 3:19 and 26:20, where *metanoeō* and *epistrephō* (turn) are used in the same sentence, translators often revert to a Latin influence and use *nicham* (remorse) to translate *metanoeō* and *shuv* is correctly used to translate *epistrephō*. There is an inappropriate inconsistency in this.

[45] My own hunch is that John did not use a single word when he was preaching in Hebrew or Aramaic. A clue might be found in Isaiah 6:9-10 (the opening words of Isaiah's commissioning text), which is quoted in the New Testament by Jesus and Paul (Matthew 13:14-15; Acts 28:26-27), in which the LORD said to Isaiah that people will not '… understand with their hearts, and turn and be healed'. 'Understand with your heart' is a very Hebrew idea that John might have used. In the way that we seem to need a phrase to translate *metanoeō* into English, it is possible that this might be true for Hebrew as well. There is also in Isaiah 6:9-10 a clear distinction between understanding and turning.

[46] Other phrases that might be used to translate *metanoeō* are, let this dawn on your mind; realise this truth; grasp this truth; take heed of what I say; be mindful of what I say; think differently. In Acts 3:19 The Voice renders *metanoeō*: 'rethink everything'.

[47] Definitions of *metanoia* in English dictionaries – Oxford online dictionary: 'change in one's way of life resulting from penitence or spiritual conversion'. Collins online dictionary: 'a fundamental change in character or outlook, esp repentance'. Merriam-Webster online dictionary: 'transformative change of heart, *especially,* a spiritual conversion'. Dictionary.com: 'a profound, usually spiritual,

transformation; conversion".

48 There is not yet a verbal form of *metanoia* in English, but *metanoy* would be a good one. It is an imperative form of the verb and some translations use an exclamation mark. Perhaps *Metanoy!* is appropriate.

49 In the time of the tabernacle and the temple, animals were sacrificed as sin offerings, but it was never the case that everyone was required to sacrifice every time they sinned (otherwise everyone would be visiting the temple to sacrifice every day) as people were also forgiven when a person realised the error of their way and confessed their sins, turning to God and away from sin.

50 Luke 24:47.

51 In John 1:19-28 John was quizzed by some envoys from Jerusalem. They had not been through John's preparation of *metanoia* and baptism so, while he told them that there was a Coming One, he did not tell them what the Coming One would do.

52 This is the literal translation of this verse from Chapter 4.

53 Translation by C. Croll.

54 Luke 1:17.

55 Translation by C. Croll.

56 In the New Testament it is also maintained that Christian baptism is prefigured by two events in the Old Testament: at the flood (1 Peter 3:20f) and at the crossing of the Red Sea (1 Corinthians 10:2).

57 John 3:26 and 4:1.

58 In Mark 1:4, 6:14,24 a participle of the verb *baptizō* is used rather than the noun *baptistēs*.

59 Mark 7:4,8. As we saw in Chapter 2, Jews ritually cleanse dishes for kosher cooking. This involves immersion in water.

60 Acts 8:36-39. The text does not tell us whether Philip physically immersed the Ethiopian eunuch or simply accompanied him into the water.

[61] *Wars of the Jews* 2.160-161 (2.18.13). 1 Corinthians 12:23 refers to the kind of modesty that this represents.

[62] Matthew 3:6; Mark 1:5.

[63] Dionysiou Monastery, Mount Athos, Greece. Used with permission.

[64] Today, sadly, it is not just muddy but polluted by sewage and the run-off of fertilisers, pesticides and herbicides from the intensive agriculture practised in the Jordan valley. In the last four decades of the twentieth century the flow of water in the river was reduced from 1.3 billion cubic metres per annum to 100 million cubic metres – a reduction of over 90 per cent – leading to a lowering of the Dead Sea.

[65] Library of Congress, 'No known restrictions on publication'. See http://www.loc.gov/pictures/resource/matpc.05914/ (accessed 3.4.19).

[66] Public domain. (By Fallaner – Own work, CC BY-SA 4.0, https://commons.wikimedia.org/w/index.php?curid=69682294 [accessed 1.5.19])

[67] Photograph from the Jordan Tours web site. Used with permission.

Chapter 4: Baptism in the Holy Spirit

[1] Translation by C. Croll.

[2] I once did a MPhil in textual criticism of the New Testament and have thirteen Greek New Testaments in my study, each with slight variations representing different textual theories and editorial judgements made by different exponents of those theories. Of these, eight say that there is no one greater than John and five say that there is no prophet greater than John.

There is a textual criticism 'rule' (textual criticism rules are more like guidelines or 'rules of thumb') that scribes had a tendency to harmonise readings. It is reasonable to think that a scribe copying the New Testament, having found Jesus saying that there is 'no one greater than John' in Matthew's Gospel, could have decided to harmonise Luke's Gospel with this, or even to have done this unconsciously, and this is reflected in that small handful of manuscripts of Luke 7:28 that say that there is no one greater than John.

3   Matthew 11:9; Luke 7:26.

4   Luke 1:17; Luke 1:76.

5   Matthew 16:13f.

6   Public domain. From the collection of the Metropolitan Museum of Art. Auguste Rodin's father's first name was Jean-Baptiste, which may have sparked his interest in the subject.

7   Paul also paraphrased John's expression in Titus 3:5b-6, which we will also look at in Chapter 9.

8   C.F.D. Moule, *An Idiom Book of New Testament Greek* (Cambridge: CUP, 1979), p. 77.

9   W. Bauer, tr. W. F. Arndt and F. W. Gingrich, *A Greek-English Lexicon of the New Testament and Other Early Christian Literature*, revised and edited by F.W. Danker (Chicago, IL and London: University of Chicago Press, 2000, 3rd ed.). Entry on ἐν, pp. 326-330. Thayer's and Liddell & Scott's older nineteenth-century Greek-English lexicons, both in the public domain and accessible online, are in broad agreement with Bauer on ἐν.

10   In a similar way, the Oxford English Dictionary's entry for *in*, the basic meaning of *en*, also has multiple definitions and sub-divisions.

11   Bauer, op. cit., category 5 (Thayer category I.5.c; Liddell & Scott category III). There is often a corrective footnote in modern versions that says, 'Or in'.

12   As an example of this compare the section on baptism in the first edition with the last edition of Calvin's *Institutes of the Christian Religion*. It balloons in size and becomes increasingly vitriolic.

13   The American Standard Version, the Amplified Bible, the Complete Jewish Bible, the Douay-Rheims Bible, the Jubilee Bible 2000, *The*

Message, The New Testament: A Translation (by David Bentley Hart [New Haven, Ct: YUP, 2018]), The Orthodox Jewish Bible, The Voice and the World English Bible are the exceptions that use 'in', as did the Revised Version of 1881, the precursor of the Revised Standard Version of 1946, and its subsequent revisions, which use 'with'.

[14] John 14:17. Jesus was talking here about the Holy Spirit being in us rather than us being in the Holy Spirit, which is what John's prophecy was about, but the principle remains the same.

[15] Genesis 1:1-2 (NASB). This is a bird-like image and there are echoes of this when Jesus was in the River Jordan and the Holy Spirit anointed him by coming down to him in the form of a dove. It is a moot point whether to use the pronoun 'he' for the Holy Spirit or to use something else – 'he' is preferred in this book.

[16] Genesis 2:7.

[17] E.g. Exodus 31:5; Judges 6:14-16; 15:14-15.

[18] E.g. Jeremiah 31:31-34; Ezekiel 36:25-27; 37:1-14; 47:1-12; Joel 2:28-29.

[19] E.g. Luke 1:14-15,35,41,67; 2:25-27.

[20] E.g. Luke 4:1,14,18.

[21] E.g. Matthew 10:1.

[22] E.g. John 7:37-39; 14:15-18.

[23] John 20:22; Luke 24:49.

[24] Acts 1:4,5,8.

[25] The aorist imperative active second person plural of *metanoeō* (μετανοήσατε) is used to record what Peter said.

[26] In 1 Corinthians 12:13 it is just πνεύματι (Spirit) without ἁγίῳ (Holy).

[27] Matthew 3:11; Luke 3:16. Translation by C. Croll.

[28] The rules of grammar are different in Greek in which there is no indefinite article, so the lack of definite article does not mean John is saying 'a Holy Spirit.' Another example of a definite article not

being used is in John 20:22, when Jesus breathes on his disciples and says, "Receive Holy Spirit."

[29] Acts 2:3.

[30] John speaks of judgement in Luke 3:9. C.H. Kraeling is one of those who say John's mention of fire is to do with judgement in *John the Baptist* (New York: Scribners, 1951), pp. 63f. For ritual cleansing after childbirth, see Leviticus chapter 12 (cf. Luke 2:22-24); for ritual cleansing after leprosy, see Leviticus chapter 14 (cf. Mark 1:40-45). See also Numbers 31:21-23. For refining, see Malachi 3:2-3; 1 Corinthians 3:13-15.

[31] See Hebrews 10:22, where our washing is in the 'pure water' of the Holy Spirit.

[32] E.g. John 7:37-39; 1 Corinthians 12:13.

[33] Acts 1:5; Luke 24:49.

[34] Curiously, it appears that sprinkling only emerged as a widespread baptismal practice in England in the seventeenth century, with the rubric of the service for infant baptism in *The Book of Common Prayer*, published in 1662, still calling for the infant to be dipped, unless the godparents certified that the child was weak. Henry VIII's children were all dipped for baptism in the sixteenth century. It is a custom that can be seen carved in stone on unspoiled medieval seven sacrament fonts.

[35] The mitre that a bishop wears at such occasions is symbolic of the tongues of fire of the Holy Spirit on the heads of those present on the day of Pentecost (Acts 2:3).

[36] Because Christian baptism in or with water is normally thought of as a one-off event it is not unnatural to think of baptism in the Spirit as a one-off event too. But this may not be the best way to think of it, it may not be the way John thought of it. Thinking of it as immersion in the Spirit rather than baptism in the Spirit might help to free our thinking.

[37] John 1:29-34. True to form the fourth Gospel does not record the baptism of Jesus. As discussed in Chapter 6 John is thought to have said this when Jesus returned to see him after his forty-day fast in the wilderness.

[38] In Matthew 11:2-3, John hears 'about the deeds of the Christ'.

[39] John 3:28.

[40] John 1:29. In John 1:41 Andrew, after being introduced to Jesus by John as the Lamb of God (v. 36), told his brother Simon that he had 'found the Messiah'.

[41] The expression comes from the Greek verb *erchomai* (ἐρχόμαι). John is recorded using the present nominative masculine singular participle, *erchomenos* (ἐρχόμενος), in Matthew 3:11; 11:3; Luke 7:19,20; John 1:27, and the indicative present third person singular, *erchetai* (ἔρχεται), in Mark 1:7; Luke 3:16.

[42] Compare John 7:30 and 8:20 to John 12:23f, 13:1 and 17:1.

[43] Malachi 3:1, quoted in Matthew 23:39; Mark 11:9; Luke 13:35 and John 12:13.

[44] *Talmud, Ketubot* 96a.

[45] Josephus, *Antiquities* 18.116 (18.5.2), translated by H. St. John Thackeray. His works are readily available on the internet in various translations. There is more information on Josephus on my website johnthebaptistbook.com. There are two numbering systems for the writings of Josephus, the newer Niese system that is broken down into smaller paragraphs and looks like this: 18.109-119, and the older Whiston system that looks like this: 18.5.1-2 (or xviii.5.1-2). For convenience this book uses both systems like this: 18.109-119 (18.5.1-2).

[46] Josephus, *Life* 2. Banus is sometimes spelled Bannus.

[47] Josephus, *Antiquities* 18.63-64 (18.3.3), known as the *Testimonium Flavianum*. The text may have been corrupted.

[48] Acts 19:1-7. This passage is discussed in Chapter 9.

[49] Translation by C. Croll.

Chapter 5: Make Straight the Way of the LORD

[1] Matthew 3:2. In Matthew 4:17 they are also the first words of Jesus' ministry.

[2] Genesis 12:3; 22:18; Acts 3:25; Romans 4:16; 1 Corinthians 12:13; Galatians 3:8-9,14.

[3] Galatians 3:29. Some Jewish expectations of the kingdom included the idea that Gentiles would be subject to a coming judgement. John, though, turned the spotlight on the Jews themselves.

[4] Cf. Isaiah 7:14; Luke 1:31,34,35; Galatians 4:4. Jesus also used the phrase 'brood of vipers' in Matthew 12:34.

[5] Malachi 3:1ff. Part of this passage is quoted by Mark to introduce John to his readers (Mark 1:2): 'Behold, I send my messenger before your face, who will prepare your way.' In a number of modern translations this is introduced as being a quote from Isaiah when clearly it is not, which makes Mark out to be ignorant. This is taken from a questionable textual variant, found in only a small handful of manuscripts, and is best explained by someone at some point writing a marginal note referring to the next sentence, which does quote Isaiah, which became incorporated in the text by a subsequent unwitting copyist as if it applied to both quotes. The insistence on attributing this Malachi quote to Isaiah is a clumsy and inappropriate use of the textual criticism rule about preferring the harder reading (*difficilior lectio potior*). Textual criticism rules are more like guidelines or 'rules of thumb', and textual criticism is as much an art as a science, so this 'rule' should be no more than a guide to be used discerningly.

A better reading is, 'As it is written in the Prophets', as it is found in, for instance, the NKJV.

[6] Jeremiah 11:16.

7 The threshing floor image was used in Isaiah 41:15-16, which is very close to John's commissioning text in chapter 40. Describing the wicked as chaff was a familiar Old Testament image – cf. Job 21:18; Psalm 1:4; 35:5, Isaiah 17:13; 29:5 and Hosea 13:3. In Revelation 14:14-16 Jesus is described as having a sickle in his hand to harvest the earth.

8 Isaiah 40:4 (NKJV). Luke quotes Isaiah 40:3-5 a few verses earlier in Luke 3:4b-6.

9 *Midrash* is a way of interpreting Scripture to provide answers for contemporary practical (*aggadah*) and theological (*halakhah*) questions that may not have been current when the Bible was written. John's interpretation of Isaiah 40:3-5 was a *midrash aggadah*.

10 In John 3:26 his disciples call him 'Rabbi'.

11 Luke 19:1-10.

12 Luke 3:11,13. He must have been at least reasonably honest to be able to make such an offer. If he had been dishonest then an offer to repay four times as much would have broken him financially.

13 Matthew 22:21 (The Voice).

14 C.H. Scobie, op. cit., p. 86.

15 J.E. Taylor speculates that they continued their trade and that Jesus and John thereby legitimised prostitution (op. cit., pp. 119ff). John legitimised tax collectors and soldiers, despite their unpopularity, and spoke to them about conducting their professions ethically, but he did not do this for prostitutes.

16 Luke 1:17; Malachi 4:6. These are the closing words of the Old Testament.

17 Mark 1:11, Luke 3:22. Matthew 3:17 records it in the third person: 'This is my beloved Son, with whom I am well pleased.'

18 As predicted by Jesus in Matthew 24, Mark 13 and Luke 21:5ff.

19 1 Kings 17-21.

20 Matthew 21:23-32; Mark 11:27-33; Luke 20:1-8. There are some

commentators who suggest that these temple delegates were interested to know what authority he had to baptize, in the same way that Church authorities might ask that question today. This, though, is not actually the question they ask.

21 Deuteronomy 18:15ff.

22 John 1:29-34.

23 Luke 1:17. Some say that he saw himself not so much as Elijah, but as Elisha, who had the spirit of Elijah. While this is straining the evidence a little too much, there is a parallel – both were described as having the spirit of Elijah, with Elisha having a double portion (2 Kings 2:9). There are some conspiracy theorists who want to take this further and, without any evidence, maintain that John saw himself as Elisha ushering in Elijah, but the Church hijacked John's reputation and put words into his mouth to make out that he authenticated Jesus as more than Elijah.

24 John 3:30.

25 Matthew 11:14; 17:10-13; Mark 9:11-13; Malachi 4:5. One of the settings at which Jesus set the record straight was just after the transfiguration, when Moses and Elijah appeared with him.

Chapter 6: The Baptism of Jesus

1 This is the literal translation of this verse from Chapter 4.

2 There are some lesser known inter-testamental Jewish writings (1 Enoch 49:3; Psalms of Solomon 17:42 [or 37]) that say that the Messiah was to be the bearer of God's Spirit. Some commentators say that this is where John got his idea, but it is not really credible that he would base his life's work on something so obscure, and the sign he was promised was much more specific and his prophecy much more powerful.

3 Isaiah 61:1 which Jesus quoted in the synagogue in Nazareth shortly after his baptism (Luke 4:18).

4 Luke 3:2.

5 The Greek verb *eudokeō* is here translated 'well pleased,' but some translations say the Father is delighted with Jesus, or very happy with him, or that he gives him great joy or pride: 'That's my boy! I love him, and I'm so proud of him.'

6 Jesus' baptism provides an excellent text for Trinity Sunday.

7 Bearing in mind that the baptismal site is beside where the Brook Cherith was thought to be, there is another bird parallel with the Old Testament: Elijah was fed at the Brook Cherith by ravens (1 Kings 17:1-6). Another Elijah parallel is that the chariot of fire came down for Elijah and a double portion of Elijah's spirit came down on Elisha near where the Spirit came down on Jesus and remained on him (2 Kings 2).

8 Ezekiel 47:1-12.

9 This is an unusual expression used by Isaiah on only three occasions and elsewhere only once: Isaiah 1:20; 40:5; 58:14; Jeremiah 9:12.

10 Chapters 13 to 17.

11 Day one in verses 19-28; day two in verses 29-34; day three in verses 35-42; day four in verses 43-51; and the wedding in Cana three days later – on day seven – in chapter 2 verses 1-11.

12 Following Jesus' baptism and forty-day fast, this is his first day back with John.

13 Verse 33 is the literal translation from Chapter 4.

14 Matthew 3:15 (NRSV). In the KJV it is rather beautifully rendered, 'It becometh us …'

15 It is only Matthew's Gospel that records Jesus saying that he must 'fulfil all righteousness'. Fulfilling the law and the prophets is a theme of Matthew's Gospel and by being righteous according to God's standards Jesus was uniquely fulfilling the law. In Essene thought, 'righteousness' was understood to mean God's plan for the world.

[16] 2 Chronicles 4:2-6 describes the laver in the temple in which the priests were cleansed and the ten smaller lavers in which sacrificial animals were cleansed. Jesus was both priest and sacrifice.

[17] Some call this Jesus' Pentecost, which has some truth in it, but does not do full justice to what happened.

[18] The dove is almost invariably shown as white, although there is nothing in the text to tell us the colour. At the baptismal site today, the Greek Orthodox Church nurtures a small flock of imported white doves, although the local doves are grey. Elsewhere in Scripture there is no association of a dove with the Holy Spirit. It is unique to this event, although in Genesis 1 the Spirit does hover over the primeval waters of creation like a bird. In Matthew 10:16, Jesus tells us to be 'harmless as doves' (NKJV), using a Greek work (*akereios*) that can mean harmless or pure. Perhaps this is how we should think of this manifestation. It is, of course, appropriate that it should be a dove coming down on the Prince of Peace.

[19] 'Went up' in Matthew and 'came up' in Mark is *anabainō* (ἀναβαίνω) in Greek. The same verb is used in Acts 8:39 of the Ethiopian eunuch's baptism.

[20] Matthew 4:1-11; Mark 1:12-13; Luke 4:1-13; John 1:29-51. The Mount of Temptation, the traditional site of Jesus' temptations, can be seen from the baptismal site and vice versa.

[21] Verses 31 and 33 have been translated by C. Croll.

[22] Isaiah 53:7; Acts 8: 32; 1 Peter 1:18-19; Revelation 5:6-14; 17:14 (cf. Testaments of the Twelve Patriarchs: Joseph 19:8-9). *Amnos* is the Greek word used by John and others, while *arnon* is used in Revelation, but the connection is still valid.

[23] Malachi 3:1; Luke 1:76.

[24] John 1:34

[25] 'After me comes a man who ranks ahead of me', occurs in its variant forms in Matthew 3:11; Mark 1:7; Luke 3:16; John 1:15,27,30; Acts 13:25.

[26] See John 1:31. The Greek verb used here for 'reveal' is *phaneroō*, which is related to the composite noun *epiphaneia* from which Epiphany is derived. 'Epiphany' means manifestation or revelation and reflects this saying of John's that he baptized in water in order that Jesus might be 'revealed' (made manifest) to Israel. In the West the feast of Epiphany has traditionally celebrated the visit of the Magi or the appearance of the star to the Magi, but latterly the revised common lectionary has alternated Magi readings with baptism readings.

[27] John 1:35-45. If this unnamed fifth disciple was John the Evangelist, it makes him uniquely qualified to record the events of this extraordinary week.

[28] In the sense of 'Judea beyond the Jordan' (Matthew 19:1; Mark 10:1).

[29] Andrew is the patron saint of evangelists because of this.

[30] Nathanael appears only here and after the resurrection, in John 21:2, where we learn that Cana was his home town.
The volume of water Jesus turned into wine was approximately the amount needed to fill a *mikvah*. John fasted in the wilderness and Jesus feasted at a wedding (cf. Matthew 11:18-19; Luke 7:33-35).

[31] John 3:22-24.

[32] Matthew 4:12-22; Mark 1:14-20; Luke 3:19-20 and 5:1-11.

[33] This way of relating to scripture is sometimes called Ignatian meditation (or contemplation).

[34] It is in this passage that John is called Rabbi (v. 26).

[35] E.g. C.M. Murphy, *John the Baptist: Prophet of Purity for a New Age* (Collegeville, MN: Liturgical Press, 2003), pp. 38, 82.

[36] For example, Mary is thought to have been an important witness for Luke.

[37] I have said that literary tools can be 'overapplied'. However, with some of these critics one gets the impression that they go out of their way to choose an interpretation that makes the Gospel writers

look incompetent or dishonest. J.P. Meier (op. cit.), for example, does this all the way through his book.

On pages 284-286 of his biography of Paul, Tom Wright critiques some of the Pauline critics, saying that some of their assertions are 'generated by ideology rather than historical study' (T. Wright, *Paul: A Biography* [SPCK, London, 2018]). It is a fair point.

Sixty years ago, C.S. Lewis told a cautionary tale about literary criticism during an address to ordinands at Cambridge entitled 'Fern Seeds and Elephants' since published in a book of the same name, which is still in print (London: Fount, new edition 1998). It is worth reading.

[38] J.P. Meier, op. cit., p. 21. Meier is the extreme advocate of this theory.

[39] John 1:28; John 3:23.

[40] John 3:23 (NIV UK 2011).

[41] The story of the woman at the well starts in John 4:4. It is stretching a point, but this site could still geographically be considered part of the wilderness of Judea, although it was not politically so at that time, being in Samaria, except that both were ruled at this time by the Roman Procurator Pontius Pilate.

[42] 1 Kings 17:3-6. See Chapter 3, note 7.

[43] Public domain. Taken from a photograph on Wikimedia: (By No machine-readable author provided. Disdero assumed [based on copyright claims]. – No machine-readable source provided. Own work assumed [based on copyright claims]. https://commons.wikimedia.org/w/index.php?curid=1723325 [accessed 1.5.19]).

[44] Herod Antipas was one of the sons of Herod the Great and was appointed tetrarch of Galilee and Perea. Perea is the territory to the east and north east of the Dead Sea, including the east bank of the River Jordan opposite Jericho where Bethany beyond the Jordan is found, and this possible site of Aenon near Salim. The

site near Scythopolis was in the territory of Decapolis, ruled from Damascus, and the site near Shechem was in Samaria, ruled from Caesarea Maritima by the Roman Procurator Pilate.

45 See Chapter 3, note 7.

46 Joshua 3:15 refers to the annual flooding of the River Jordan, so does Jeremiah 12:5 in some versions (e.g. NKJV).

47 Clemens Kopp offers this as a possibility in his book *The Holy Places of the Gospels*, tr. R. Walls (New York: Herder and Herder, 1963), p. 126.

48 In an age of changing political boundaries, some evidently thought of this area as being part of Judea even though it was at that time in Perea. A few years previously it had all been part of Herod the Great's kingdom.

49 John 3:26.

50 'Beyond the Jordan' in NASB, NKJV, RSV. 'East of the Jordan' in CEV. The seven uses of *peran tou Iordanou* are Matthew 4:15,25; 19:1; Mark 3:8; 10:1; John 1:28; 3:26 and 10:40.

51 John 3:29. On another occasion Jesus referred to his disciples as friends of the bridegroom (Mark 2:18-20).

Chapter 7: Bound and in Prison

1 Herod the Great was given his honorific title retrospectively, mainly because it helps us to distinguish him from the other members of his family called Herod who succeeded him.

2 Ambrosius Theodosius Macrobius, *Saturnalia*, Book 2, chapter 4:11. Some think that Augustus may have been speaking Greek when he said this because of the word play: pig is *hus* in Greek and son is *huios*.

3 Ethnarch and tetrarch are Greek terms used by the Romans in the east of their empire. Technically, ethnarch means ruler of a people and is senior to tetrarch, which means ruler of fourth part of a

region: Herod the Great's kingdom had been divided among four heirs. Cf. Luke 3:1; Acts 13:1.

4 Antipas' wife is sometimes called Phasaelis in books and articles but, while we know from inscriptions and coins that Aretas IV had a child called Phasael (the modern equivalent is Faisal), we also know that he had other sons and daughters and there is no record of which one married Antipas (N.I. Khairy, 'A New Dedicatory Nabatean Inscription', *PEQ* 113.1, 1981, pp. 19-26). Herod Antipas had a half-sister who married someone called Phasaelus, and this may be the source of the confusion (Josephus, *Antiquities* 18.130-142 [18.5.4]). King Aretas is mentioned in 2 Corinthians 11:32.

5 As the Rose Red City, this is a famous tourist destination in the Hashemite Kingdom of Jordan. Petra is the Greek word for rock and is an appropriate name for a city carved from the cliffs.

6 Sometimes known as Mariamme II, she was the daughter of Simeon the high priest and is not to be confused with Herod the Great's second wife who was also called Mariamme.

7 'Herod' in Josephus, *Antiquities* 18.130-142 (18.5.4), and 'Philip' in Matthew 14:3 and Mark 6:17. Luke 3:19 does not name him. The only record of his name is in the Gospels. See the article about Josephus on my website johnthebaptistbook.com for an example of Josephus simply using the Herod family name. It was common to do this, and it is sometimes done in the New Testament, for example Antipas is called Herod in Matthew 14:3; Mark 6:17; Luke 3:19 and Agrippa 1 is called Herod in Acts 12:20-21. Berenice is sometimes called Bernice.

8 In books and articles, he is variously called Herod, Herod II, Philip, Herod Philip, Herod [Philip] and Herod-Philip. It is because of the other son of Herod called Philip that some claim that the Gospel writers were confused. There was, however, a lot of repeating of

names in the Herod family. Philip, meaning 'lover of horses' in Greek, was a popular name in the ancient Hellenistic world. It was the name, for instance, of Alexander the Great's father.

9 Josephus, *Antiquities* 17.68-78 (17.4.2).

10 Herodias was simultaneously her husband's half-niece by her father and first cousin once removed by her mother.

11 We know her name from Josephus, *Antiquities* 18.130-142 (18.5.4), not from the Bible. Salome is the Greek rendering of the Hebrew name Shlomit, which is derived from Shalom, meaning peace. The other Salome mentioned earlier in this chapter, Herod the Great's sister, who inherited some territory from him, was this Salome's great-aunt on her father's side and grandmother on her mother's side. Similarly, Herod the Great was both her great-uncle and grandfather. She is not to be confused with Jesus' disciple Salome, who was present at his crucifixion (Mark 15:40; 16:1).

12 Josephus, *Antiquities* 18.109-115 (18.5.1).

13 Bernice (a.k.a. Berenice), after being widowed twice and leaving her third husband, became mistress to Titus who commanded the Roman armies that destroyed Jerusalem in AD 70. Ironically, Herod the Great built the temple and his great-granddaughter stood with the man who destroyed it. When Titus succeeded his father as emperor Bernice was controversially able to join him in Rome.

14 Deuteronomy 25:5-10 (cf. Luke 20:28) describes the duty to marry a dead brother's wife. Leviticus 18:16 and 20:21 forbid such a marriage if the brother is alive, and the resulting union was expected to be childless. Josephus adds that it was against the laws of the Jews for a woman to divorce her husband (*Antiquities* 18.130-142 [18.5.4]). Philip/Herod and Antipas were half-uncles of Herodias, which makes them uncomfortably closely related, but it seems to have been the habit of Herod's family to engage in this sort of inbreeding and it does not appear to be this that provoked criticism from John.

[15] Luke 3:19. He was a prophet and will have had lofty ideals about the behaviour of rulers.

[16] Josephus, *Antiquities* 18.116-119 (18.5.2). It is from Josephus that we learn that John was taken to Machaerus. Its name is derived from the Greek word for a sword: *machaira* (μάχαιρα. Machaerus is Μαχαιροῦς in Greek). When the fourth-century historian Eusebius quoted this text from Josephus' *Antiquities* in his *Ecclesiastical History* (1.11.4-6) he added the detail that John was taken to Machaerus in chains, a later addition that may or may not be true but has nevertheless found its way into a number of histories of John. Matthew 14:3 simply says that Antipas 'bound him'.

[17] One of its qualities as a defensive fortress was that it could be seen from far away and could therefore signal news of an invasion from the south to the other Herodian fortresses. In fact, the fortresses at Masada and Alexandreion, that did not have a clear line of sight to Jerusalem, could send signals there via Machaerus. The most visible feature of Jerusalem from Machaerus was the smoke from the burnt offerings, followed by the gleaming gold-clad temple (G. Vörös, op. cit., vol. 1, pp. 152ff. and 354). Cf. Josephus, *Wars of the Jews* 5.224 (5.5.6).

[18] Photograph from the Hiking in Jordan website, www.hiking-in-jordan.com. Used with permission.

[19] Since 2009 Győző Vörös has led a team of archaeologists at Machaerus, and this reconstruction is from volume one of his report (G. Vörös, op. cit., vol. 1, fig. 511, p. 337). Used with permission. There is also a volume two (2015) and a volume three (2019) of his report, by the same publishers. In vol. 3 this reconstruction has been amended (pp. 164-5). A shorter report can be found in *Biblical Archaeology Review* (September/October 2012, volume 38.5, pp. 30-41).
Pliny the Elder described Machaerus as the most strongly fortified place in Judea after Jerusalem (Pliny, *Natural History* 5.15).

20 G. Vörös, op. cit., vol. 1, fig. 506, p. 331. Used with permission.

21 Mark 6:19-20. The lower part of the fortress, described by Josephus as 'the lower part of the city' in Whiston's translation, and as 'the town below' in Williamson's translation (*Wars of the Jews* 7.163-209 [7.6.1-4]), was built on terraces on the north-east side of the hill. John was beheaded 'in the prison' (Mark 6:27), but that does not necessarily mean he was held there – he could have been taken there for his execution. If he was held under house arrest, it may have been like that enjoyed by Paul in Rome, described in Acts 28. The popularity of the subterranean dungeon idea goes back to Oscar Wilde's play *Salome* and he in turn got it from a false inference by H.B. Tristram, who visited the site in the nineteenth century. He had incorrectly assumed that the Herodian cistern that he could see was the dungeon (G. Vörös, vol. 1, op. cit., p.344f.).

22 Matthew records that John heard about 'the deeds of the [Messiah] Christ', but John is never recorded as having called Jesus 'Messiah', or 'Christ', although he might have done. John is consistently recorded referring to Jesus as the 'Coming One' (NKJV) ('the one who is to come' [ESV], 'he who is coming after me' [Matthew 3:11, ESV]) or the Lamb of God ('who takes away the sin of the world').

23 The Greek verb translated here as 'offended' is *skandalizō* and means 'to cause someone to stumble'.

24 See note 23.

25 'Truly, I say to you' is a formula Jesus used sometimes when he was saying something particularly important. 'Truly' is *amēn* in Greek, a transliteration from Hebrew.

26 As noted in Chapter 4, most ancient manuscripts and some translations record Jesus saying that there was no greater prophet than John.

27 For more detail see, for example, D. Guthrie, op. cit., pp. 409ff.

28 Jesus was quoting from Isaiah chapters 35 and 61, both of which inform his ministry.

[29] Daniel 7:13.

[30] Luke 1:17; Malachi 4:5-6.

[31] There is a fable attributed to Aesop about an oak and a reed in which the reed bends with the wind, but the oak refuses to do so. In a gale, the oak ends up being blown down by the wind because it would not bend. John was an oak of a man.

Some commentators point out that Antipas' coins had a reed on the obverse and that Jesus was also making a reference to this, which is a nice story except that the design on the coins is generally thought to be a palm branch, not a reed.

[32] There is a story told by Josephus in *Jewish War* 1.478-480 (1.24.3) of the sons of Herod the Great by his second wife Mariamme I, whom he had executed, complaining when Herod gave her court finery to his later wives. They threatened to wear hair cloth as a protest that Herod was depriving them of what was rightly theirs.

[33] This popular quote, often attributed to Tertullian, is not exactly what he wrote, although it is nevertheless true. Tertullian wrote, 'the blood of Christians is the seed' (*semen est sanguis christianorum*), *Apologeticus* 50.

[34] Matthew 5:1-12; Matthew 11:6 and Luke 7:23.

[35] Cf. 2 Timothy 3:10-12.

[36] Mark 6:20; Luke 9:7; Matthew 14:5.

[37] Matthew 25:36,44. In Matthew 4:12 we read that Jesus withdrew up north to Galilee when he heard of John's arrest.

Chapter 8: Head on a Plate

[1] R. Buth, 'That Small-fry Herod Antipas, Or When a Fox Is Not a Fox' (*Jerusalem Perspective* 40, September/October 1993, pp. 7-9).

[2] Luke 13:31-34. This is the only time Jesus is reported criticising a politician.

[3] Mark 6:19-20.

⁴ The details of this can be found in Josephus' *Antiquities* 18.109-142 (18.5.1-4), see my website johnthebaptistbook.com for the text. The other reason cited for the dispute concerned their boundaries.

⁵ G Vörös, op. cit., vol. 1, pp. 21, 35, 43, vol. 2, pp. 502-513, vol. 3, pp. 514-516. It was later fortified as a garrison by the Romans but seized by the Jews during the revolt that broke out in AD 66, to be finally destroyed by the Romans in AD 71.

⁶ Herod Philip became Herodias' son-in-law when he married Salome after John's execution. Agrippa I was made king in AD 37-38 after Herod Philip died in AD 34. His territory also included Abila, which had been ruled by the tetrarch Lysanias (Luke 3:1). Agrippa I was Antipas' half-nephew and is mentioned in Acts 12:20-23. See the family tree in Chapter 7.

⁷ In *Antiquities* 18.240-256 (18.7.1-2) Josephus says Antipas was exiled to Lyons but in *Wars of the Jews* 2.183 (2.9.6) he says he was exiled to Spain. Antipas' exile was brought about because Agrippa I, Herodias' brother, sent a messenger to Caligula to accuse Antipas of planning sedition. To rub salt in the wound, Agrippa, who was a personal friend of Caligula, was then given Antipas' territory of Galilee to add to his kingdom.

⁸ Josephus, *Antiquities* 18.255 (18.7.1). Josephus was a man of his time!

⁹ 1 Kings 17–2 Kings 9. See also Revelation 2:20.

¹⁰ Matthew 14:5; 21:26 and Mark 11:32.

¹¹ Matthew 14:5.

¹² Mark 6:19-20.

¹³ Matthew 14:1-2; Mark 6:14-16; Luke 9:7-9. These texts are examined in Chapter 9.

¹⁴ Luke 23:6-12.

¹⁵ Josephus, *Wars of the Jews* 7.163-209 (7.6.1-4). There is a lengthy description of Machaerus in this chapter. The Hasmonean

Alexander Jannaeus originally built it as a frontier fortress in about 90 BC, but the Roman Gabinius later destroyed it. It was Herod the Great who rebuilt it sumptuously.

[16] Josephus, *ibid.*

[17] Mark 6:21. In John 4:46-53 there is a story of Jesus healing the son of a Galilean nobleman and it is intriguing to wonder if he was one of those present at this party. There are some who assume that it was a palace in Galilee that John was taken to, hence the reference to the presence of aristocrats from Galilee, but that is to draw the wrong inference from the story: the Galileans were mentioned because they were not in Galilee. There is, nevertheless, a tomb that is said to be John's in Sebaste in Galilee – one of many (see note 40).

[18] C.J. Humphreys, *The Mystery of the Last Supper* (Cambridge: CUP, 2011). This study, based on recently available astronomical calculations, is very convincing, although there are those who argue for an earlier date. There is more information about the calculation of John's dates in the Appendix.

[19] Acts 13:24f.

[20] Agrippa II helped Josephus in later life with many reminiscences. He was Salome's first cousin by her second marriage and she was also related to him by her mother and father, and she named her second son after him.

[21] Mark 5:21-43.

[22] Cf. Luke 8:42.

[23] Matthew 9:24,25.

[24] The English word gynaecology is derived from *gynē*.

[25] Josephus, *Antiquities* 18.130-142 (18.5.4).

[26] Both Matthew and Mark refer here to Antipas as king. The Gospel writers knew he was a tetrarch as elsewhere he is referred to by this title (Matthew 14:1; Luke 3:1,19; 9:7), so they were probably using ironic language, as he later tried to become a king and failed, ending up in exile. He behaved at the party in a very high-handed

way. There is a parallel to this sort of promise in Esther 7:2.

27 The internal dimensions of each dining room are approximately 9.6 metres square = 92 m2, 990 sq. ft. (G. Vörös, op. cit., vol. 1, p. 224). From the cutaway illustration in Chapter 7 it can be seen that the dining rooms are thought to have been on the first floor.

This is similar to the scenario in Esther 1:8-9.

28 G. Vörös, op. cit., vol. 1, pp. 318, 332-335.

29 There is a record of a self-proclaimed Jewish prophet being beheaded by the procurator Fadus in AD 46 (Josephus, *Antiquities* 20.97-98 [20.5.1]).

While there is no record in the ancient world of a head being produced on a plate, it was not unheard of for a decapitated head to be produced as proof that someone was dead. For example, when the Emperor Tiberius instructed Vitellius to confront Antipas' erstwhile father-in-law, Aretas, in battle a few years later, he ordered that if Aretas was killed his head was to be brought to him (Josephus, *Antiquities* 18.115 [18.5.2]).

30 G. Vörös, op. cit., vol. 1, p. 289, fig. 349. Used with permission. In vol. 3 this ground plan has been amended (pp. 170ff).

31 Josephus, *Antiquities* 18.255 (18.7.2), *Wars of the Jews* 2.183 (2.9.6).

32 Uniquely, there are two feast days for John in the calendar of the Western Church, his birth on 24 June and his beheading on 29 August. Jesus' birthday is celebrated just after the winter solstice and his cousin John's just after the summer solstice. In times past John was known as the Midsummer Saint and the eve of St John's day was widely celebrated with bonfires and dancing and lots of fun. It still is in some Nordic countries. There are more feast days for him in the Eastern Church where he is venerated alongside Mary (S. Bulgakov, tr. B Jakim, *The Friend of the Bridegroom* [Grand Rapids, MI: Eerdmans, 2003]).

[33] T. Bentley, *Sisters of Salome* (New Haven, Ct.: YUP, 2002).

[34] Described this way by Lynne Truss in a review of Sisters of Salome, ibid. that can be found at www.lynnetruss.com/journalism/sisters-of-salome (accessed 17.4.19).

[35] The 1953 film *Salome*, with Rita Hayworth in the title role, is more historical travesty. Jean Steinman in his book *Saint John the Baptist in the Desert Tradition* (op. cit.) says she danced naked!

[36] As E. Lohmeyer points out in his commentary of Mark's Gospel, *Das Evangelium des Markus* (Göttingen: Dandenhoed & Ruprecht, 1953), pp. 119f. 'Portraying a princess as a prostitute, entertaining with her dance the men gathered round her, has no parallel or antecedent', G. Vörös, op. cit., vol. 1, p. 350.

[37] Josephus, *Antiquities* 18.130-142 (18.5.4), Tacitus, *Annals* 13:7 and 14:26. Aristobulus was Salome's mother's nephew (son of her mother's brother Herod and Mariamme who was a cousin of both Herodias and Salome). Aristobulus was also nephew of Herod Agrippa I of Acts 12:20-23 and first cousin of Agrippa II of Acts 25:13–26:32. See the Herod family tree in Chapter 7. According to Josephus, Herod's descendants, not surprisingly, died out through inbreeding (*Antiquities* 18.120-129 [18.5.3]). Coincidentally, Armenia was later to become the first kingdom to declare itself Christian.

[38] It is unusual for a coin from this time to have an image of a queen on it, which, together with her fame, may account for the price of $160,000 US that one of these coins was recently sold for at auction. There are extant likenesses of the emperors Augustus, Tiberius and Claudius, and of Herod Philip, Agrippa I and Agrippa II, all of whom get brief mentions in the New Testament, but Salome is the only female New Testament figure for whom we have a contemporary likeness. And we have likenesses of both her husbands.

[39] Photograph from Classical Numismatic Group, Inc. (www.cngcoins.com/Coin.aspx?CoinID=30045 [accessed 1.5.19]). Used with permission.

[40] There evidently was once a grave for John, but it is long since lost, although there are Herodian graves near to Machaerus, which accord with Jewish custom (G. Vörös, vol. 1, op. cit., pp. 143ff, vol. 2, op. cit., pp. 100ff). In later centuries legends would develop about the location of John's head and body. In AD 361-2 Julian the Apostate had a grave dug up at Sebaste that was supposed to have contained John's headless body, which he burned. Nevertheless, there is still a tomb for John at Sebaste, which, according to J. Murphy O'Connor dates to the second-third centuries (J. Murphy O'Connor, *The Holy Land: An Archaeological Guide from Earliest Times to 1700* [Oxford: OUP, 1992, rev. ed.], pp. 403-406). There is also a mosque in Damascus, the Umayyad Mosque, built over a pre-existing church dedicated to John, which has in it a tomb reputed to contain John's head. There are other supposed tombs, including one in Egypt and another in Italy. The chances of any of them being John's resting place are vanishingly small as he would almost certainly have been buried within a day at or near Machaerus. The place of his burial makes not a scrap of difference – in fact, Jesus criticised the scribes and Pharisees for venerating tombs (Matthew 23:29) and it seems fitting that, as with Elijah and Moses, we do not know where his physical remains lie.

[41] From the context, we can see that Jesus was in a wilderness somewhere in Galilee, or perhaps in Herod Philip's tetrarchy.

Chapter 9: Postmortem

[1] Matthew chapter 14 (cf. Mark 6:30ff).

[2] Josephus, *Antiquities of the Jews*, 18.118-119 (18. 5. 2). See the article on Josephus on my website johnthebaptistbook.com for the full text.

[3] Luke 23:6-12.

[4] Some speculate that there may have been a family likeness – that Jesus looked like John – which added to the confusion (G. Vörös,

op. cit., vol. 1, p. 360).

5 The first time he said John was Elijah was in Matthew 11:14.

6 Matthew 6:9-13. On the two occasions the prayer is recorded for us it is in a slightly different form, which is an indication that it is the substance of the prayer (i.e. the sorts of things that are prayed for and perhaps the order in which they are prayed), rather than the exact form that is important.

7 Matthew 7:7-11.

8 Tabernacles is also known as the Feast of Booths and *Sukkot*.

9 Matthew 3:2; 4:17.

10 Matthew 3:10; Luke 3:9.

11 John in Matthew 3:8 and Luke 3:8, and Jesus in, for example, John 15:16.

12 John in Matthew 3:7 and Luke 3:7, and Jesus in Matthew 12:34 and 23:33 (cf. John 8:44).

13 John in Matthew 3:9 and Luke 3:8, and Jesus in John 8:33-39.

14 John in Matthew 3:12 and Jesus in Luke 3:17; Matthew 13:24-30 and 36-43.

15 C.M. Murphy (op. cit.) provides an example of this school of thought.

16 John 3:30.

17 Matthew also records this last visit of Jesus to the baptismal site, but his account omits Jesus' last Judean and Perean ministry described in the third and fourth Gospels, so he merely says, 'He departed from Galilee and came to the region of Judea beyond the Jordan' (Matthew 19:1), referring to Bethany beyond the Jordan.

18 Luke 12:50; Matthew 20:22f; Mark 10:38f. One of the symbolisms of baptism is to identify with the death, burial (being submerged under water) and resurrection of Jesus (Romans 6:3-13).

19 We owe this insight to G. Vörös, op. cit., vol. 1, pp. 343-361 and 152-175.

[20] G. Vörös, op. cit., vol. 1, fig. 161, p.175. Used with permission.

[21] Acts 1:5 is the literal translation from Chapter 4.

[22] Acts 1:21-27.

[23] Those who are sprinkled with water at their baptism instead of being immersed are experiencing a symbol of a symbol. In the same way that we are in the Spirit we are also in Christ and in the Father, as Jesus prayed on the night of his betrayal (John 17:20-23). Hebrews 6:2 refers to the doctrine of baptisms (plural), which seems to mean both baptism in water and baptism in the Spirit.

[24] There is another Gospel passage that is sometimes cited in discussions about baptism: John 3:1-8 records a conversation that Jesus had with Nicodemus in which he said a person must be born again. Nicodemus responded by asking whether that means going back into one's mother's womb. To which Jesus replied that one must be born of water and the Spirit. In context that must mean the water of the womb, given that he provides a parallel by talking about being born of the flesh and of the spirit. However, it is sometimes maintained that the water means the water of baptism, which is a very questionable assertion given that there is nothing in that context to support it.

[25] The washing away of sins by immersion in water would have been a very foreign idea to the Jerusalem Jews Paul was addressing.

[26] John 1:31b.

[27] Acts 1:22.

[28] Acts 2:38. Translation by C. Croll.

[29] Translation by C. Croll. With the sound of a rushing mighty wind and the tongues of fire there is a parallel with Elijah, who went up to heaven in a whirlwind with a chariot of fire.

[30] Luke 3:11; Acts 2:44f.

[31] Acts 2:41; 8:12,13,36-38; 9:18; 10:47-48; 16:15,33; 18:8; 22:16.

[32] Verse 16b is the literal translation from Chapter 4.

[33] Wright, op. cit., p. 118.

[34] Wright, op. cit., p. 433.

[35] Cf. 1 Corinthians 14:21-22; Isaiah 28:11-12.

[36] Acts 18:24-26.

[37] Acts 13:24; Luke 16:16.

[38] This is the literal translation from Chapter 4.

[39] Paul used the term 'Greeks' to denote all other races, as since the time of Alexander the Great Greek culture was the omniculture of that part of the world.

[40] Whether it is baptism of a believer by immersion or by a symbolic sprinkling, or by infant baptism that is later confirmed as an adult.

[41] John 4:7-14; 7:37-39. Cf. Ezekiel 47:1-12. Paul wrote about the Israelites drinking the same spiritual drink in 1 Corinthians 10:4 (Cf. Mark 10:38-39).

[42] 1 Corinthians 11:17-34.

Chapter 10: Postscript

[1] John 1:6.

[2] Matthew 11:11.

[3] Europe, N. America, S. America, Australia/Oceania and Africa (which became majority Christian in the first decade of the twenty-first century). Asia is the exception; it is home to Islam, Buddhism and Hinduism and has no majority religion. 157 countries are majority Christian.

[4] Matthew 28:19.

[5] Luke 11:9-13.

[6] John 1:8.

Appendix

[1] C.J. Humphreys, 'The Star of Bethlehem, a Comet in 5 BC and the Date of Christ's Birth', *Tyndale Bulletin*, 43.1, 1992, pp. 31-56. Humphreys' conclusion is based on new astronomical evidence.

2 Luke 1:24.

3 Luke 1:36.

4 Luke 1:56. Jesus' annunciation took place in the sixth month of Elizabeth's pregnancy (Luke 1:36). Depending on how long it took for Mary to sort things out with Joseph and travel to Ein Kerem, her three-month stay at the home of Elizabeth and Zechariah will probably have started some time in Elizabeth's sixth or seventh month.

5 J. Finegan, *Handbook of Biblical Chronology* (Peabody, MA: Hendrickson, revised edition 1998), pp. 340f, section 583. Dionysius followed the same convention, beginning to count from 1 January in the year after Jesus was thought to have been born.

6 E.g. R. Riesner, *Paul's Early Period: Chronology, Mission Strategy, Theology* (Grand Rapids, MI: Eerdmans, 1998) p. 39ff.

7 Riesner, ibid., p. 40.

8 Luke 3:1. The verb *hēgemoneuō* (ἡγεμονεύω) is used of Pontius Pilate in the same verse. *Hēgemonia* is the root of the English word 'hegemony'.

9 Luke 1:5.

10 Finegan, op. cit., p. 338, section 580. It is not something that has occurred to any Bible translator of this passage and has the air of a special-pleading, out-of-context word study.

11 Luke 20:20-26.

12 Finegan, op. cit., p. 338, section 580.

13 C.J. Humphreys and W. G. Waddington, 'The Jewish Calendar, a Lunar Eclipse and the Date of Christ's Crucifixion', *Tyndale Bulletin,* 43:2, Nov. 1992, pp. 331-351; C.J. Humphreys and W.G. Waddington, 'Dating the Crucifixion' *Nature,* 306 (1983), 743-6; C.J. Humphreys and W.G. Waddington, 'The Date of the Crucifixion', *Journal of the American Scientific Affiliation,* 37 (March 1985), pp. 2-10; C.J. Humphreys, *The Mystery of the Last Supper,* op. cit.,

p. 168. There were earlier attempts at using astronomy to recreate first-century Jewish calendars, such as J.K. Fotheringham, 'The Evidence of Astronomy and Technical Chronology for the Date of the Crucifixion', *Journal of Theological Studies*, 34 (1934), pp. 146-162, that could not achieve the accuracy of Humphreys and Waddington. When working out ages of people AD who were born BC, it is important to remember that there is no year zero in the calendar.

[14] C. J. Humphreys, *The Mystery of the Last Supper*, op. cit., pp. 72-73. It is generally reckoned that Luke included this detail to show that Jesus was old enough to enter the Levitical priesthood, for which one had to be thirty years of age (Numbers 4:3,23,30, etc.).

[15] C.J. Humphreys and W.G. Waddington, 'The Jewish Calendar, a Lunar Eclipse and the Date of Christ's Crucifixion', *Tyndale Bulletin*, pp. 337f; C.J. Humphreys, *The Mystery of the Last Supper*, op. cit., pp. 63-66.

Made in the USA
Coppell, TX
11 December 2020

44248417R00154